D0554437

The Informational Role
of Prices

The Wicksell Lectures

The Informational Role of Prices

Sanford J. Grossman

The MIT Press
Cambridge, Massachusetts
London, England

© 1989 Massachusetts Institute of Technology
All rights reserved. No part of this book may be reproduced in any form by any electronic or mechanical means (including photocopying, recording, or information storage and retrieval) without permission in writing from the publisher.

This book was set in Palatino by Asco Trade Typesetting Ltd., Hong Kong, and printed and bound by Halliday Lithograph in the United States of America.

Library of Congress Cataloging-in-Publication Data

Grossman, Sanford J.
  The informational role of prices.

  (Wicksell lectures)
  Includes index.
  1. Stocks—Prices—United States. 2. Prices.
I. Title. II. Series.
HG4636.G94   1989   332.63'222   88-27146
ISBN 0-262-07121-5

Contents

Series Foreword

In 1958 The Wicksell Lecture Society, in cooperation with the Social Science Institute of Stockholm University, the Stockholm School of Economics, and the Swedish Economic Association, inaugurated a series of lectures to honor the memory of Knut Wicksell (1851–1926). Until 1975 lectures were given each year. After a period of dormancy the series was reinaugurated in 1979 by the Swedish Economic Association. Starting with the 1982 lectures, a set of lectures will be offered every two years;

Source Acknowledgments

Chapter 2

Reprinted, with revisions, by permission from *Review of Economic Studies*, Vol. 48, October 1981, pp. 541–559. An earlier version appeared as NBER Working Paper No. 800, which was reprinted by permission from *Journal of Public Economics*, Vol. 18, 1982, pp. 139–159. Copyright © 1982 North-Holland Publishing Company.

Chapter 3

Reprinted, with revisions, by permission from *Journal of Economic Theory*, Vol. 18, 1978, pp. 81–101. Copyright © 1978 Academic Press, Inc.

Chapter 4

Reprinted, with revisions, by permission from *Review of Economic Studies*, Vol. 44, 1977, pp. 431–449. Copyright © 1977 Society for Economic Analysis Limited.

Chapter 5

Reprinted, with revisions, by permission from *American Economic Review*, Vol. 70, 1980, pp. 393–408. Copyright © 1980 American Economic Association.

Chapter 6

Reprinted, with revisions, by permission from *Journal of Business*, Vol. 61, 1988, pp. 275–298. Copyright © 1988 The University of Chicago.

Chapter 7

Reprinted, with revisions, by permission from *Journal of Finance*, Vol. 36, 1981, pp. 253–270. Copyright © 1981 American Finance Association.

Chapter 8

Reprinted, with revisions, by permission from *Journal of Law and Economics*, Vol. 24, 1981, pp. 461–483; copyright © 1981 The University of Chicago.

Chapter 9

Reprinted, with revisions, by permission from *Journal of Political Economy*, Vol. 91, 1983, pp. 907–928; copyright © 1983 The University of Chicago.

To Aviva, Naava, and Shulamite

The Informational Role
of Prices

1   Introduction

1.1   Introduction

The chapters brought together herein are related by the common theme that the very activity of trading conveys information that affects the outcome of the activity. Some of the chapters focus on this theme by explaining the informational role of prices (chapters 2–7), while others focus on the informational role of contracts (chapters 8 and 9). Rather then summarizing the chapters, I shall present my interpretation of the ideas in them in the light of recent developments in financial markets, and selected contributions to this literature since they were written. The reader will find a critical review and summary of many of the chapters in Kreps (1988).

1.2   The Informational Role of Prices

It is a common theme of most discussions of the competitive price system that prices convey information. Hayek (1945, p. 527) wrote, "We must look at the price system as ... a mechanism for communicating information if we want to understand its real function.... The most significant fact about this system is the economy of knowledge with which it operates, or how little the individual participants need to know in order to be able to take the right action ... by a kind of symbol, only the most essential information is passed on...." However, the models of competitive allocations developed by Marshall and Walras do show how people use the information contained in prices. No one learns anything from prices; people are merely constrained by prices. In their framework, prices determine the costs and benefits of various activities, and thus provide incentives to economize on the use of (or to increase the production of) relatively scarce resources. In some ways these models treat people like rats in a maze. Prices are like the walls that the rats are bumping into, which produce pain and thus guide them in the right direction. The rats (presumably) do not get statistically useful information about the structure of the maze when they bump into a wall.

I have elaborated a model of economic equilibrium that is based upon the idea that prices have a dual role: They constrain behavior by affecting the costs or benefits of acts, but they also convey information about what will be the costs and benefits of the acts.

An example of such a model is one where an individual's demand for shares of a security depends upon his information about the future payoffs to holders of the security. Each individual knows that others have information about the security's future payoff. In the standard Walrasian model each consumer i, with information y_i, would have a demand function $x_i(p; y_i)$, and the Walrasian market clearing price would be a number p that depends on $y = (y_1, y_2, \ldots)$, say, $p(y)$, such that the sum of the x_i equals the total stock of the security. If this price really clears the market, then there should be no desire to recontract away from the allocations associated with the price. This is what "market clearing" must mean. However, I shall now argue that there *will* be a desire to recontract after all the consumers learn that a particular price $p(y)$ is "market clearing." Just consider a consumer, say Mr. 1, who observed a signal y_1 that indicated that the payoff to the security is likely to be unusually high. His Walrasian demand would then specify that at each price p, a large amount of the security is desired. But suppose that other traders observe very bad news about the payoff to the security. This will cause the "market clearing" price to be very low. Consumer 1 will infer from the fact that a very low price "cleared the market" that his information is an outlier. He would thus revise his desired holdings downward after observing a very low "market clearing" price.

A trader is induced to adjust his "demand" function to reflect the fact that the price at which a market clears conveys information. Hence, his "demand" should be expressed as a function $x_i(p; y_i, p(y))$, which states his desired quantity of shares if the market clearing price process $p(y)$ takes on a particular value p. It is a statement about how much is desired at prices that are market generated, rather than at arbitrary prices as in the Walrasian approach.

The Walrasian demand function is derived by finding the x that maximizes expected utility subject to each unit of x having a cost of p. The demand function specifies a desired level of holdings of the security at each particular price p, irrespective of whether or not p is a market clearing price. It is the outcome of a thought experiment in which the consumer imagines that he faces a particular price p chosen at random, and then decides how much of the security to purchase given that it will cost p. The crucial deviation from this framework, which I have focused upon, assumes that the consumer faces a price that is a real offer of another person, or the outcome of a market process. Hence the fact that a particular price is offered is itself information about what someone else thinks about the future payoff[1] (see chapters 7 and 8).

The classical notion of a demand schedule should be contrasted with demand schedules that are actually used in real securities markets. The New York Stock Exchange sets the opening price (each morning), for each stock based upon a procedure that solicits demand schedules, and then determines the price where excess demand is zero. A common method by which demand is expressed is through the use of "limit orders." A single limit order (to buy shares) specifies, for example, that a particular quantity $q(p)$ will be bought at a price of p or lower. The submission of a list of such orders will generate (by summation) a statement about how much of the security the person is willing to buy, say, $Q(p)$, for each price p. These orders state that if the market clearing price is p, then he will accept $Q(p)$ shares. No statement is implied about what he would accept at a "price" p that was not a market clearing price. An extreme type of limit order is a "market order" for q shares that specifies that a person is willing to buy q shares at any price, as long as it is the market clearing price.[2] A person who submits these types of orders takes into account that the price at which his trade is executed will incorporate the information possessed by other traders.

Once the Walrasian notion of "demand" is modified to be an expression of desired holdings at prices that are "market clearing," it is easy to define a notion of "market clearing" in which there is no desire to recontract after observing that a particular price is the market clearing price. To do so, define a Rational Expectations (R.E.) price function $p(y)$ such that, for each y, if $p(y) = p$, then the total market demand equals total supply given that each individual chooses his demand at p to maximize his expected utility conditioned on both his private information *and on the information contained in the event that p is a market clearing price (i.e., that $p(y) = p$).*

The crucial characteristic of an R.E. equilibrium is that each consumer forms his demand as if he possessed far more than his own information. I have shown that $p(y)$ can be a sufficient statistic for the information of all traders; i.e., if individuals form their demands cognizant of the fact that the prices at which their trades will be executed represent market clearing prices, then the final allocations are as if each person possessed *all* of the economy's information.

The R.E. model is capable of capturing the idea that prices *inform* individuals as well as *allocate* resources. It has been used to formalize the idea that if markets are complete, but information is dispersed throughout the economy, then there exists an R.E. equilibrium that yields allocations that could not be Pareto dominated by a central planner in possession of all the economy's information [see Grossman (1981) and chapter 2]. This is a much stronger theorem than the fundamental theorem of welfare economics for Walrasian equilibrium, and it summarizes the idea that prices convey information that has an impact on the resource allocation process.

The ability of prices to aggregate information perfectly is limited by the extent to which individuals must be able to earn a return for resources they expend on information collection. If prices fully aggregate information, why would any individual expend resources on information collection? If securities prices are perfectly efficient in the sense that *everyone* should hold the market portfolio no matter what the prices of individual securities may be, then who will collect the information to price individual securities appropriately? The answer to these questions is that the excess demand for a security varies for noninformational reasons (some of which are elaborated below) that obscure the informational movements in prices. The supply of traders with costly-to-collect information adjusts to make prices noisy signals for information to an extent necessary to reward, at the margin, information collection and processing [see chapter 5 and Admati (1985), Diamond and Verrecchia (1981), and Verrecchia (1982)].

1.3   Interpreting a Financial Panic

The enormous stock price volatility during October 1987 provides an interesting example of the informational role of prices, and the failure of the Walrasian notion of demand. It is a tautology that the value of a stock is determined by (1) information about expected future payouts (such as dividends), (2) uncertainty about the size of the payouts, (3) the opportunity cost of holding a risky asset (as represented, for example, by the return on a riskless asset), and (4) the premium that the marginal investor must be paid to bear risk rather than hold a relatively riskless asset. If the stock market falls, then economists tend to search for news iterms about the size of expected payouts. Often this search is fruitless.[3] It is now well established that the short term volatility of the stock market cannot be attributed to volatility in the expectation of future payouts.[4] Some have suggested that this is strong evidence against investor rationality, and point to the October 1987 episode as another example of irrational behavior. In contrast, I think that these events and the excessive volatility of stock prices relative to the volatility of expected payouts are evidence in favor of the type of "rationality" embodied in the R.E. approach outlined above, rather than evidence for irrationality. As I argue below, once the Walrasian notion of demand is eliminated, the volatility phenomena can be seen as an expression of a sophisticated trading strategy (used by relatively uninformed individuals) rather than irrationality.

The R.E. models of the stock market explored in chapters 2–5 assume that a stock exists for two dates, and that there is uncertainty and asymmetric information regarding the value of the stock's payoff at the final date. At the first date traders receive information about the size of the final payoff. The information, denoted by y (as above), is one of the determinants of the price at date 1. It is assumed that there is another determinant of the price, namely, the excess demand of traders (henceforth called uninformed traders) who are trading for reasons unrelated to information about the date 2 payoff, and this factor is denoted by n.[5] Therefore the date 1 price, p, is some function of y and n, say, $p(y, n)$.

In this model, suppose a price $p(y, n)$ is observed by a trader i, whose information y_i about the final payoff is, say, pessimistic. He does not know whether this price is high because uninformed traders have a high demand or because other informed traders (observing variables other than y_i) have a high demand. Trader i wants to disentangle these two sources because the latter source of high demand indicates that there is very optimistic information about the final payoff, while the former source of high demand indicates nothing about the final payoff. Put differently, if most of the variability in $p(y, n)$ is due to variability in y rather than in n, then a high value of p indicates that the final payoff on the stock is likely to be high. In this case, the trader will find it optimal to send a limit order to the market expressing a willingness to buy even at a price somewhat higher than average (since he knows that if his order is executed at a high price, then this will be a state of nature where the stock will have a final payoff higher than average). In contrast, if most of the variability in $p(y, n)$ is due to variability in n, then a trader with pessimistic information would not be willing to buy the stock at a price higher than average since he knows that the price is probably high only because uninformed traders have a high excess demand for it. He might instead offer to sell the stock when its price is unusually high.

The above discussion is somewhat artificial since it posits a two-period world, and gives no hint as to why there is noninformation based trading. I believe that a major source of noninformation based trading derives from the use of dynamic trading strategies that exist precisely because there are many trading periods. In much of the literature on multiperiod consumption and portfolio optimization, there is no clear focus on preferences that require systematic, nonlinear, portfolio rebalancing. Quite to the contrary, there is a strong focus on homothetic preferences, where it is optimal to invest a constant proportion of wealth in stocks [see, e.g., Merton (1971)]. This should be contrasted with preferences that exhibit a desire for "portfolio insurance" [see Leland (1980)]. An example of such preferences is given by an objective such as, Maximize end-of-horizon expected utility of wealth *subject to the constraint that wealth surely remains above a predetermined "floor."*[6] If a floor is chosen such that it can be achieved if all the portfolio wealth is invested in a risk free asset at the initial date, then this objective is meaningful and is achieved as follows. When wealth is substantially above the floor, a large fraction of the portfolio is invested in risky assets (such as common stock) to expose the portfolio to the high expected returns offered by risky assets. However, if wealth falls toward the floor, then risky assets are replaced by risk free assets, so that the portfolio is invested exclusively in risk free assets as wealth reaches the floor. If the risky asset value follows a logarithmic Brownian motion, then the optimal strategy is to trade the asset dynamically so as to synthesize the payoff of a put option with a strike price given by the floor.

In 1987, prior to October, approximately $70 billion worth of equity was managed by a dynamic trading strategy involving the synthesis of put options.[7] On October 19, 1987, approximately $5 billion in equity was sold pursuant to the above strategy.[8] This may well be the "tip of the iceberg." It is possible that a substantial number of investors have preferences that lead them to follow less formal "portfolio insurance" trading strategies. This strategy is a formalization of a classic risk management strategy that attempts to lock in capital gains by selling after each fall in the stock market, so that the exposure to downside risk is limited. Unfortunately, these types of strategies cause investors to respond to price moves in a highly correlated manner that can cause an enormous rise in volatility. It is obviously impossible for all investors to lock in capital gains by selling when the stock market reaches a particular level. Their attempts to do so will cause the price to jump down below that level. Dynamic trading strategies that cause an investor to want to hold less of a risky asset as the price falls, and more as it rises, obviously raise the sensitivity of the market clearing price to news about underlying asset payoffs. Chapter 6 discusses this in more detail and explains how the use of "strategies" (such as those designed to synthesize a put option), rather than the direct trading of appropriate contingent claims, can raise volatility. In particular, securities that are redundant in the Black-Scholes (1973) model are actually not redundant because of the important informational role of real securities prices.

I believe that a major component of a financial panic is the desire of a large fraction of equity holders to reduce their equity exposure at the same time (after observing a fall in price). They do so not because they are informed about future payoffs, but simply to limit their exposure to risk. It should be noted that on October 19, 1987, over 600 million shares were traded on the New York Stock Exchange, and this was almost three times the previous record high volume day. This suggests that a primary component of a panic is not only the revaluation of the worth of equities but a desire to reallocate substantially the holding of risky assets in the economy.

How do these remarks relate to Rational Expectations? As noted earlier, an investor with private information looks to price for a summary of the information of other traders. At the instant at which a large number of sell orders arrive at the market, a trader does not know whether this represents strongly negative information about future payoffs or merely the fact that some equity holders have become more risk averse (say, through the implementation of a dynamic trading strategy) after receiving minor bad news about payoffs.[9] The pessimistic component of the information in the observed selling event tends to lower the value that an investor who observes no other negative information puts on equity payoffs, because a large current sell imbalance at the last price is always partially a signal that some traders currently possess information indicating that the last price overvalued the stocks' payoffs. Thus, the fact that investors extract information from price makes a rational expectations price $p(y, n)$ much more sensitive to n (i.e., to preference related shifts in the demand for equities) than occurs in the standard Walrasian model.

A panic is therefore the compounding of two phenomena. First, even if all investors have the same information, then the use of "portfolio insurance" types of trading strategies will greatly increase the sensitivity of the market clearing price to small amounts of news when that price is near the desired "floor" of investors. Second, if investors do not all share the same information, then even an investor who does not have "portfolio insurance" preferences will have a demand function very sensitive to small price movements when he rationally attempts to infer information from price movements. Ex-post, we label an event a "panic" when a group of investors has shifted out of equities for noninformational reasons, and this shift has caused substantial numbers of other investors to shift out of equities because they think that the price has moved for informational reasons. Of course, at the time the "panic" occurred, the uninformed investors actually used their rational expectations to infer that the price move had its normal informational component; they did not know that it actually represented a shift in risk aversion by some other group in the economy.

Notes

1. See the following for discussions of models where the assumption of perfect competition is dropped but the same type of idea is used: Kyle (1984), Milgrom (1981), Milgrom and Stokey (1982).

2. What would happen if *everyone* submitted "market orders"? The market clearing price would be indeterminate. Indeed, the R.E. models where price fully aggregates information [e.g., Grossman (1976) and chapters 2 and 3] often have the property that demand (evaluated at the market clearing price) is independent of the realization of $p(y)$. As Hellwig (1980) has pointed out, such models should be considered as the limiting case of models where price does not fully aggregate information, and thus where each person's demand varies with price and his private information.

3. See, e.g., Roll (1986).

4. See, e.g., Shiller (1987). Though some writers have criticized Shiller's assumptions, e.g., Marsh and Merton (1986); no one has succeeded in explaining short term stock price variability.

5. These traders are (with unjust condescension) called "noise" traders by Kyle (1985) and Black (1986).

6. See Rubinstein (1985).

7. See Leland and Rubinstein (1988, p. 46).

8. See Gammill and Marsh (1988, p. 29). To put these numbers in perspective, note that a New York Stock Exchange average trading volume of 175 million shares, and an average price per share of $35, gives a dollar volume of $6.125 billion.

9. They have become more risk averse, not because their preferences have shifted, but because at values of wealth close to their desired "floor" on wealth, their indirect utility function of wealth exhibits higher risk aversion.

References

Admati, Anat R. "A Noisy Rational Expectations Equilibrium for Multi-Asset Securities Markets," *Econometrica*, Vol. 53 (May 1985), 629–657.

Black, Fischer. "Noise," *The Journal of Finance*, Vol. 41 (July 1986), 529–540.

Black, F., and M. Scholes. "The Pricing of Options and Other Corporate Liabilities," *Journal of Political Economy*, Vol. 81 (May–June 1973), 637–659.

Diamond, Douglas W., and Robert E. Verrecchia. "Information Aggregation in Noisy Rational Expectations Model," *Journal of Financial Economics*, Vol. 9 (September 1981), 221–235.

Gammill, J. F., and T. Marsh. "Trading Activity and Price Behavior in the Stock and Stock Index Futures Markets in October 1987," *Journal of Economic Prespectives*, Vol. 2, No. 3 (Summer 1988), 25–44.

Grossman, S. "On the Efficiency of Competitive Stock Markets Where Traders have Diverse Information," *Journal of Finance*, Vol. 31, No. 2 (May 1976), 573–584.

Grossman, S. "Future Results on the Informational Efficiency of Competitive Stock Markets," *Journal of Economic Theory*, Vol. 18, No. 1 (June 1978), 81–101.

Grossman, S. "An Introduction to the Theory of Rational Expectations under Asymmetric Information," *Review of Economic Studies*, Vol. 68 (1981), 541–559.

Grossman, S., and J. Stiglitz. "Information and Competitive Price Systems," *American Economic Review*, Vol. 66, No. 2 (May 1976), 246–253.

Hayek, F. "The Use of Knowledge in Society," *American Economic Review* (September 1945).

Hellwig, M. "On the Aggregation of Information in Competitive Markets," *Journal of Economic Theory*, Vol. 22 (1980), 477–498.

Kreps, D. M. "In Honor of Sandy Grossman, Winner of the John Bates Clark Medal," *Journal of Economic Perspectives*, Vol. 2, No. 2 (Spring 1988), 111–135.

Kyle, Albert S. "Continuous Auctions and Insider Trading," *Econometrica*, Vol. 53 (November 1985), 1315–1335.

Leland, H. "Who Should Buy Portfolio Insurance?" *Journal of Finance*, Vol. 35 (May 1980), 581–594.

Leland, H. and M. Rubinstein. "Comments on the Market Crash: Six Months After," *Journal of Economic Perspectives*, Vol. 2, No. 3 (Summer 1988) 45–50.

Merton, Robert C. "Optimum Consumption and Portfolio Rules in a Continuous-Time Model," *Journal of Economic Theory*, Vol. 3 (December 1971), 373–413.

Milgrom, P. "Rational Expectations, Information Acquisition, and Competitive Bidding," *Econometrica*, Vol. 49 (1981), 921–944.

Milgrom, Paul, and Nancy Stokey. "Information, Trade and Common Knowledge," *Journal of Economic Theory* Vol. 26 (January 1982), 17–27.

Roll, R. "Orange Juice and Weather," *The American Economic Review* Vol. 74, No. 5, 861–880.

Rubinstein, M. "Alternative Paths to Portfolio Insurance," *Financial Analysts Journal* (July–August 1985), 42–52.

Shiller, R. "Do Stock Prices Move Too Much to be Justified by Subsequent Changes in Dividends?" *American Economic Review*, Vol. 71 (June 1981), 421–436.

Shiller, R. "Investor Behavior in the October 1987 Stock Market Crash: Survey Evidence" National Bureau of Economic Research Working Paper No. 2446 (November 1987).

Verrecchia, R. "Information Acquisition in a Noisy Rational Expectations Economy," *Econometrica*, Vol. 50 (1982), 1415–1430.

2

An Introduction to the Theory of Rational Expectations under Asymmetric Information

2.1 Introduction

Every good economics textbook contains the cliché that market prices provide signals that facilitate the allocation of resources to their best use. In a world not subject to random shocks, consumers and producers when faced with competitive prices need look no further than their own preferences or production technology to be able to make a decision. They need give no thought to the tastes, endowments, or technology of other agents. However, in a world subject to random shocks, this is no longer the case. Agents are faced with the problem of forecasting future states of nature and, more important, of forecasting the impact of these states on the actions of other agents. Rational expectations theories provide a model of how agents make those forecasts.

In a world subject to random shocks, it will be the case that agents acquire (or at least attempt to acquire) information about the future realization of the shocks. It will, in general, be the case that different agents have access to different information. The fact that information is dispersed throughout the economy has the potential to cause a misallocation of resources relative to what would be the case if all agents knew everything. An efficient allocation of resources will in general require the transfer of information from consumers who have some information about their future demands to producers who can take current actions to mitigate avoidable scarcities or surpluses.

Though many classical and neoclassical writers emphasize the informational role of prices, the standard Marshallian or Walrasian model of competitive equilibrium does not involve prices transferring information across traders. The purpose of this chapter is to show that rational expectations models are radically different from Walrasian models in an economy where traders have diverse information. This is demonstrated by showing that unlike what occurs in a Walrasian equilibrium of an economy with hetero-geneous information, if there is a complete set of insurance markets and utility is additively separable over time, then there exists a rational expec-tations equilibrium that gives consumers the same allocation as if each consumer has access to all of the economy's information. This implies that, under the above assumptions, a central planner with all the economy's information could not Pareto dominate the competitive allocation achieved when traders have diverse information and rational expectations.

This chapter makes *no* attempt to survey the literature on rational expectations. The reader is referred to Shiller (1978), Barro (1981) for a survey of macroeconomics and rational expectations, and Radner (1980) for a survey of the microeconomics and mathematical theory of rational ex-pectations. This chapter will, however, try to outline the evolution of the rational expectations concept from a notion of optimal forecasting to a virtually complete departure from the Walrasian model of equilibrium. The rest of this section is devoted to a discussion of prerational expectations ideas.

Expectations are a natural subject for analysis in problems where there is a lag in production. For example, a farmer desires to plant corn "today." The corn is harvested "tomorrow." In order to decide how much to plant, the farmer must estimate the price of corn tomorrow. Most nineteenth century economists attempted to treat this as a problem in capital theory and invoked the idea of a stationary state. In the stationary state, prices are always constant so tomorrow's price will be today's. Uncertainty was ignored or treated as if there were certainty. Alfred Marshall, in contrast, did attempt to deal with uncertainty and price expectations.

Marshall had two distinct expectational theories: a theory for the "short run" and another for the "long run." His long-run theory is captured in the following description of how a cloth manufacturer forms expectations about the future wages he will have to pay workers. Marshall notes that the manufacturer "in estimating the wages required to call forth an ade-quate supply of labour to work a certain class of looms he might take the current wages ... or he might argue ... that looking forward over several years so as to allow for immigration he might take the normal rate of wages at a rather lower rate than that prevailing at the time ... or [the cloth manufacturer] might think that wages of weavers ... were abnormally low ... in consequence of a too sanguine view having been taken of the prospects of the trade a generation ago" (book V, chapter V, section 1).

The above passage is extraordinary because the cloth manufacturer is thinking about the determinants of future wages. He is estimating future wages by estimating the determinants of wages. Even more extraordinary, the manufacturer has a very simple Marshallian model for the determinants of future wages; e.g., a large supply of immigrants will drive down wages. As we shall see below, the essence of rational expectations (R.E.) is that agents have some economic model of the economy that relates the exogenous variables to the endogenous variables that he is interested in forecasting. Marshall defined the "normal price" to be the price where the supply curve intersects the demand curve. When, e.g., the demand curve undergoes a permanent shift, the normal price will change. Marshall's "short-run" analysis assumed that firms will not directly observe the factors that shift the demand curve. Instead, firms (assumed to produce with a lag) see that the price they get for their usual output changes. When this occurs, firms have static expectations; i.e. today they invest expecting tomorrow's price to be the same as today's. This will lead to a new output tomorrow and a new market clearing price. The new price will not be the price that firms expected, since they expected price to be unchanged. Further, the expectations that firms hold at t about the price at $t + 1$ lead to production decisions at t and output at $t + 1$ which determine the actual price at $t + 1$.[1]

Hicks (1939, p. 132) suggested the term perfect foresight for the situation where producers anticipate a price and then engage in production decisions with the property that the actual price which comes about is the anticipated price. The key point that Hicks emphasized is that the expectations held by firms about future *endogenous* variables (such as tomorrow's price of corn) actually help determine the true value of the future endogenous variables. Thus perfect foresight is an equilibrium concept rather than a condition of individual rationality.

After Hicks, uncertainty was explicitly introduced into models. In section 2.2 we shall review some of the ideas that surrounded econometric modeling of expectations. Then the applied economic theories that introduced "rational expectations" will be covered along with the simultaneous generalization of Hicks's perfect foresight idea to the case of uncertainty. Section 2.3 introduces a simple model with asymmetric information and argues that markets will not clear at the standard Walrasian equilibrium prices if traders have rational expectations. Section 2.4 proves the chapter's main theorem: If there is a complete set of markets and utility is additively separable over time, then a rational expectations equilibrium always exists that completely aggregates all traders' information and leads to allocations that are as if each trader had all of the economy's information. Section 2.5 contains conclusions.

2.2 Rational Expectations

In econometric modeling, R.E. grew out of dissatisfaction with *ad hoc* models of expectation formation. Perhaps one of the first *ad hoc* models of expectation formation to be estimated was by Irving Fisher (1930) in his celebrated work on inflationary expectations and their relationship to nominal interest rates. In what was to become standard practice for many years, Fisher assumed that the expected rate of inflation for year T was a weighted average of the actual rate of inflation in years previous to T (i.e., the rate of inflation acticipated for year T is a distributed lag of the actual rates in previous years). This *ad hoc* approach to expectations was refined and modified throughout the next two decades. For example, Nerlove (1958) used the "adaptive expectations" model where the period t corn price anticipated by a farmer p_t^a satisfies

$$p_t^a = p_{t-1}^a + \eta(p_{t-1} - p_{t-1}^a),$$

where p_{t-1} is the actual spot price at time t and $0 < \eta < 1$. This is, of course, just another distributed lag model:

$$p_t^a = \eta \sum_{j=0}^{\infty} (1 - \eta)^j p_{t-j-1}.^2 \tag{1}$$

Since econometric studies rarely had enough data to estimate arbitrary distributed lags with any confidence, it became essential to put some *a priori* restrictions on the form of the lag structure. One restriction, suggested by Muth (1960), was that the distributed lag should be "rational." By this he meant that if the sequence of actual prices $\{p_t\}_{t=-\infty}^{t=+\infty}$ is a particular stochastic process, then the anticipated period t price p_t^a, as of period $t - 1$, should be given by $p_t^a = E[p_t | p_{t-1}, p_{t-2}, \ldots]$. That is, if the farmer knows the stochastic structure generating prices, then the price he expects (i.e., anticipates) for time t is the conditional expectation of p_t given all past realizations of the stochastic process. The farmer is being rational in that he is correctly computing the true conditional expectation. For example, in the adaptive expectations model, the distributed lag that defined p_t^a is given without any reference to the actual stochastic process generating $\{p_t\}$. In particular, suppose that

$$p_t = \begin{cases} 1 & \text{for} \quad t \leq 1 \\ 2 & \text{for} \quad t \geq 2. \end{cases}$$

Then under adaptive expectations

$p_2^a = 1, \qquad p_3^a = 1(1 - \eta) + 2\eta,$

$p_4^a = (1 + \eta)(1 - \eta) + 2\eta, \qquad \ldots, \qquad \lim_{t \to \infty} p_t^a = 2.$

While under a rational lag structure,

$p_2^a = E[p_2 | p_1, p_2, \ldots] = 2 \qquad \text{since} \quad p_2 \equiv 2.$

Under adaptive expectations, it takes time for people to learn that price has changed from 1 to 2 because all they do is look at past prices. Under R.E., people know the price process, so in this simple example they know that price has changed permanently from 1 to 2 after $t = 1$. Note that this sort of R.E. is not an equilibrium concept. It is merely a statement of internal consistency. If an agent thinks the price process is $\{p_t\}$, then the expected price as of $t - 1$ is $E[p_t | p_{t-1}, p_{t-2}, \ldots]$. For it to be anything else, the agent would have to know more than past prices (i.e., have some other source of information about p_t) or he would have to have forgotten $p_{t-1}, p_{t-2}, \ldots$.

From the above, it may seem as if R.E. assumes that agents know a lot more about the process generating prices than does the adaptive expectations model. This is true but misleading. Agents know something. Whatever it is that they are uncertain about can be modeled from a Bayesian point of view using the R.E. approach.[3] The problem with an *ad hoc* model such as adaptive expectations is that it assumes that agents have *too little* uncertainty about the structure. Agents act as if they are *certain* that the stochastic process generating prices has some *ad hoc* form, such as equation (1).

Quite naturally, the next question to arise in the literature was, Where does the stochastic process $\{p_t\}$ come from? The assumption that agents use a rational lag structure does not help econometric estimation by adding reasonable a priori restrictions because the econometrician must still make some a priori assumption (which he has too little data to check) about the stochastic process $\{p_t\}$. This problem generated the next contribution, which was a return to, and generalization of, Hicks's perfect foresight idea. In a seminal paper, Muth (1961) presented a perfect foresight model of a stochastic economy. Muth's basic idea can be described by the following simple model. Let a single firm's output q_t in period t have a cost of production $C(q_t)$. Assume that there are many firms. Suppose that at time t the market demand for the firm's product is

$$\tilde{p}_t = D(Q_t, \tilde{\varepsilon}_t), \qquad (2)$$

where $\tilde{\varepsilon}_t$ is a random variable summarizing the stochastic factors affecting demand at t, while p_t is the price at which the total output Q_t will be demanded. Throughout this chapter, we shall put a "˜" above a symbol to indicate that it is a random variable. For a given Q_t, $\tilde{p}_t$ is a random variable because $\tilde{\varepsilon}_t$ is stochastic. Muth assumed that firms, acting as price takers, maximize expected profit

$$E\tilde{\pi}_t = E\tilde{p}_t q_t - C(q_t) \tag{3}$$

Assume that production takes place with a lag so that q_t must be chosen at time $t - 1$. Then the optimal q_t for the firm will be a function of $E\tilde{p}_t$, say, $q_t = H(E\tilde{p}_t)$, where $H(\cdot)$ is the inverse of the marginal cost function. If there are N identical firms, then total supply is $Q_t = NH(E\tilde{p}_t)$, and the actual market price will be given by the random variable

$$\tilde{p}_t = D(NH(E\tilde{p}_t), \tilde{\varepsilon}_t). \tag{4}$$

Equation (4) makes clear the point emphasized by Hicks, namely, the expected period t price held by firms at $t - 1$ (i.e. $E\tilde{p}_t$) determines their production decision and hence total output at t, which in turn determines the actual spot price at t. Suppose there is a number p^* such that

$$p^* = ED(NH(p^*), \tilde{\varepsilon}_t), \tag{5}$$

where the expectation in (5) is taken with respect to the distribution of $\tilde{\varepsilon}_t$. If p^* solves (5), then it is a perfect foresight equilibrium because firms anticipating a price of p^* make production decisions $NH(p^*)$ so that next period's spot price is a random variable $D(NH(p^*), \tilde{\varepsilon}_t)$ with mean (i.e., expected value of) p^*. Muth called p^* the rational expectations equilibrium price. Note that the equilibrium price is a random variable $D(NH(p^*), \tilde{\varepsilon}_t)$ not a number. Muth, by assuming risk neutrality and nonstochastic production, was able to provide a model that used certainty equivalents, and thus avoided the invention of the idea of a stochastic equilibrium.

Note that rational expectations is an equilibrium concept. It is a stochastic equilibrium, where the prices are random variables rather than numbers as in a Walrasian equilibrium. To see this more clearly, consider a model where certainty equivalent prices will not work. Assume that production is random. Let l_{t-1} denote the inputs chosen at time $t - 1$, and let $C(l_{t-1})$ be their cost. Further, let output at t be given by $\tilde{q}_t = f(l_{t-1}, \tilde{v}_t)$, where $\tilde{v}_t$ is a random shock affecting the production of all firms, such as the weather. The market-clearing price at time t will be some function of the random shocks affecting supply and demand, say, $p(\tilde{\varepsilon}_t, \tilde{v}_t)$. A rational expectations equilibrium is a price function $p^0(\tilde{\varepsilon}_t, \tilde{v}_t)$ such that

if l_{t-1}^0 solves max $Ep^0(\tilde{\varepsilon}_t, \tilde{v}_t) f(l_{t-1}, \tilde{v}_t) - C(l_{t-1})$, then $\quad$ (6a)
$\quad\quad\quad\quad l_{t-1}$

$$p^0(\varepsilon_t, v_t) = D(Nf(l_{t-1}^0, v_t), \varepsilon_t) \quad\quad \text{for all} \quad (\varepsilon_t, v_t). \quad\quad (6b)$$

Condition (6a) requires that firms choose l_{t-1} to maximize expected profit, acting as price takers with respect to the price random variable $p^0(\tilde{\varepsilon}, \tilde{v})$. Condition (6b) requires that the anticipated price random variable $p^0(\tilde{\varepsilon}_t, \tilde{v}_t)$ is the actual market-clearing price for every realization of $(\tilde{\varepsilon}_t, \tilde{v}_t)$. Since realized output $f(l_{t-1}^0, \tilde{v}_t)$ is correlated with $p^0(\tilde{\varepsilon}_t, \tilde{v}_t)$, firms need to know more than the average price next period. A firm needs to know the whole equilibrium price distribution, in order to find its optimal l_{t-1}.

R.E. is a condition of market equilibrium rather than being only a condition of individual rationality. However, the information requirements it makes on traders are no different from those in models with rational distributed lags. The latter models assume that traders know the stochastic process generating prices and use this knowledge in their decision problem. In an R.E. equilibrium, the information requirements are no greater; traders need only know the stochastic process generating the equilibrium price. Though the theory of market-clearing tells the *economist* about the underlying structural factors that determine price (such as the forms of the cost and demand functions), in equilibrium *traders* need not know anything about the structural form of the economy. They need only know the relationship between price and the stochastic factors that determine output. Of course, the theory does not explain how equilibrium comes about.

2.3   Equilibrium under Asymmetric Information

Thus far we have considered situations where production decisions are made at $t - 1$ and uncertainty is resolved at date t. We have assumed that at $t - 1$ all traders have the same information about the various stochastic factors that determine price and output at date t. However, it is likely to be the case that traders will not have the same information. An individual producer will in general have more information about the demands of his own customers and the productivity of his own land than he has about those of other producers. Thus information is likely to be distributed throughout the economy.

A useful way to model information is to imagine that at time $t - 1$ trader i observes the realization of a random variable $\tilde{y}^i$. In the previous section, $\tilde{\varepsilon}_t$ denoted uncertainty about the state of demand at time t. Therefore $\tilde{y}^i$ will provide information about $\tilde{\varepsilon}_t$ if the two random variables are correlated. For example, let $\tilde{\varepsilon}_t$ represent the amount of rainfall at time t and let $\tilde{y}^i$ represent the wind velocity and humidity observed by agent i at time $t - 1$. Let

$$\tilde{\mathbf{y}}_{t-1} = (\tilde{y}^1, \tilde{y}^2, \tilde{y}^3, \ldots)$$

be the vector of all traders' information at $t - 1$ about $\tilde{\varepsilon}_t$. For the model described in the last section, firm i will choose a production level at $t - 1$ that depends on its information $l_{t-1}(\tilde{y}^i)$. Thus the total input at $t - 1$, say $L_{t-1}(\mathbf{y}_{t-1}) \equiv \sum_i l_{t-1}(\tilde{y}^i)$, will depend on $\mathbf{y}$. Hence the output at t will depend on $\mathbf{y}_{t-1}$. This implies that the market-clearing price at t, say, $P_t(\mathbf{y}_{t-1}, \tilde{\varepsilon}_t, \tilde{v}_t)$, will depend on $\mathbf{y}_{t-1}$ as well as $\tilde{\varepsilon}_t$ and $\tilde{v}_t$. Thus P_t reveals some information about $\mathbf{y}_{t-1}$. This is because $P_t(\mathbf{y}_{t-1}, \tilde{\varepsilon}_t, \tilde{v}_t)$ will be correlated with $\mathbf{y}_{t-1}$.

Unfortunately, the information transmitted by P_t about $\mathbf{y}_{t-1}$ is too late in coming to affect production at $t - 1$. Each producer at $t - 1$ would like to learn the information possessed by other traders at $t - 1$. What market forces are there that will allow producers to use each other's information at time $t - 1$ when they need it? Grossman (1975b) pointed out that whenever traders have heterogeneous beliefs there are incentives to open speculative markets, which, as we shall see below, tends to homogenize their beliefs. In the above example, traders have different information about $\tilde{\varepsilon}_t$, so $EP_t(\mathbf{y}_{t-1}, \tilde{\varepsilon}_t, \tilde{v}_t)$ will in general differ across the traders. These traders thus have different price expectations as of $t - 1$ and this creates an incentive for the opening of a futures market at time $t - 1$, where they can bet against each other. The futures price at $t - 1$ will transmit some information across traders at $t - 1$.

The notion that current prices can convey current information is quite complex. This notion was first used by Lucas (1972).[4] The fundamental insight presented in his remarkable model can be understood as follows. He considered an economy with a storable commodity (money). The current price of the commodity p is determined by a variable α that represents *permanent* increases in the supply of the commodity, and also by the current *temporary* demand for the commodity, denoted by β; denote this price function by $p(\alpha, \beta)$. Traders do not observe α and β directly. However, a trader would like to know what α is because it affects the future value of the storable commodity. In our previous discussions of R.E., traders were trying to forecast a future endogenous variable by forecasting its exogenous determinants [e.g., traders went from their knowledge about the probability distribution of $(\tilde{\varepsilon}, \tilde{v})$ to knowledge of $p_t(\tilde{\varepsilon}, \tilde{v})$]. Lucas, in an extraordinary insight, reversed the logic. He argued that if traders observe the current price p and know the relationship between p and α, β, then they can use their observation of p to learn about the current realization of α and β.

Green (1973) used the same equilibrium concept but in the context of traders with heterogeneous information. In Green's model there is a class of traders (called informed traders) who have some information, say, α, about the future value of the commodity. Another group of traders (called uninformed) do not know α. There may be other temporary factors denoted by β affecting the current spot price of the commodity. Hence the current price is some function $\hat{p}(\alpha, \beta)$. As in Lucas, uninformed traders observe the current price $\hat{p}$ and try to learn something about α.

Clearly, in a world subject to uncertainty and asymmetric information, traders will attempt to use their information in a speculative market to earn profit. In so doing, information can get transmitted across agents. To model this in the clearest way, we shall model an economy with uncertainty and a complete set of (speculative) state-contingent futures markets. Let $\tilde{s}$ be a random variable that takes on n values $s_1, s_2, \ldots, s_n$. Let there be (without loss of generality) two periods. In the first period, firm f makes a production decision that leads to an output at the second period of $z_f(s, l_f)$, which depends on the realized state s and the amount of input in the initial period l_f. For notational simplicity, assume that z_f and l_f are scalars. Each consumer h has a von Neumann–Morgenstern utility function $u^h(C_1^h, C_2^h, s)$ over consumption in the two periods (where C_1^h and C_2^h are scalars) that can be state-dependent. Further, each consumer has an endowment in the initial period e_1^h, and a date 2 endowment $e_2^h(s)$.

In the above economy, uncertainty enters preferences, endowments, and production opportunities. Let there be H consumers and F firms. We shall assume that each trader h has information y^h about s. That is, the vector $(\tilde{y}^1, \tilde{y}^2, \ldots, \tilde{y}^H, \tilde{s}) \equiv (\tilde{y}, \tilde{s})$ has some well-defined joint distribution, with $\pi_i(y)$ defined to be the conditional probability that $\tilde{s} = s_i$ given that $\tilde{y} = y$. Consumer h observes y^h at date 1 and uses this to make inferences about the realization of $\tilde{s}$ at date 2.

We first consider the usual Walrasian equilibrium for the economy described above. In the first period, consumers can trade the current consumption good for promised delivery of a good in each of the states s. Let p_i be the price in terms of the date 1 consumption good for the delivery of the date 2 good if and only if $\tilde{s} = s_i$. For example, $\sum_{i=1}^{n} p_i$ is the current price of a good to be delivered with certainty tomorrow, and

$$R_f \equiv \sum_{i=1}^{n} p_i z_f(s_i, l_f) \tag{7}$$

would be the market value at date 1 of firm f. Each consumer h endowed with shares $\tilde{\Theta}^h_f$ of firm f will choose to purchase state-contingent consumption

$$C^h_1, C^h_{21}, C^h_{22}, C^h_{23}, \ldots, C^h_{2n}) \equiv C^h_1, \tilde{C}^h_2)$$

to maximize his expected utility subject to his budget constraint: choose $(C^h_1, \tilde{C}^h_2)$ to maximize

$$E[u^h(C^h_1, \tilde{C}^h_2, \tilde{s}) | y^h] \equiv \sum_{i=1}^{n} u(C^h_1, C^h_{2i}, s_i) \pi^h_i(y^h) \tag{8a}$$

subject to

$$C^h_1 + \sum_{i=1}^{n} C^h_{2i} P_i \leq e^h_1 + \sum_{i=1}^{n} e^h_{2i} P_i + \sum_{f=1}^{F} \bar{\Theta}^h_f(R_f - l_f). \tag{8b}$$

The expectation in (8a) is evaluated using the conditional probability that $\tilde{s} = s_i$ given that $\tilde{y}^h = y^h$, $\pi^h_i(y^h)$. Let $\mathbf{P} \equiv (P_1, P_2, \ldots, P_n)$. We can denote the solution to (8) by $C^h_1(\mathbf{P}, y^h)$, $\tilde{C}^h_2(\mathbf{P}, y^h)$, which represents the consumers' demand function for current consumption and state-contingent claims. For example, if the consumer has information indicating that state s_j is very likely relative to its cost P_j, then he will buy a lot of consumption in that state. When many consumers have information that a state is very likely, they will demand a lot of consumption in that state and this will tend to bid up the price. Thus the "market-clearing" price $\mathbf{P}$ will be some function of traders' information $\mathbf{P}(\mathbf{y})$.

To define the "market-clearing" price, assume that each firm f chooses l_f to maximize profit:

$$l_f(\mathbf{P}) \text{ solves } \max_{l_f} R_f - l_f.^5 \tag{9}$$

Note that realized output is a random variable, but all risks are priced so the firm faces a simple nonstochastic optimization problem. Let

$$\tilde{z}_f(\mathbf{P}) \equiv (z_f(s_1, l_f(\mathbf{P})), z_f(s_2, l_f(\mathbf{P})), \ldots, z_f(s_n, l_f(\mathbf{P}))) \tag{10}$$

be the supply function of f.

We now define the usual Walrasian equilibrium where supply equals demand for all the commodities.[6] $\mathbf{P}(\mathbf{y})$ is a Walrasian equilibrium if and only if, for each y,

$$\sum_{h=1}^{H} C^h_1(\mathbf{P}(\mathbf{y}), y^h) = \sum_{h=1}^{H} e^h_1 - \sum_f l_f(\mathbf{P}(\mathbf{y})), \tag{11a}$$

$$\sum_{h=1}^{H} \tilde{C}_1^h(\mathbf{P}(\mathbf{y}), y^h) = \sum_{h=1}^{H} \tilde{e}_2^h + \sum_{f=1}^{F} \tilde{z}_f(\mathbf{P}(\mathbf{y})). \tag{11b}$$

Equation (11a) requires that supply equal demand at date 1. Equation (11b) requires that, for each state s, supply equals demand. Recall that $\tilde{C}_1^h$ is a vector with the ith component being trader h's consumption in state i at date 2. Note that since demand $\sum_h C_2^h(\mathbf{P}, y^h)$ depends on $\mathbf{y}$, the market-clearing price vector will depend on $\mathbf{y}$. Thus, (11) is to be interpreted as, For each $\mathbf{y}$ compute a Walrasian equilibrium price vector—denote the $\mathbf{P}$ that corresponds to a given $\mathbf{y}$ by $\mathbf{P}(\mathbf{y})$.[7]

Note that $\mathbf{P}(\mathbf{y})$ reflects information about $\mathbf{y}$ in the sense that a trader or an econometrician who observes that $\mathbf{P}(\mathbf{y}) = \mathbf{P}$ can make an inference about $\mathbf{y}$. If traders have information indicating that $\tilde{s} = s_i$ is very likely, then they will bid up the price (at date 1) of the consumption good that is to be delivered at date 2. Thus $P_i(\mathbf{y})$ is likely to be high when there is information that the event $\tilde{s} = s_i$ has high probability, i.e., when $\pi_i(\mathbf{y})$ is high. Conversely, if a particular trader observes a high $P_i(\mathbf{y})$, then he can infer (to some extent) that other traders must have information that $\tilde{s} = s_i$ is likely [i.e., that $\pi_i(\mathbf{y})$ is high].

The fact that prices reveal information is not remarkable. It is, however, remarkable that the traders in the economy described by (11) ignore the information in prices. The standard Walrasian equilibrium assumes that traders form their demands based upon their own private information [see equation (8)]. Traders totally ignore the fact that $\mathbf{P}(\mathbf{y})$ reveals something about $\mathbf{y}$. This can lead to allocations that are quite poor relative to what would arise if economists modeled traders as if they could learn from prices.

These points might be clearer from an example. Suppose that all traders have utility functions given by

$$u^h(C_1, C_{2i}, s) \equiv \alpha^h \ln C_{2i} + C_1, \qquad \alpha^h > 0, \tag{12a}$$

and further that there is no social risk in this economy; i.e.

$$\sum_{h=1}^{H} e_{2i}^h = 1 \qquad \text{for all } i = 1, 2, \ldots, n. \tag{12b}$$

Trader h's demand for consumption in state i can be found to be

$$C_{2i}^h(\mathbf{P}, y^h) = \alpha^h \pi_i^h(y^h) \div P_i. \tag{13}$$

Suppose production is separable across states, so that if a firm puts l_i units of the date 1 consumption good into the activity of producing in date

2-state i consumption, this leads to a date 2-state i output of $f(l_i)$, where $f(\cdot)$ is strictly concave. Thus profit maximization will imply that total output supplied for state i will be some increasing function of P_i, say $q(P_i)$. Therefore "supply equals demand" is given by

$$\sum_h C_{2i}(\mathbf{P}, y^h) = \sum_{h=1}^H e_{2i}^h + q(P_i).$$
(14)

Combining (12)–(14) yields that there is some increasing function $H(\cdot)$ so that the equilibrium price is given by

$$P_i(\mathbf{y}) = H\left(\sum_{h=1}^H \alpha^h \pi_i^h(y^h) \right).$$
(15)

Thus in Walrasian equilibrium the price of state i goods and hence the production of state i goods depends on the weighted sum of the probabilities that each agent puts on the event that $\tilde{s} = s_i$. This might seem like a great job of aggregating trader information. However, that is false. The term $\sum_h \alpha^h \pi_i^h(y^h)$ does not in general completely summarize traders' information. It is an *ad hoc* function of the observation $\mathbf{y} = \{y^h\}$. Further, even if it did completely summarize traders' information, it is being ignored by them when they form their demands.

To be more precise, consider an example where each trader has a little piece of information about $\tilde{s}$, but all the traders' information together completely reveals $\tilde{s}$. For example, let y^h be given by

$$y^h = s + \varepsilon_h,$$
(16a)

where

$$\sum_{h=1}^H \varepsilon_h = 0.$$
(16b)

Then a person who observed $\sum_h y^h$ would know exactly which state would occur at date 2.

It is of some value to compare the Walrasian equilibrium with an economy where each trader has private information to the Walrasian equilibrium that would arise if each trader had all of the economy's information. The economy where each trader is given all the information $\mathbf{y}$ is an artificial device for comparing the quality of the private information equilibrium with what would arise if everyone could observe $\mathbf{y}$. Thus we define

Definition An artificial, fully informed economy equilibrium is a price vector $\mathbf{P}^a(\mathbf{y})$ with demands $C^h(\mathbf{P}, \mathbf{y})$ chosen to maximize $E[u^h(C_1^h, \tilde{C}_2^h, \tilde{s})|\mathbf{y}]$

subject to the budget constraint (8b), such that supply equals demand at $\mathbf{P}^a(\mathbf{y})$. The only difference between the Walrasian equilibrium and the artificial economy equilibrium is that each trader h gets to observe $\mathbf{y}$ (the whole economy's information), which he uses to form his demands in the artificial economy.

In the example given by (12), (13), and (16), the artificial, fully informed equilibrium is very simple. Since $\mathbf{y}$ reveals s exactly, there is no risk given information. If $\tilde{s} = s_i$, then everyone knows this and $P_j^a(\mathbf{y}) = 0$ for $j \neq i$. Thus there will be no production of state $j \neq i$ goods. Note that this is very efficient (in a way that will be made precise below). This is to be compared with the Walrasian equilibrium. In the actual Walrasian equilibrium, each trader h observes only y^h, so $\pi_j(y^h)$ will not be zero for $j \neq i$, even though $\pi_j(\mathbf{y}) = 0$ for $j \neq i$ when $\tilde{s} = s_i$. Therefore there will be some goods with positive prices and resources devoted to their production at date 1 simply because traders had diverse information. The Walrasian equilibrium does not model the idea that diverse information across traders is aggregated in such a way that the allocation is as if each trader possessed all of the economy's information.

The Walrasian equilibrium not only leads to poor allocations under asymmetric information, but also is a bad positive model of equilibrium. A good model of equilibrium prices $\mathbf{P}(\mathbf{y})$ should have the property that, at $\mathbf{P}(\mathbf{y})$, traders have no desired to recontract. We shall now show that sophisticated traders will desire to recontract at the Walrasian price, and thus it is not even market-clearing when traders have rational expectations. To see this, imagine that the Walrasian equilibrium in (7)–(14) is OK and that the economy described above is replicated many times so that each trader h observes many realizations of $(\mathbf{P}(\tilde{\mathbf{y}}), \tilde{y}^h, \tilde{s})$. By replication, we mean that people and commodities live for two periods for a particular draw of $\tilde{\mathbf{y}}, \tilde{s}$. Then new people are born and there is another draw of $\tilde{\mathbf{y}}, \tilde{s}$, etc. Each generation remembers its parents' information. Then eventually traders of family h will come to know the joint distribution of $\tilde{s}$ given $\tilde{y}^h, \tilde{\mathbf{P}}$. A trader will in general find that $\text{Prob}(\tilde{s}|y^h) \neq \text{Prob}(\tilde{s}|\mathbf{P}(\mathbf{y}), y^h)$; i.e. observing $\tilde{\mathbf{P}}$ will lead each trader to change his beliefs because it gives him new information. After traders learn this, they will desire to recontract after observing $\mathbf{P}(\mathbf{y})$, (A smart trader might even say to himself, "Let all the other traders trade naively using their own information. I will wait until the market clears, and after observing the current realization of $\mathbf{P}(\mathbf{y})$, make my purchases of C_1^h, C_{2i}^h to maximize $E[u^h(C_1^h, \tilde{C}_2^h)|y^h, \mathbf{P}(\mathbf{y})]$. Since I am a price taker I will expect to do better than by trading now and maximizing $E[u^h(C_1^h, \tilde{C}_2^h)|y^h]$.")

When traders observe $\mathbf{P}(\mathbf{y})$ and then compute their optimal choices so as to maximize $E[u^h(C_1^h, \tilde{C}_2^h)|y^h, \mathbf{P}(\mathbf{y})]$, $\mathbf{P}(\mathbf{y})$ will no longer, in general, be the market-clearing price that corresponds to $\tilde{\mathbf{y}} = \mathbf{y}$. This is because $\mathbf{P}(\mathbf{y})$ is the market-clearing price when each trader forms his demands naively looking only at his own information, i.e., maximizing $E[u^h|y^h]$. It is important to note that in an economy where all traders have the same information, there is no desire to recontract at the Walrasian equilibrium price. That is exactly why we think of it as a true equilibrium. However, in our situation, traders come to the market with different information. Because of this, the price at which the market clears is itself a very important piece of information to each trader (in that it reveals the information of other traders).

A proper definition of an equilibrium price $\mathbf{P}^0(\mathbf{y})$ is one where there is no desire to recontract when each trader gets what he demands at $\mathbf{P} = \mathbf{P}^0(\mathbf{y})$ after he is informed that the market-clearing price is $\mathbf{P}^0(\mathbf{y})$. At what price $\mathbf{P}^0(\mathbf{y})$ will there be no desire to recontract after traders observe that $\mathbf{P} = \mathbf{P}^0(\mathbf{y})$? This price must have the property that the allocation that each trader h gets is what he demands, when his demand is formed by conditioning on y^h and $\mathbf{P}^0(\mathbf{y})$. This is precisely the property that Lucas (1972) requires of rational expectations under asymmetric information.

A rational expectations equilibrium is a mapping $\mathbf{P}^0(\mathbf{y})$ such that if each consumer h forms his demand $C^h(y^h, \mathbf{P})$ to solve

$$\max E[u(C_1^h, \tilde{C}_2^h, \tilde{s})|\tilde{y}^h = y^h, \mathbf{P}^0(\mathbf{y}) = \mathbf{P}], \quad \text{subject to}$$

$$C_1^h + \sum_{i=1}^n C_{2i}^h P_i \le e_1^h + \sum_{i=1}^n e_{2i}^h P_i + \sum_{f=1}^F \bar{\Theta}_f^h(R_f - l_f),$$

$$(17)$$

and each firm chooses l_f to maximize R_f in (7), then demand equal supply; i.e., for each $\mathbf{y}$

$$\sum_h C_1^h(y^h, \mathbf{P}^0(\mathbf{y})) = \sum_h e_1^h - \sum_f l_f, \qquad (18a)$$

$$\sum_h C_2^h(\mathbf{y}, \mathbf{P}^0(\mathbf{y})) = \sum_h e_{2i}^h + \sum_f z_f(s_i, l_f), \qquad i = 1, 2, \ldots, n. \qquad (18b)$$

In (17), consumer h is assumed to know the joint distribution of $\tilde{s}$, $\mathbf{P}^0(\tilde{\mathbf{y}})$, $\tilde{y}^h$. He then observes a particular realization of $\tilde{\mathbf{P}}^0$ and $\tilde{y}^h$, namely $\mathbf{P}$, y^h. He uses this to compute the conditional probability that $\tilde{s} = s_i$ given that $\mathbf{P}^0(\tilde{\mathbf{y}}) = \mathbf{P}$ and $\tilde{y}^h = y^h$, say $\pi_i^h(\mathbf{P}, y^h)$. Next he chooses the $n + 1$ dimensional vector $(C_1^h, C_{21}^h, C_{22}^h, \ldots, C_{2n}^h)$ to maximize $\sum_{i=1}^n u(C_1^h, C_{2i}^h, s_i)\pi_i^h(\mathbf{P}, y^h)$, subject to his budget constraint. Condition (18) requires that, when $\tilde{y} = y$, $\mathbf{P}^0(\mathbf{y})$ gives the price vector that clears all markets. It is essential to note that consumers will have no desire to recontract after being told that $\mathbf{P}^0(\mathbf{y})$ is the market-clearing price; their demands at $\mathbf{P}^0(\mathbf{y})$ already reflected the knowledge that $\mathbf{P}^0(\mathbf{y})$ tells them about $\tilde{s}$. This equilibrium concept is not subject to the criticism to which the standard Walrasian model is subject. As pointed out earlier in standard Walrasian equilibrium, the fact that $\mathbf{P}(\mathbf{y})$ is a market-clearing price provides traders with new information about $\tilde{s}$ and hence leads them to change their demands at that price—which is equivalent to the statement that they would desire to recontract the instant the market cleared at $\mathbf{P}(\mathbf{y})$ [equivalently, the market simply will not clear at the Walrasian price $\mathbf{P}(\mathbf{y})$].

We shall see in the next section that a rational expectations equilibrium has a remarkable property—it leads to allocations that are as if each trader has *all* of the economy's information. This can be seen very easily for the example given in (12)–(16). The following is a rational expectations equilibrium

$$
\mathbf{P}_i^0(\mathbf{y}) = \begin{cases} 0 & \text{if } \sum_{h=1}^H y^h \neq s_i \\[2mm] H\left(\sum_h \alpha^h\right) & \text{if } \sum_{h=1}^H y^h = s_i. \end{cases}
\tag{19}
$$

That is, $\mathbf{P}^0(\mathbf{y})$ is a price vector with zeros in all of its components except for the component j with the property that $\sum_{h=1}^H y^h = s_j$. Consumers faced with a price vector like (19) will know that there is exactly one state that will occur for sure: state $\sum_{h=1}^H y^h$. Therefore, their demands in that state will be given by (13), where $\pi_i^h(y^h) = 1$ for that state. Hence the price where supply equals demand is given by (15). In this example, the current information of the whole economy $\mathbf{y}$ is sufficient to predict the realization of $\tilde{s}$ exactly. When traders observe a price vector with zeros everywhere except in its ith component, this tells them that $\tilde{s} = s_i$, and the economy is reduced to a Walrasian economy with two goods C_1 and C_{2i}, where everyone has full information. In other words, the allocation for the rational expectations economy where traders begin with heterogeneous information will be the same as that for the artificial, fully informed economy defined previously. We shall see in the next section that this result is true under arbitrary information structures and more general preferences than that considered for the example in (12)–(16).

2.4   The Existence and Information Content of Rational Expectations Prices

In the previous section we showed that, in situations of heterogeneous information, the usual Walrasian equilibrium does not lead to outcomes that are as if all traders in the economy shared their information freely. The Walrasian allocations are not the same as those that occur in an artificial economy where everyone was fully informed. Walrasian prices simply do not transmit information. We now show that the rational expectations equilibrium price can transmit an enormous amount of information. In particular, our theorem is, If $\{\mathbf{P}(\mathbf{y}), C^h(\mathbf{y}), z_f\}$ is a Walrasian equilibrium for the artificial economy where everyone is fully informed (i.e., where each trader observes all of the economy's information), and each trader has additively separable utility, then $\{\mathbf{P}(\mathbf{y}), C^h(\mathbf{y}), z_f\}$ is a rational expectations equilibrium for the economy where traders have heterogeneous information (i.e., where each trader h only observes component h of $\mathbf{y}$). Note that the Walrasian equilibrium for the fully informed artificial economy cannot be Pareto dominated by a planner who observes all the economy's information. Thus our theorem implies that a planner with all of the economy's information could not Pareto dominate the allocations that arise in a competitive economy where each trader has only a little information, but all traders have rational expectations.

The proof of the theorem is slightly technical, so we provide some intuitive motivation. Define the n-dimensional vector $\boldsymbol{\pi}(\mathbf{y}) = (\pi_1(\mathbf{y}), \pi_2(\mathbf{y}), \ldots, \pi_n(\mathbf{y}))$, where $\pi_i(\mathbf{y})$ is $\mathrm{Prob}(\tilde{s} = s_i|\mathbf{y})$. Thus $\boldsymbol{\pi}(\mathbf{y})$ is the probability beliefs possessed by a trader with all of the economy's information. Note the following simple fact:

$$\mathrm{Prob}(\tilde{s} = s_i|\boldsymbol{\pi}(\mathbf{y})) = \mathrm{Prob}(\tilde{s} = s_i|\mathbf{y}). \tag{20}$$

That is, the vector $\boldsymbol{\pi}(\mathbf{y})$ completely summarizes the information about $\tilde{s}$ contained in $\mathbf{y}$.[8] Next note that in the artificial economy, where all traders observe $\mathbf{y}$, each trader's demand $C^h(\mathbf{P}, \mathbf{y})$ comes from maximizing $E[u^h|\mathbf{y}]$. But by (20) this is equivalent to maximizing $E[u^h|\boldsymbol{\pi}(\mathbf{y})]$. Therefore we can write his demand as a function of $\mathbf{P}$ and $\boldsymbol{\pi}(\mathbf{y})$: $C^h(\mathbf{P}, \boldsymbol{\pi}(\mathbf{y}))$. The competitive equilibrium price sets supply equal to demand. Therefore the competitive price depends on $\mathbf{y}$ only through $\boldsymbol{\pi}(\mathbf{y})$. So we can write the artificial equilibrium price vector $\mathbf{P}^0(\mathbf{y})$ as $\mathbf{P}^a\boldsymbol{\pi}(\mathbf{y}))$.

Note that there are $n + 1$ commodities $(C_1, C_{21}, \ldots, C_{2n})$ in this economy. Thus there are n relative prices given by the n-vector $\mathbf{P}^a(\boldsymbol{\pi})$. There are n states of nature with probabilities which sum to one. So $\mathbf{P}^a(\boldsymbol{\pi})$ is a function from R^{n-1} into R^n. Suppose that it is an invertible function. Then a trader observing $\mathbf{P}^a(\pi)$ would be able to learn π. This implies that $\mathbf{P}^a(\pi)$ is a rational expectations equilibrium for the economy where trader h observes only y^h amd $\mathbf{P}^a$. To see this, note that trader h forms his demands by solving $\max E[u^h|y^h, \mathbf{P}^a(\pi(y))]$. But since $\mathbf{P}^a(\pi)$ is invertible, this is equivalent to maximizing $E[u^h|y^h, \pi(y)]$, which by (20) is equivalent to maximizing $E[u^h|y]$. Thus trader h's demands would be exactly the same as in the artificial economy. Hence markets will clear at $\mathbf{P}^a(y)$ for the rational expectations economy.

It remains to argue that $\mathbf{P}^a(\pi)$ is invertible in π. That is, we want to argue that if π changes and $\mathbf{P}^a$ stays the same, then all markets will not clear in the artificial fully informed economy. If $\mathbf{P}^a$ stays the same, then when, e.g., π_i, goes up, this is like increasing the quality of the state contingent commodity C_{2i}. This tends to raise everyone's demand for C_{2i}. However, note that when π_i goes up, some other probability π_j must go down. But this only reinforces the increase in demand for C_{2i} because, with von Neumann-Morgenstern utility, goods in mutually exclusive states are substitutes. Complications arise in this story because (a) more than two probabilities may change, and (b) initial period consumption C_1 may change. As the following theorem shows, (a) is not a problem. However, (b) is a problem. For example, if C_1 is a substitute for C_{2i} for some people, and a complement for other people, then there is the possibility that C_1 goes up for some people in such a way that C_{2i} is unchanged, and C_1 goes down for other people in such a way that C_{2i} is unchanged. Presumably for some "knife edge" cases the rise in demand for C_1 exactly offsets the fall in demand for C_1, so that markets clear at unchanged prices where π changes. To avoid this problem, the theorem below assumes that utility is additively separable over time.

We now prove the main theorem, which states that $\mathbf{P}^a(\pi)$ is essentially invertible. Let $(\mathbf{P}^a(\mathbf{y}), C^h(\mathbf{y}) \equiv C^h(\mathbf{P}^a(\mathbf{y}), \mathbf{y}))$ denote the competitive equilibrium to the artificial fully informed economy (See the definition given after (16)].

Theorem 1   *Assume that traders are nonsatiable and, for all traders h and i, $u^h(C_1, C_{2i}, s_i)$ is a strictly concave differentiable function of the argument (C_1, C_{2i}) and that $u^h(C_1, C_{2i}, s_i)$ is additively separable in initial period consumption; i.e. $u^h(C_1, C_{2i}, s_i) = u_1^h(C_1) + u_2^h(C_{2i}, s_i)$. Assume that, for each $\mathbf{y}$, $\pi_i(\mathbf{y}) > 0$ for $i = 1, 2, \ldots, n$, and that each firm's profit maximizing input-output vector is a function (not a correspondence) of market prices. Consider any two realizations of $\tilde{\mathbf{y}}$, say, $\mathbf{y}$ and $\bar{\mathbf{y}}$, which lead to $\pi = \pi(\mathbf{y})$ and $\bar{\pi} = \pi(\bar{\mathbf{y}})$,* *which are distinct (i.e., $\pi \neq \bar{\pi}$). If there exists a trader h such that $C^h(\mathbf{y}) \neq C^h(\bar{\mathbf{y}})$, then $\mathbf{P}^a(\mathbf{y}) \neq \mathbf{P}^a(\bar{\mathbf{y}})$.*

Proof By contradiction. Suppose $\mathbf{P}^a(\mathbf{y}) = \mathbf{P}^a(\bar{\mathbf{y}}) \equiv P$; consider trader h who holds different consumption bundles in the two cases. Since the production decisions of firms depend only on the price vector $\mathbf{P}$ that they face, their market value is unchanged when $\mathbf{y}$ changes to $\bar{\mathbf{y}}$. Hence *all* traders have the same incomes under $\mathbf{y}$ and $\bar{\mathbf{y}}$. Let $(C_1^h, C_{2i}^h)_i \equiv C^h(\mathbf{y})$ and $(\bar{C}_1^h, \bar{C}_{2i}^h)_i \equiv C^h(\bar{\mathbf{y}})$. By revealed preferences for trader h

$$\sum_i u^h(C_1^h, C_{2i}^h, s_i)\pi_i > \sum_i u^h(\bar{C}_1^h, \bar{C}_{2i}^h, s_i)\pi_i. \tag{21}$$

Since $u^h(\cdot, \cdot, s_i)$ is a concave function,

$$u^h(C_1^h, C_{2i}^h, s_i) - u^h(\bar{C}_1^h, \bar{C}_{2i}^h, s_i) \leqq \frac{\partial u^h(\bar{C}_1^h, \bar{C}_{2i}^h, s_i)}{\partial C_1}(C_1^h - \bar{C}_1^h)$$

$$+ \frac{\partial u^h(\bar{C}_1^h, \bar{C}_{2i}^h, s_i)}{\partial C_{2i}}(C_{2i}^h - \bar{C}_{2i}^h). \tag{22}$$

Let $\partial \bar{u}_i^h / \partial C$ denote $\partial u^h(\bar{C}_1, \bar{C}_{2i}, s_i)/\partial C$, and combine (21) and (22) to get

$$\sum_i \left[\frac{\partial \bar{u}_i^h}{\partial C_1}(C_1^h - \bar{C}_1^h) + \frac{\partial \bar{u}_i^h}{\partial C_{2i}}(C_{2i}^h - \bar{C}_{2i}^h) \right]\pi_i > 0. \tag{23}$$

Note that from the first-order conditions to the consumers h's optimization problem when $\mathbf{y} = \bar{\mathbf{y}}$, there exists a number $\bar{\lambda}^h > 0$ such that

$$\sum_i \frac{\partial \bar{u}_i^h}{\partial C_1}\pi_i \leqq \bar{\lambda}^h \qquad \text{with equality if} \quad \bar{C}_1^h > 0; \tag{24a}$$

$$\frac{\partial \bar{u}_i^h}{\partial C_{2i}}\bar{\pi}_i \leqq \bar{\lambda}^h P_i \qquad \text{with equality if} \quad \bar{C}_{2i}^h > 0. \tag{24b}$$

Combining (23) and (24) yields

$$(C_1^h - \bar{C}_1^h) \sum_{i=1}^n \frac{\partial \bar{u}_i}{\partial C_1}\pi_i + \bar{\lambda}^h \sum_{i=1}^n P_i(C_{2i}^h - \bar{C}_{2i}^h)\frac{\pi_i}{\bar{\pi}_i} > 0, \tag{25a}$$

where we have used the fact that if $\bar{C}_1^h$ or $\bar{C}_{2i}^h$ is zero, then it contributes nothing to the sum. Note that the assumption of additively separable utility implies that

$$\sum_{i=1}^n \frac{\partial \bar{u}_i}{\partial C_1}\pi_i = \sum_{i=1}^n \frac{\partial \bar{u}_i}{\partial C_1}\bar{\pi}_i. \tag{25b}$$

Note that since $\bar{\lambda}^h > 0$, it can divide off of both sides of (25a), which combined with (25b) leads to

$$\sum_{i=1}^{n} [(C_1^h - \bar{C}_1^h) + P_i(C_{2i}^h - \bar{C}_{2i}^h)](\pi_i/\bar{\pi}_i) > 0. \tag{26}$$

The strict inequality in (26) holds for all traders h such that $C^h(\mathbf{y}) \neq C^h(\bar{\mathbf{y}})$. The left-hand side of (26) clearly equals zero for any trader with $C^h(\mathbf{y}) = C^h(\bar{\mathbf{y}})$. Therefore we can sum (26) over all traders and conclude

$$\sum_{i=1}^{n} \left[\sum_{h=1}^{H} (C_1^h - \bar{C}_1^h) + P_i\left(\sum_{h=1}^{H} (C_{2i}^h - \bar{C}_{2i}^h) \right) \right] (\pi_i/\bar{\pi}_i) > 0. \tag{27}$$

However, aggregate demand must equal aggregate supply for all commodities with positive prices. Note that aggregate supply is the same under $\mathbf{y}$ as under $\bar{\mathbf{y}}$, since prices are the same and firms' supply decisions only depend on prices. Therefore, $\sum_h C_1^h = \sum_i \bar{C}_1^h$ and $P_i \sum_{h=1}^{H} (C_{2i}^h - \bar{C}_{2i}^h) = 0$, so (27) is impossible.   QED

As noted in the two paragraphs introducing theorem 1, an immediate consequence of the invertibility of $\mathbf{P}^a(\boldsymbol{\pi})$ is that $\mathbf{P}^a(\boldsymbol{\pi}(\mathbf{y}))$ is a rational expectations equilibrium.

Theorem 2   *Under the assumptions of theorem 1, if there exists a Walrasian equilibrium $P^a(\boldsymbol{\pi}(\mathbf{y}))$ to the artificial fully informed economy, then $\mathbf{P}^a(\boldsymbol{\pi}(\mathbf{y}))$ is a rational expectations equilibrium for the economy where each trader h only observes $\mathbf{y}$.*

Proof   If $\mathbf{P}^a(\boldsymbol{\pi})$ is invertible, then consumers who maximize $E[u^h|y^h, P^a(\pi)]$ will have the same demands as those who maximize $E[u^h|\mathbf{y}]$. Hence $\mathbf{P}^a(\boldsymbol{\pi}(\mathbf{y}))$ will clear markets when $\tilde{\mathbf{y}} = \mathbf{y}$.

If $\mathbf{P}^a(\boldsymbol{\pi})$ is not invertible, we show by contradiction that it must also be a rational expectations equilibrium. Suppose it is not and there exists some consumer h for whom

$$E[u^h|\mathbf{P}^a(\boldsymbol{\pi}), y^h] \neq E[u^h|\mathbf{y}]. \tag{28}$$

However, by theorem 1, if $\mathbf{P}^a \equiv \mathbf{P}^a(\boldsymbol{\pi}) = \mathbf{P}^a(\bar{\boldsymbol{\pi}})$ and $\boldsymbol{\pi} \neq \bar{\boldsymbol{\pi}}$, then *every* consumer must be indifferent between the artificial economy allocations he gets when $\boldsymbol{\pi}(\tilde{\mathbf{y}}) = \boldsymbol{\pi}(\mathbf{y})$ and $\boldsymbol{\pi}(\tilde{\mathbf{y}}) = \boldsymbol{\pi}(\bar{\mathbf{y}})$; i.e.,

$$E[u^h(C_1^h(\mathbf{P}^a, \mathbf{y}), \tilde{C}_2^h(\mathbf{P}^a, \mathbf{y}))|\mathbf{y}] = E[u^h(C_1^h(\mathbf{P}^a, \bar{\mathbf{y}}), \tilde{C}_2^h(\mathbf{P}^a, \bar{\mathbf{y}}))|\bar{\mathbf{y}}].$$

But this equation holds for all $\mathbf{y}$, $\bar{\mathbf{y}}$ such that $\mathbf{P}^a(\pi(\mathbf{y})) = \mathbf{P}^a(\pi(\bar{\mathbf{y}}))$. This contradicts (28). QED

The fact that $\mathbf{P}^a(\pi)$ is a rational expectations equilibrium has a very important welfare implication. By the fundamental theorem of welfare economics, the allocations in a Walrasian equilibrium cannot be Pareto dominated by a central planner. Thus, by theorem 2, there is a rational expectations equilibrium for the economy with diverse information that cannot be Pareto dominated by a planner with all of the economy's information. This immediately implies

Theorem 3 *Define a consumption allocation to be feasible if there exists a technologically feasible production vector $(\hat{l}_f, \hat{z}_f)$ such that*

$$\sum_h [\hat{C}^h_{2i} - e^h_1] \leqq -\sum_f \hat{l}_f$$

and

$$\sum_h [\hat{C}^h_{2i} - e^h_{2i}] \leqq \sum_f \hat{z}_{fi}$$

for $i = 1, 2, \ldots, n$. Under the assumptions of theorem 2, there exists a rational expectations equilibrium $\mathbf{P}^a(\pi(\mathbf{y}))$ with associated consumption allocations $(C^h)_h$ and production allocations $(z_f)_f$ such that, if $(\hat{C}^h)_h$ is any other feasible consumption allocation, then, for each $\mathbf{y}$, it is impossible to have

$$\sum_i u^h(\hat{C}^h_1, \hat{C}^h_{2i}, s_i)\pi_i(\mathbf{y}) \geqq \sum_i u^h(C^h_1, C^h_{2i}, s_i)\pi_i(\mathbf{y})$$

for all h and strict inequality for some h.

Theorem 3 is a much stronger statement about the optimality of competitive allocations than the usual theorem. The standard optimality result essentially says that in an economy where markets are complete and *all* consumers have identical information, then a planner with the same information cannot Pareto dominate the competitive allocations. Theorem 3 states that in an economy where traders may have arbitrarily diverse information, the allocations brought about by competitive prices are as if each trader had all the information. Hence these allocations cannot be Pareto dominated.

The assumption that there is one good in each state is for notational convenience only. The reader may easily verify that theorems 1–3 are true if there are many goods per state. The assumption of a complete set of markets is, however, essential. I do not know whether the assumption that utility is additively separable over time is essential given complete markets. The reader can easily convince himself that theorem 1 is true if there is no consumption in the initial period, i.e. $u_1^h(C_1) = 0$. That is, in an economy with only n commodities and thus $n - 1$ relative prices, the price vector will be essentially invertible in π. It seems quite strange that by adding another price (which is what occurs when C_1 is put back into the utility function), the larger equilibrium price vector might no longer be invertible. The theorem works because, with complete markets, traders' demands tend to "respond in the same way" to changes in probability beliefs. I would conjecture that there is some simple assumption about $u(C_1, C_{2i})$ much more general than additive separability, which leads people's demands to respond in the same direction to changes in probabilities.

The next section explores the implications of theorems 1–3 in some detail. We close this section with a discussion of related proofs of existence of rational expectations equilibrium.

Lucas (1972) proved existence and uniqueness of equilibrium for the example mentioned in the previous section. His technique is difficult to extend in that it relies heavily on there being only one type of consumer with a nondegenerate allocation decision. Green (1973) had a model close to the one of this section except that he had only two types of traders; one type, called the "uninformed," observe nothing, and all members of the other, called "informed," observe the same thing. As we do, Green assumed a complete set of markets. He showed that, for each price vector, the demand function of the informed trader is an invertible function of the probability vector π. This implies that the artificial economy's price vector is invertible because there are only two types of traders with the uninformed observing nothing. Green's proof of the invertibility of demands was wholly different (it involved showing that the matrix of derivatives of demands with respect to π was a "$\mathbf{P}$" matrix) from that presented here. I do not know whether his techniques can be extended to the case where there are more than two types of traders, since the sum (over traders) of invertible functions need not be invertible.

Radner (1979) and Allen (1979) consider economies without a complete set of markets. For example, there are k securities markets, but all realizations of the probability vector $\pi(y)$ form an $m = n - 1$-dimensional space. If we let $\mathbf{P}^a(\pi)$ be the mapping from $R^m \to R^k$ that gives the prices of the k securities, then, if m satisfies $m \geq k + 1$, Allen shows that $\mathbf{P}^a(\pi)$ is generically invertible [i.e. if $\mathbf{P}^a(\pi)$ is not invertible for the given preferences, then change preferences just a little and the new function will be invertible].

If the assumption of complete markets is dropped, then there are counter examples to the existence of equilibrium by Kreps (1977) and Green (1977). See also Radner (1980) for more counter examples and a much more detailed discussion of the literature on the existence of rational expectations.[9]

2.5 The Informational Role of Prices: Conclusions

Prices are often referred to as signals. However, in nonstochastic economies, they clearly play no formal role in transferring information. No one learns anything from prices. People are constrained by prices (often in just the right way so that individual rationality is transformed into collective rationality); however, they are not informed by prices in the classical Walrasian or Marshallian models. Nevertheless, it is an old idea that prices contain information. Perhaps the clearest statement appears in Hayek (1945, p. 527): "We must look at the price system as ... as mechanism for communicating information if we want to understand its real function.... The most significant fact about this system is the economy of knowledge with which it operates, or how little the individual participants need to know in order to be able to take the right action ... by a kind of symbol, only the most essential information is passed on...."

Hayek wrote the above in criticism of the planning literature of the 1940s. That literature, taking the mathematical models of Walras, and the welfare theorems of Lange, literally, assumed that the State could set prices in such a way as to induce an efficient allocation and also the income distribution desired by the Leaders of the State. (The fundamental theorem of welfare economics assures us that, assuming convexity, any Pareto optimum can be supported by a competitive price system.) Hayek argued (in a vague way) that such arguments miss the point of price competition and the invisible hand. Each trader knows something about his own customers and neighborhood. No one knows everything about the economy. Each individual's little piece of information gets aggregated and transmitted to others via trading. The final competitive allocations are as if an invisible hand with all the economy's information allocated resources. However, a planner without all of that information could not have done as well.

In section 2.3, we showed that the standard Walrasian equilibrium concept is insufficient to capture the above idea. In an economy with diverse information, the Walrasian equilibrium does not lead to allocations that are as if each trader had all of the economy's information. Further, we argued that in the long run markets will not clear at the Walrasian equilibrium prices because traders observing those prices will extract information and thus revise their demands. We argued that the logical conclusion of this recontracting, i.e. the price vector at which no one desires to recontract, is the rational expectations equilibrium (R.E.) price vector. In section 2.4, we showed that this price vector, in the presence of complete securities markets, and additively separable utility over time, has the remarkable property that Hayek suggested; in an economy where traders have diverse information the R.E. allocations are as if each trader has all of the economy's information. That is, in an economy where traders begin with diverse information but have rational expectations, the allocations are as if they were generated by a Walrasian equilibrium for an artificial economy where each trader has all of the economy's information. That R.E. price is, in a formal sense, a sufficient statistic for all of the economy's information.[10]

In section 2.4, we showed that the above R.E. equilibrium leads to allocations that cannot be Pareto dominated by a planner with all of the economy's information. This is a powerful extension of the fundamental theorem of welfare economics to economies with diverse information. Like the Walrasian welfare theorems, it requires the assumption of complete markets. However, the reader is cautioned that there may be multiple R.E. equilibria. Theorem 3 states only that as long as there are complete markets and additively separable utility, there will exist *some* R.E. equilibrium that cannot be Pareto dominated by a fully informed planner.

The reader should also be cautioned against accepting the notion that the usual Walrasian equilibrium is useless as a tool for thinking about how goods are allocated under asymmetric information. It is only when there is diverse current information about the future that affects current prices that the Walrasian equilibrium seems unsuitable. For example, consider an economy with no production decisions, where people live for a single period and are endowed with apples and oranges. Suppose a planner or any single trader does not know who has what goods, or what individual preferences are for those goods. However, the existence of a market will lead people to allocate themselves to goods so that marginal rates of substitution are equalized. No one tries to learn anything from prices since there is nothing for any individual to learn. Walrasian prices constrain individuals in such a way that goods get drawn to people who value them. In this example, the mere existence of a market conveys all the information that a trader wants—namely, it tells him where he can find someone with whom to trade, and what are the terms of trade. This example should be contrasted with the example considered in section 2.3. In the example considered in section 2.3, the worth of a risky consumption stream, or of a current production decision, to a particular agent h depends on what other agents know about the economy. The current relative value of "risky production decision a" versus "production decision b" depends upon all the current information possessed about the probability distribution of payoffs. In such an economy, current prices of securities will convey information to traders and affect their current decisions—if traders have rational expectations. The Walrasian model is inappropriate in situations where the current worth to trader h of a future income stream depends on other traders' current information. The Walrasian model is appropriate in the apples and oranges one-period example mentioned above because all consumers know what the value of an apple and orange is to them. They have no need to look to others to figure out how much utility they will get from their own consumption. This is to be contrasted with what would arise if currently consumers are buying land and are uncertain about the harvest on land. There the utility they currently get out of land depends on their information about the future income flows the land gives. They would like to know the information other traders possess about the flows to better compute their expected utility.

The fact that we have assumed that there are a complete set of futures markets for our results deserves further emphasis. In Grossman (1977), and Grossman and Stiglitz (1980), it was shown that when information is privately costly then R.E. prices cannot be fully revealing. Some markets must close until there are few enough prices that an uninformed trader cannot completely free-ride on the informed trader's information by inverting $\mathbf{P(y)}$ for the information $\mathbf{y}$. That is, if a trader who bears no costs can, by looking at prices, learn all the information that other traders produce, then this will destroy the incentives for the production of information. Thus it is incorrect to expect prices to be fully revealing of information that is costly for individuals to acquire. However, there is information that would be costly for an arbitrary individual to acquire, but that was costless to the acquiree. For example, each trader h collects some information y^h in the ordinary course of his business. A shoe seller learns a little about the demand for shoes, for free, from his customers. That is, information is often produced complementary with the production and distribution of other commodities. Each trader can for free learn something about his own demanders and suppliers. This is the situation where $\bar{y}^h$ is free to trader h, but $\bar{\mathbf{y}} = (y^1, y^2, \ldots, y^H)$ is costly or impossible to acquire. In this case, when $\bar{P}^0(\mathbf{y})$ is a sufficient statistic, no disincentives to acquire $\bar{y}^h$ are generated (since it is free), but yet every trader is being given information by $\bar{P}^0$ that he could not obtain otherwise, except at great cost. This is the sense in which an R.E. equilibrium in a complete market captures Hayek's idea that a fundamental role of competitive prices is the aggregation of information.

Rational expectations (or perfect foresight) models began as an attempt to generalize the competitive equilibrium concept to economies subject to uncertainty. In the ordinary Walrasian model of an economy not subject to uncertainty, there is a price P^e such that if all traders believe the market will clear at P^e, then it will clear at P^e, where P^e is the competitive equilibrium price. Under uncertainty, if traders make decisions today anticipating that the market price tomorrow is some function $P^e(\bar{\varepsilon})$ of the exogenous random disturbance $\bar{\varepsilon}$, then those decisions will lead tomorrow's market clearing price to be $P^e(\varepsilon)$ when $\bar{\varepsilon} = \varepsilon$. This is not a radical departure from the competitive equilibrium under certainty paradigm. The quote in section 2.1 from Marshall indicates that he thought of traders forming their expectations about endogenous variables via a model of how these variables are determined by exogenous forces. These models give one the idea that uncertainty does not make much difference.

It is macroeconomic phenomena such as unemployment that are the most difficult to reconcile with the "competitive equilibrium under certainty" paradigm. Thus it is in models in this area where we should expect the most radical departure from that paradigm. Lucas (1972) in attempting to model unemployment implicitly made the innocuous-looking remark that if traders could have a model $P^e(\varepsilon)$ that allowed them to forecast future prices, why not assume they have a model of the determination of the current price as a function of its exogenous determinants, say $\mathbf{P}^0(\varepsilon)$. Each trader can then learn something about ε by inverting $\mathbf{P}^0(\varepsilon)$ after he observes the current price.

This is a radical departure because it allows us to model the role of prices as creating an externality by which a given individual's information gets transmitted to all other traders. That is, one of the determinants of current price is the information that traders possess about future states of nature. An uninformed trader can invert the current price to learn something about the informed traders' information. Thus the R.E. paradigm can be used to model the idea that a fundamental role of competitive markets (especially speculative markets) is to provide a mechanism by which traders can earn a return on information collection, while the information gets transmitted and aggregated along with other traders' information.[11]

Given that the R.E. paradigm is such a radical departure from the standard Walrasian model, it is important to have some empirical evidence as to its validity. Unfortunately, there is very little available. Plott (1980) has engaged in some experiments that indicate that the R.E. allocations can be generated experimentally. Further, there is one observation that provides some evidence to distinguish the Walrasian model from the R.E. model. In a Walrasian model, people trade and at the equilibrium price vector have no desire to trade further. Thus, if the next day there is a big change in a price and a person has no change in preferences or income, he will in general trade away from his position. Many people hold shares of stock. The stock price varies enormously from day to day. Yet many people do not trade. For example, I come home at the end of the day and learn that the price of a stock that I own has gone up 20%. No other news has impacted on me. If there is no information in the event that the price has gone up 20%, then I would surely sell, since yesterday I was indifferent at the margin and transaction costs are only 2%. I do not sell when I get the news of the price rise because it contains information about the payoff for the stock that leads me to change my preferences for it. In section 2.3, the R.E. equilibrium was constructed to have just this property: People should have no desire to recontract after observing the equilibrium price.

Notes

1. It is interesting to note that Marshall did not apply R.E. to his short-run dynamics. In the discussion of his dynamic process (book V, chapter III), he seems totally unaware of the fact that if the economic agents knew the process, then the market-clearing price would come about immediately (i.e., Marshallian dynamics would not be observed if agents anticipate Marshallian dynamics). See Arrow (1959). Another way of putting this is that firms are continually observing that they were wrong to have static expectations (since tomorrow's price is not today's price), unless they actually expect tomorrow's price to be the new Normal price (corresponding to the new state of demand).

2. See Nerlove (1972) for a survey of distributed lag models.

3. See, e.g., Grossman (1975a) or Cyert and DeGroot (1974).

4. It is also suggested in Radner (1967). Radner did not model the idea that traders use current prices to revise their current demands and did not define an equilibrium of this process.

5. It is convenient to model the firm as if there is some feasible convex set, say, T, of input-output combinations $(z_f(s_1), z_f(s_2), \ldots, z_f(s_n), l_f) \equiv (\bar{z}_f, l_f)$. So (9) should be interpreted as: choose a $(\bar{z}_f, l_f) \in T$ to maximize $R_f - l_f$.

6. See Debreu (1959), Arrow (1964), and Radner (1968).

7. For notational convenience, we define equilibrium to require that supply equal demand for all goods. This is, of course, too strong and should be interpreted as permitting goods with zero prices to be in excess supply.

8. To see this, let $F(s)$ be any function of s and let $\bar{Q}(\mathbf{y}) = E[F(s)|\mathbf{y}] = \sum_s F(s)$ $\mathrm{Prob}(s|\mathbf{y}) \equiv Q(\pi(\mathbf{y}))$. Hence $E[F(s)|\mathbf{y}]$ depends on $\mathbf{y}$ only through $\pi(\mathbf{y})$. But $E[F(s)|\pi(\mathbf{y})] = E\{E[F(s)|\mathbf{y}]|\pi(\mathbf{y})\} = E[Q(\pi(\mathbf{y}))|\pi(\mathbf{y})] = Q(\pi(\mathbf{y})) \equiv E[F(s)|\mathbf{y}]$. The result now follows if we set $F_i(s) = 1$ if $s = s_i$ and $F_i(s) = 0$ otherwise.

9. Jordan (1980) considers an equilibrium concept different from the rational expectations models discussed above. An example of his framework is as follows. Let $C_a^h(\mathbf{y})$ denote the consumption allocation that trader h has in the *fully* informed Walrasian economy, but one *without* a complete set of securities markets. Jordan assumes that, in the economy with heterogeneous information, an agent maximizes his expected utility given prices *and* also given his own consumption bundle. Therefore a trader can always imagine that his consumption bundle is $C_a^h(\mathbf{y})$ and it will be the case that the solution to $\max_c E[u^h | C_a^h(\mathbf{y}), y^h, \mathbf{P}^a(\mathbf{y})]$ will be $C_a^h(\mathbf{y})$. Thus the equilibrium to the artificial economy is always a "public prediction equilibrium" (as Jordan calls it) for the economy with heterogeneous information. This result does not require a complete set of markets as does theorem 2. I do not see what its relationship is to the rational expectations equilibrium. It seems to be the statement that if we could all know what our consumption would be if we are fully informed, then indeed we can act as if we are fully informed. The rational expectations model, on the other hand, states that, with enough markets, prices will give traders enough information so that they become fully informed.

10. See Grossman (1976, 1978), Kihlstrom and Mirman (1975). Hellwig (1980) provides some important insights regarding equilibrium prices that are sufficient statistics. He resolves the following paradox: If price is a sufficient statistic, then each trader ignores his own information. But if each trader ignores his own information, how does any information get into prices?

11. See Bray (1981), Danthine (1978), and Futia (1981) for interesting R.E. models of futures markets that reach a somewhat different conclusion.

References

Allen, B. (1979), "Generic Existence of Completely Revealing Equilibria for Economies with Uncertainty when Prices Convey Information" (Working Paper N° 79-07, Center for Analytic Research in Economics and the Social Sciences, Dept. of Econ., University of Pennsylvania).

Arrow, K. J. (1959), "Toward a Theory of Price Adjustment," in Abramovitz M. *et al.* (eds.) *The Allocation of Economic Resources* (Stanford University Press) 41–51.

Arrow, K. J. (1964), "The Role of Securities in the Optimal Allocation of Risk-Bearing," *Review of Economic Studies*, 31, 91–96.

Barro, R. J. (1981), "The Equilibrium Approach to Business Cycles," in Barro, R. J. (ed.) *Money Expectations and Business Cycles* (New York: Academic Press).

Bray, M. (1981), "Futures Trading, Rational Expectations and the Efficient Market Hypothesis," *Econometrica*, 49 (3), 575–596.

Cyert, R., and DeGroot, M. (1974), "Rational Expectations and Bayesian Analysis," *Journal of Political Economy* 82, 521–536.

Danthine, J. (1978), "Information, Futures Prices, and Stabilizing Speculation," *Journal of Economic Theory*, 17, 79–98.

Debreu, G. (1959) *Theory of Value* (New York: John Wiley).

Fisher, L. (1930) *The Theory of Interest as Determined by Impatience to Spend Income and the Opportunity to Invest It* (New York: Macmillan).

Futia, C. A. (1981), "Rational Expectations in Stationary Linear Models," *Econometrica*, 49 (1), 171–192.

Green, J. R. (1973), "Information, Efficiency and Equilibrium" (Discussion Paper N° 284, Harvard Institute of Economic Research, Harvard University).

Green, J. R. (1977), "The Non-Existence of Informational Equilibria," *Journal of Economic Studies*, 44, 451–463.

Grossman, S. (1975a), "Rational Expectations and the Econometric Modeling of Markets Subject to Uncertainty," *Journal of Econometrica*, 3, 255–272.

Grossman, S. (1975b), "The Existence of Futures Markets, Noisy Rational Expectations and Informational Externalities" (from Ph.D. dissertation, Dept. of Econ., University of Chicago).

Grossman, S. (1976), "On the Efficiency of Competitive Stock Markets Where Traders Have Diverse Information," *Journal of Finance*, 31 (2), 573–585.

Grossman, S. (1977), "The Existence of Futures Markets, Noisy Rational Expectations and Informational Externalities," *Review of Economic Studies*, 64 (3), 431–449.

Grossman, S. (1978), "Further Results on the Informational Efficiency of Competitive Stock Markets," *Journal of Economic Theory*, 18 (1), 81–101.

Grossman, S. J., and Stiglitz, J. E. (1980), "On the Impossibility of Informationally Efficient Markets," *American Economic Review*, 70 (3), 393–408.

Hayek, F. H. (1945), "The Use of Knowledge in Society," *American Economic Review*.

Hellwig, M. F. (1980), "On the Aggregation of Information in Competitive Markets," *Journal of Economic Theory*, 22, 477–498.

Hicks, J. R. (1939) *Value and Capital* (London: Oxford University Press).

Jordan, J. (1980), "On the Predictability of Economic Events," *Econometrica*, 48 (4).

Kihlstrom, R. E., and Mirman, L. J. (1975), "Information and Market Equilibrium," *Bell Journal of Economics*, 6 (1), 357–376.

Kreps. D. M. (1977), "A Note on Fulfilled Expectations Equilibria," *Journal of Economic Theory*, 14, 32–44.

Lucas, R. E. (1972), "Expectations and the Neutrality of Money," *Journal of Economic Theory*, 4 (2), 103–124.

Muth, J. R. (1960), "Optimal Properties of Exponentially Weighted Forecasts," *Journal of the American Statistical Association*, 55, 229–305.

Muth, J. R. (1961), "Rational Expectations and the Theory of Price Movements," *Econometrica*, 24, 315–335.

Nerlove, M. (1958), "Adaptive Expectations and Cobweb Phenomena," *Quarterly Journal of Economics*, 73, 227–240.

Nerlove, M. (1972), "Lags in Economic Behavior," *Econometrica*, 40 (2).

Plott, C. R., and Sunder, S. (1980), "Efficiency of Experimental Security Markets with Insider Information: An Application of Rational Expectations Models" (Social Science Working Paper N° 331, California Institute of Technology).

Radner, R. (1967), "Equilibrium of Spot and Futures Markets Under Uncertainty" (Technical Report N° 24, April, Center for Research in Management Science, University of California, Berkeley).

Radner, R. (1968), "Competitive Equilibrium Under Uncertainty," *Econometrica*, 36, 31–56.

Radner, R. (1972), "Existence of Equilibrium in Plans, Prices, and Price Expectations in a Sequence of Markets," *Econometrica*, 40 (2), 289–303.

Radner, R. (1979), "Rational Expectations Equilibrium: Generic Existence and the Information Revealed by Price," *Econometrica*, 47 (3), 655–678.

Radner, R. (1980), "Equilibrium Under Uncertainty," in Arrow, K. J., and Intriligator, M. D. (eds.) *Handbook of Mathematical Economics* (North-Holland Inc.) Vol. II, Chapter 20.

Shiller, R. (1978), "Rational Expectations and the Dynamic Structure of Macroeconomic Models: A Critical Review," *Journal of Monetary Economics*, 4, 1–44.

3 Further Results on the Informational Efficiency of Competitive Stock Markets

3.1 Introduction

If traders have diverse information about the returns on risky assets, then the competitive equilibrium asset prices will, to some extent, aggregate their information. Grossman [7, 8] gives an example of an economy with one risky and one risk free asset, where consumers have constant absolute risk aversion utility functions. Therein, it is shown that the equilibrium price of the risky asset perfectly aggregates the information of traders. Thus, in this economy where traders have diverse information sources, the equilibrium price produces allocations that are as if each trader had all the economy's information. The purpose of this chapter is to extend and elaborate the above results to an economy with many risky assets where no special assumption is made about trader utility functions. This leads to a strong implication about the form of the "Capital Asset Pricing Model" in "informationally efficient markets."

The structure of the chapter is as follows. In section 3.2 we give a model of an economy where traders obtain diverse information about the payoff on risky assets. We show that this economy can be thought of as being equivalent to an artificial economy where each trader has all the economy's information, if and only if the equilibrium price random variable in one of the economies is a sufficient statistic. (The appendix contains some results on conditional expectations and sufficient statistics that are used throughout this chapter.) This is closely related to the result of Kihlstrom and Mirman [11], who implicitly show that the two economies are equivalent if the price is sufficient in the sense of Blackwell, and only one type of trader has information. The remainder of the section is devoted to showing that under the assumption of Normality, price will be a sufficient statistic if the market portfolio of risky assets is not a Giffen good.

Section 3.3 generalizes the welfare result in Grossman [8]. It is shown that if the competitive equilibrium price is a sufficient statistic in the economy where traders have diverse information sources, then the competitive allocations cannot be Pareto dominated by a central planner with *all* of the economy's information. This demonstrates that the appropriate notion of an "efficient capital market" is one in which price is a sufficient statistic.

In section 3.4 it is shown that the results in section 3.2 can be used to extend the Capital Asset Pricing Model of Sharpe [15] and others to an economy where traders have diverse information sources. That is, under the assumption of joint Normality (which is standard in the above literature), a strong version of the capital asset pricing model holds when traders have diverse information.[1] The model has the property of being easier to test empirically than the standard model as well as being consistent with "capital market efficiency."

Section 3.5 points out that if information is costly, then markets cannot be informationally efficient. However, the main purpose of the section is to show how the above problem can be resolved. We show that when the stock market is informationally efficient, many markets are irrelevant and will close down if trade is costly. When some markets close down two things happen: (a) Traders observe a price that has lower dimensionality and thus reveals less information, and (b) a new source of uncertainty is added to the model due to the existence of supplies of nontraded goods, and this further reduces the informational content of the equilibrium price. Thus, when information and trade are costly, equilibrium must involve some markets that are too thin to operate competitively and an equilibrium price in competitive markets that is not a sufficient statistic.

3.2   The Model and the Main Theorem

The appendix contains a review of some statistical results that are used in this section.

The economy has $N + 1$ goods. The first N goods are shares of risky assets, and the last good is a risk free asset, i.e., a bond. All assets pay off in the same commodity, namely, "money." The economy lasts for two periods. In period 0 consumers trade shares of assets and bonds among themselves but do not consume. In the final period there is no trade, and each consumer consumes his pro rata share of the output of each of the assets.

In the initial period consumers do not know what the payoff on the N risky assets will be. Let u_j denote the payoff per share of risky asset j, for

$j = 1, \ldots, N$. Let R denote the payoff per bond on bonds. Let $u \equiv \{u_j\}_{j=1}^N$. Let (Ω, S, v) be a probability space. Let $\tilde{u}: \Omega \to \mathbb{R}^N$ be a random variable on this space (where $\mathbb{R}^N$ is the N-dimensional Euclidean space). The event $\tilde{u} = u$ occurs when the payoff per share on the risky assets is u.

The economy has T consumers (called traders). Each consumer collects information, before the market opens, about what realization of $\tilde{u}$ will be observed in the final period. That is, trader t observes the realization of a random variable $\tilde{y}_t: \Omega \to \mathcal{Y}_t$ defined on (Ω, S, v), where $\mathcal{Y}_t$ is a subset of a finite dimensional Euclidean space. Trader t observes the realization of $\tilde{y}_t$ before the period 0 market opens. Thus, trader t will use the conditional distribution of $\tilde{u}$ given $\tilde{y}_t = y_t$ when he decides on his optimal portfolio. Thus, since $\tilde{u}$ and $\tilde{y}_t$ are correlated random variables, we say "$\tilde{y}_t$ provides information about $\tilde{u}$."

Let $\tilde{y} \equiv \{\tilde{y}_t\}_{t=1}^T$, and let $\mathcal{Y} = \mathsf{X}_{t=1}^T \mathcal{Y}_t$. Except for the proof of lemma 1, we shall assume that

$$(\tilde{u}, \tilde{y}) \text{ has a joint Normal distribution.} \tag{1}$$

That is, $\text{Prob}(\tilde{u} \leqslant u, \tilde{y} \leqslant y) \equiv v\{\omega \in \Omega \mid \tilde{u}(\omega) \leqslant u \text{ and } \tilde{y}(\omega) \leqslant y\}$ is a Normal distribution function.

Following Lucas [13], Green [6], and others, we define a Rational Expectations competitive equilibrium where prices convey information to traders as an *equilibrium price* random variable $\tilde{P}: \mathcal{Y} \to \mathbb{R}_+^N$ such that if for $t = 1, 2, \ldots, T$,

$x_t(y_t, P) \in \mathbb{R}^N$, $B_t(y_t, P) \in \mathbb{R}$ is a solution to

$$\max_{x_t, B_t} E[U_t(\tilde{u} \cdot x_t + B_t R) \mid \tilde{y}_t = y_t, \quad \tilde{P}(\tilde{y}) = P(y)], \tag{2}$$

subject to

$$P(y)x_t + B_t \leqslant P(y)\bar{x}_t + \bar{B}_t \equiv W_{0t}, \tag{3}$$

then

$$(\forall y \in \mathcal{Y}) \quad \sum_{t=1}^T x_t(y_t, P(y)) = \sum_t \bar{x}_t \equiv \bar{X}, \quad \sum_{t=1}^T B_t(y_t, P(y)) = \sum_{t=1}^T \bar{B}_t.$$

In (2), $x_t(y_t, P(y))$ is consumer t's holdings of risky assets when the consumer maximizes his expected utility given observations on the price (i.e. $\tilde{P} = P$) and the private information variable $\tilde{y}_t$. In (3), $\bar{x}_t$ is the vector pf initial endowments of risky assets while $\bar{B}_t$ is the endowment of the risk free asset owned by trader t. Thus, trader t has final period wealth $\tilde{u} \cdot x_t + B_t R$ that comes from his payoff on risky and risk free assets: the payoff is proportional to final holdings x_t, B_t. Equation (4) requires that the price random variable $\tilde{P}$ have realization $P(y)$ at $\tilde{y} = y$ such that all markets clear.[2]

We shall assume $\overline{X} \in \mathbb{R}^N_+$ and $\overline{X} \neq 0$. A brief motivation of the above equilibrium notion is as follows (see the above references and Grossman [8] for further discussion): Our usual notion of equilibrium involves finding demands $\hat{x}_t(y_t, P)$, $\hat{B}_t(y_t P)$ that solve max $E[U_t(\tilde{u} \cdot x_t + B_t R)| y_t]$, and a price $\hat{P}(y)$ such that $\sum_t \hat{x}_t(y_t, \hat{P}(y)) = \sum_t \overline{x}_t$ for all y. That is, our usual notion is that people bring their private information to a market and a price comes about that clears the market. This is not an expectational equilibrium in the following sense. If the above "naive" economy is replicated, then trader t will eventually learn the joint distribution of $(\tilde{u}, \hat{P}, \tilde{y}_t)$ since this is observable to him. Then, at a particular realization of $\tilde{y}$, say, y^0, the market will no longer clear at $\hat{P}(y^0)$ because trader t will not demand $\hat{x}_t(y_t^0, \hat{P}(y^0))$. Trader t will now demand, say, $\hat{\hat{x}}_t$, which solves max $E[U_t(\tilde{u} \cdot x_t + B_t R)| \tilde{y}_t = y_t^0, \hat{P}(\tilde{y}) = \hat{P}(y^0)]$ because he has additional information when he sees the market clearing price. If the market clearing price eventually comes to satisfy (2)–(4), then traders will not want to revise their holdings of assets after they observe the market clear. The equilibrium in the naive economy always leads traders to regret their holdings $\hat{x}_t$ after the market clears and thus desire to recontract, while the equilibrium in (2)–(4) never leads traders to have a desire to recontract after the market clearing price is observed. Alternatively, if our economy is like the naive economy, then "technicians" (traders who watch the ticker tape and trade based upon the information in the last trade) would make money. To the extent that the naive prices prevail, every rational trader would desire to wait until others complete their trade before making his offer.

We are interested in giving conditions under which there exists a solution to (2)–(4), $P^*(y)$, that is a sufficient statistic. There are three interesting consequences of the existence of such a solution: (a) a very strong welfare result generalizing Grossman [8]; (b) a capital asset pricing model generalizing Tobin [16], Sharpe [15] and others; and (c) implications for the thinness of markets and the nonexistence of equilibria that are sufficient statistics when information is costly.

Conditions under which there exists a solution to (2)–(4) that is a sufficient statistic can be found by analyzing the following "artificial" economy. An *artificial equilibrium* is a random variable $\mathbf{P}^a$ such that $\tilde{P}^a : \mathcal{Y} \rightarrow \mathbb{R}^N_+$ and

if for each $t = 1, \ldots, T$, $x_t^a(y, P)$, $B_t^a(y, P)$ solves

$$\max_{x_t, B_t} E[U_t(\tilde{u} \cdot x_t + B_t R)| \tilde{y} = y] \text{ such that } Px_t + B_t \leqslant \overline{B}_t + P\overline{X}_t, \qquad (5)$$

then

$$(\forall y \in \mathcal{Y}) \quad \sum_t x_t^a(y, P^a(y)) = \sum_t \bar{x}_t \equiv \bar{X}, \quad \sum_t B_t^a(y, P^a(y)) = \sum_t \bar{B}_t.^3 \quad (6)$$

In the artificial economy each trader maximizes expected utility using the conditional distribution of returns conditional on all the information (of all traders) y, rather than his own information and the price.

The following lemma provides the relevant connection between the artificial economy and the economy of interest in (2)–(4).

Lemma 1 *There exists a solution to (2)–(4) which is a sufficient statistic if and only if there is a solution to (5)–(6) which is a sufficient statistic.*

Proof Suppose there is a solution to (5)–(6), $P^a(y)$, that is a sufficient statistic. We claim that $P^a(y)$ is also a solution to (2)–(4). To see this, note that by (A1) (see appendix)

$$E[U_t \mid \tilde{y}_t, \tilde{P}^a] = E[E[U_t \mid \tilde{y}, \tilde{y}_t, \tilde{P}^a] \mid \tilde{y}_t, \tilde{P}^a]. \quad (7)$$

But if $\tilde{y}$ is given, $\tilde{y}_t$ and $\bar{P}^a$ are redundant, so

$$E[U_t \mid \tilde{y}, \tilde{y}_t, \bar{P}^a] = E[U_t \mid \tilde{y}]. \quad (8)$$

However, by (A3), since $\tilde{P}^a$ is a sufficient statistic, $E[U_t \mid \tilde{y}] = E[U_t \mid \tilde{P}^a]$. So (8) can be written as $E[U_t \mid \tilde{y}, \tilde{y}_t, \tilde{P}^a] = E[U_t \mid \tilde{P}^a]$. Substituting this in (7), we have

$$E[U_t \mid \tilde{y}_t, \tilde{P}^a] = E[E[U_t \mid \tilde{P}^a] \mid \tilde{y}_t, \tilde{P}^a]. \quad (9)$$

By (A2), $E[E[U_t \mid \tilde{P}^a] \mid \tilde{y}_t, \tilde{P}^a] = E[U_t \mid \tilde{P}^a] = E[U_t \mid \tilde{y}]$, where the last equality follows from the assumption that $\bar{P}^a$ is a sufficient statistic. Therefore (7) can be written as

$$E[U_t \mid \tilde{y}, \tilde{P}^a] = E[U_t \mid \tilde{y}]. \quad (10)$$

This proves that $\bar{P}^a$ is a solution to (2)–(4) since (10) implies that (5) is equivalent to (2) and (3).

Conversely, suppose $\tilde{P}$ is a solution to (2)–(5) and is a sufficient statistic. Then by the same argument that gave (10), we have $E[U_t \mid \tilde{y}_t, \tilde{P}] = E[U_t \mid \tilde{y}]$. Hence, (5) is equivalent to (2) and (3), and (6) is equivalent to (4), so $\tilde{P}$ is an equilibrium for the artificial economy. QED

Note that the Normality assumption (1) is not used in lemma 1. Lemma 1 is related to theorem 1 of Kihlstrom and Mirman [11, p. 364]. They assumed that $(\tilde{u}, \tilde{y})$ can take on only a finite number of values and that only one type of trader has information. They showed that the price in the artificial economy is an invertible function of the posterior distribution of $\tilde{u}$ given $\tilde{y}$ if and only if the price is *sufficient in the sense of Blackwell* for the information $\tilde{y}$. $\bar{P}$ is Blackwell sufficient for $\tilde{y}$ when all information users would prefer using $\bar{P}$ to $\tilde{y}$.

In the appendix it is shown that $\bar{P} = P(y)$ is Blackwell sufficient for $\tilde{y}$ if and only if $P(y)$ is a sufficient statistic. Thus $P(y)$ is a sufficient statistic if and only if an uninformed trader can observe the price and know the beliefs of an informed trader, in Kihlstrom and Mirman's model. However, in our model the set of posterior distribution functions will in general be infinite-dimensional as $\tilde{u}$ can take on an infinite number of realizations, so it is unlikely that P will be an invertible function on the set of posterior distributions. (In Kihlstrom and Mirman [11], there are only a finite number of unknown states, say, k, so that the set of all possible distribution functions is the k-simplex in k-dimensional Euclidean space.)

We can now give sufficient conditions under which the price in the artificial economy (and hence, an information equilibrium) is a sufficient statistic. To do this, we assume Normality, i.e., (1), and note that we have the same economy for which Tobin's [16] separation theorem applies. Following Sharpe [15] and others, it is thus possible to analyze very simply the equilibrium prices $\bar{P}^a$. Note that (1) implies that

The conditional distribution of $\tilde{u}$ given $\tilde{y} = y$ is Normal with mean, say, $m(y)$, and covariance matrix Σ.   (11)

It is essential for what follows to note that Σ does not depend on the realization of $\tilde{y}$. (This does *not* imply that the unconditional covariance matrix is identical to the conditional covariance matrix.) We assume, without loss of generality, that Σ is invertible. If it were not invertible, then there exists a linear combination of risky assets that is equivalent to the risk free asset. Eliminating portfolios of this type would not change the economy and would leave Σ invertible. The following lemma is useful.

Lemma 2   *If the Normality assumption is made, then $m(y) \equiv E[\tilde{u} \mid \tilde{y} = y]$ is a sufficient statistic.*

Proof   By (A7) it suffices to show that for any (measurable) $F(\cdot)$,

$$E[F(\tilde{u})\mid \tilde{y} = y] = E[F(\tilde{u})\mid m(\tilde{y}) = m(y)]. \tag{12}$$

This holds because $E[E[F(\tilde{u})\mid y]\mid m(y)] = E[F(\tilde{u})\mid m(y)]$ by (A1). But $E[F(\tilde{u})\mid y] = k(m(y))$ for some function $k(\cdot)$ because the conditional density of $\bar{u}$ given y depends on y only through $m(y)$. Hence, $E[F(\bar{u})|\ m(y)] = E[k(m(y))|\ m(y)] = k(m(y)) \equiv E[F(\bar{u})|\ y]$. Thus (12) holds.   QED

Lemma 2 shows that the dependence of $P^a(y)$ on y will occur only through $m(y)$. This can be seen by examining (5). If we assume Normality, lemma 2 permits us to replace (5) by

Consumer t finds $x_t^a(m(y), P)$, $B_t^a(m(y), P)$ that solves
$$\max_{x_t, B_t} E[U_t(\bar{u}\cdot x_t + B_t R)|\ m(y)] \text{ such that } Px_t + B_t = \bar{B}_t + P\bar{x}_t \equiv W_{0t}. \quad (13)$$

The necessary conditions for a maximum in (13) imply that

$$x_t^a(m, P) = k_t(m, P)\Sigma^{-1}[m - RP], \quad (14a)$$

where

$$k_t(m, P) \equiv -\frac{1}{2}\frac{\int U_t(W)(\partial f/\partial \bar{m})(W; \bar{m}(x), \bar{\sigma}(x))\, dW}{\int U_t(W)(\partial f/\partial \bar{\sigma})(W; \bar{m}(x), \bar{\sigma}(x))\, dW}, \quad (14b)$$

and where $f(W; \bar{m}(x), \bar{\sigma}(x))$ is the univariate Normal density function with mean $\bar{m}(x) \equiv E[RW_{0t} + (\bar{u} - RP)x\ |\ m(y)] = RW_{0t} + (m - RP)x$ and variance $\bar{\sigma}(x) \equiv \text{Var}(RW_{0t} + (\bar{u} - RP)x\ |\ m(y)) = x\cdot\Sigma\cdot x$. [Note that $RW_{0t} + (\bar{u} - RP)x$ is the consumer's final period wealth when he holds the vector x of risky assets derived by eliminating B_t from the budget constraint.] $k_t(m, P)$ is the consumer's marginal rate of substitution between mean-wealth and variance of wealth.

Formally, we have

Lemma 3   *If $U_t(\cdot)$ is strictly concave and strictly monotone increasing for all t, there is Normality, and if $P^a(y)$ exists, then there exists a function $\bar{P}^a: \mathbb{R}^N \to \mathbb{R}_+^N$ such that $P^a(y) = \bar{P}^a(m(y))$ for all y.*[4]

Proof   By concavity each consumer's demand function in the artificial economy satisfies (14). If

$$k(m, P) \equiv \sum_{t=1}^T k_t(m, P), \quad (15)$$

then market clearing, (6), implies

$$\bar{X} = k(m, P^a)\Sigma^{-1}[m - RP^a]. \quad (16)$$

Thus, since a market clearing price exists, we are guaranteed that it depends on y only through $m(y)$ as seen by (16) [i.e., $\bar{P}^a(m)$ is a solution to (16)].
QED

From lemma 3 it is clear that the artificial economy, and thus the informational equilibrium economy, will have a price that is a sufficient statistic if any solution to (16), $\bar{P}^a(m)$, is invertible. Grossman [8] studied a similar economy to (2)–(4) in the case where $U_t(W) = -e^{-a_t W}$, $a_t > 0$. In this case it is easy to verify that $k_t(m, P) = -1/a_t$ for all m, P. Since $k(m, P^a)$ is a constant, it follows that any solution to (16) is invertible [i.e., $\bar{P}^a(m) \equiv R^{-1}\{m - k^{-1}\Sigma\bar{X}\}$, which is clearly invertible.[5] It is easy to give a much weaker sufficient condition for invertibility. From (14) (or Tobin's separation theorem), it is clear that all traders act as if there are only two assets: (a) the risk free asset and (b) a single mutual fund of risky assets. Thus, it is as if there were just one risky asset and one risk free asset. We now show that if the risky asset is not a Giffen good (i.e., if the demand for the risky asset falls when its price rises), then there is a Rational Expectations equilibrium price, i.e., a solution to (2)–(4), that is a sufficient statistic.

To make the above notions precise, we prove a slight variant of Tobin's separation theorem.

Lemma 4 *Under the assumptions of lemma 3, if $\bar{P}^a(m)$ is a solution to (16), then the following problem leads to the same demand function as (13): Consumer t finds $z_t(\pi, \rho, W_{0t}) \in \mathbb{R}$, $B_t(\pi, \rho, W_{0t}) \in \mathbb{R}$*

that solves $\max_{z_t, B_t} E[U_t(z_t \bar{u} \cdot \bar{X} + B_t R) | m(y)]$ *subject to* $\qquad(17)$

$$\bar{P}^a \cdot \bar{X} z_t + B_t = \bar{B}_t + \bar{P}^a \cdot \bar{x}_t \equiv W_{0t},$$
where $\pi \equiv \bar{X} \cdot m$ *and* $\rho \equiv \bar{X} \cdot \bar{P}^a(m)$. $\qquad(18)$

That is, $x_t^a(m, \bar{P}^a(m)) \equiv z_t(\bar{X} \cdot m, \bar{X} \cdot \bar{P}^a(m), \bar{B}_t + \bar{P}^a(m) \cdot \bar{x}_t)\bar{X}$ *for all* m.

Proof As before, let $f(W; \hat{m}, \hat{\sigma})$ be the univariate Normal density with mean $\hat{m}$ and variance $\hat{\sigma}$. Let $\hat{m}(z) \equiv (m \cdot \bar{X} - R\bar{P}^a \cdot \bar{X})z + RW_0$ and $\hat{\sigma}(z) \equiv z^2 \bar{X} \cdot \Sigma \cdot \bar{X}$ (the mean and variance of final period wealth, using the budget constraint to eliminate B_t). A necessary and sufficient condition for z_t to be a maximizer in (17) is

$$\int U_t(W) \left\{ \frac{\partial f}{\partial \hat{m}} (W; \hat{m}(z_t), \hat{\sigma}(z_t)) [m \cdot \bar{X} - R\bar{P}^a(m) \cdot \bar{X}] \right.$$

$$\left. + \frac{\partial f}{\partial \hat{\sigma}} (W; \hat{m}(z_t), \hat{\sigma}(z_t)) (2z_t) \bar{X} \sum \bar{X} \right\} dW = 0. \qquad(19)$$

If we use the fact that $\bar{P}^a(m)$ satisfies (16), then (19) can be written

$$\int U_t(W) \left\{ \frac{\partial f}{\partial \hat{m}} (W; \hat{m}(z_t), \hat{\sigma}(z_t)) k^{-1}(m, \overline{P}^a(m)) \overline{X} \right.$$

$$\left. + \frac{\partial f}{\partial \hat{\sigma}} (W; \hat{m}(z_t), \hat{\sigma}(z_t)) (2z_t) \overline{X} \right\} dW = 0. \tag{20}$$

The necessary and sufficient condition for a maximum in (13) has the exact same form where $\overline{P}^a(m)$ satisfies (16). That is, it is exactly the same except that where x_t^a appears in the first-order condition for (13), $z_t \overline{X}$ appears in (20). QED

We shall call $z_t(\pi, \rho, W_0)$ the demand for *the* risky asset when its expected payoff is $\pi \equiv m \cdot \overline{X} \in \mathbb{R}$ and price is $\rho \in \mathbb{R}$, and trader t has initial wealth W_0. We will say that the risky asset is a Giffen good if there exist ρ_1, ρ_2 such that $\rho_1 > \rho_2$ and $z_t(\pi, \rho_1, W_0) \geqslant z_t(\pi, \rho_2, W_0)$ for some π and W_0.

It is useful to note that $z_t(\pi, \rho, W_0)$ depends on (π, ρ) only through $\pi - R\rho$; i.e., $z_t(\pi, \rho, W_0)$ can be written as $\hat{z}_t(\pi - R\rho, W_0)$. This follows (17)–(19) as the only way (for a given W_0) that π and ρ enter the maximum problem $\max_{z_t} \int U_t(W) f(W; \hat{m}(z_t), \hat{\sigma}(z_t)) dW$ is through the term $\hat{m}(z_t) \equiv (m \cdot \overline{X} - R\overline{P}^a \cdot \overline{X}) z_t + RW_0 = (\pi - R\rho) z_t + RW_0$. Since $z_t(\pi, \rho, W_0) \equiv \hat{z}_t(\pi - R\rho, W_0)$, we may equivalently state that the risky asset is a Giffen good if there exist π_1, π_2 such that $\pi_1 > \pi_2$ and $z_t(\pi_1, \rho, W_0) \leqslant z_t(\pi_2, \rho, W_0)$ for some ρ and W_0. The main theorem can now be proved.

Theorem 1 *Under the assumption of lemma 3, if the risky asset is not a Giffen good, then the Rational Expectations price random variable $\tilde{P}$ is a sufficient statistic.*

Proof By lemma 1 it is enough to show that the price in the artificial economy $\tilde{P}^a$ is a sufficient statistic. However, by lemmas 2 and 3, it is enough to show that $\tilde{P}^a(m)$ is an invertible function of m.

We show, by contradiction, that $\overline{P}^a(m)$ is invertible. Suppose there are $m_1 \in \mathbb{R}^N$ and $m_2 \in \mathbb{R}^N$ such that $m_1 \neq m_2$ and $\overline{P}^a(m_1) = \overline{P}^a(m_2) \equiv \overline{P}^a$. Let $\pi_1 \equiv m_1 \overline{X}$, $\pi_2 = m_2 \overline{X}$, and $\rho \equiv \overline{P}^a \overline{X}$.

Either $\pi_1 = \pi_2 \equiv \pi$ or they are not equal, and, say, $\pi_1 > \pi_2$. We show that $\pi_1 = \pi_2$ is impossible. From lemma 4 it is clear that if $\pi_1 = \pi_2$ then $x_t^a(m_1, \overline{P}^a) = x_t^a(m_2, \overline{P}^a)$, since initial wealth is the same for $m = m_1$ or $m = m_2$. But from (14), $k_t(m_1, \overline{P}^a) = k_t(m_2, \overline{P}^a)$ since k_t depends on m only through $\overline{m}(x_t^a) \equiv RW_{0t} + (m - RP) x_t^a(m, \overline{P}^a) = RW_{0t} + (m \cdot \overline{x} - R\overline{P}^a \overline{x}) \cdot z_t(\pi, \rho) = RW_{0t} + (\pi - R\rho) z_t(\pi, \rho)$. Since this is true for all traders,

$k(m_1, \bar{P}^a) = k(m_2, \bar{P}^a) \equiv \bar{k}$. Thus, (16) implies $\bar{x} = \bar{k}\Sigma^{-1}[m_1 - R\bar{P}^a] = \bar{k}\Sigma^{-1}[m_2 - R\bar{P}^a]$, which is impossible if $m_1 \neq m_2$.

Thus, we may assume $\pi_1 > \pi_2$. However, since the risky asset is not a Giffen good, we may use lemma 4 to note that for each t, $x_t^a(m_1, \bar{P}^a) = \hat{z}_t(\pi_1 - R\rho, W_0)\bar{X} > \hat{z}_t(\pi_2 - R\rho, W_0)\bar{X} = x_t^a(m_2, \bar{P}^a)$ (since endowments are nonnegative). Hence, it is impossible for both $\sum_t x_t^a(m_1, \bar{P}^a) = \bar{X}$ and $\sum_t x_t^a(m_2, \bar{P}^a) = \bar{X}$. Therefore, it cannot be that the market clearing price $\bar{P}^a(m)$ is the same at m_1 and m_2. QED

In summary, we showed that the Rational Expectations equilibrium price is a sufficient statistic for an economy where traders have diverse information if and only if the equilibrium price in an economy where traders have the same information (the artificial economy) is a sufficient statistic. We then showed that the vector of conditional expected returns, $m(y)$, is a sufficient statistic, and the price in the artificial economy depends on y only through $m(y)$. It was also shown that in an artificial economy, traders act as if there is only one risky asset. Finally, we showed that if the risky asset has a downward sloping demand curve, then price in the artificial economy must be invertible in $m(y)$. Therefore, there is a Rational Expectations equilibrium price that is a sufficient statistic.[6, 7]

The following corollary gives a sufficient condition for demand to be downward sloping.

Corollary *If the absolute risk aversion* $- U_t''(W)/U_t'(W)$ *of each trader is nonincreasing, then the Rational Expectations price random variable* $\bar{P}$ *is a sufficient statistic.*

Proof From Arrow[1, p. 119], the risky asset is a normal good (i.e., if π and ρ are fixed, then z_t rises with a rise in initial wealth W_{0t}) in the region where $z_t \geq 0$. Note that $\hat{z}_t(\pi - R\rho, W_{0t}) \geq 0$ if $\pi - R\rho \geq 0$ and $\hat{z}_t(\pi - R\rho, W_{0t}) \leq 0$ if $\pi - R\rho \leq 0$ because the consumer is risk averse. Since this holds for all consumers and since in equilibrium $\sum_t z_t = 1$, it must be the case that $\pi - R\rho \geq 0$. Thus, for each consumer the risky asset is a normal good. Hence, the demand for the risky asset is downward sloping. QED

The fact that there is an equilibrium price that is a sufficient statistic means that the price "perfectly aggregates traders' information." This is true in a statistical sense; however, the next section shows that it is true in an economic sense. That is, when price is a sufficient statistic for an economy where traders have diverse information, the competitive allocation cannot be improved upon by a central planner with all the information in the economy.

3.3 Welfare Implications

In this section we show that the equilibrium demonstrated in theorem 1 has very strong efficiency properties. The literature on "efficient capital markets" is somawhat vague on what is meant by efficiency. For example, Fama [5] does not distinguish between a notion that involves prices transmitting information to traders and a notion that involves Pareto optimality of allocations. His idea that prices convey information is rigorously formulated by the notion of a sufficient statistic. The following definition will be used to prove that when prices form a sufficient statistic, there is a very strong efficiency property possessed by competitive allocations.

Let $\alpha_t(y) \equiv (x_t(y), B_t(y)) \in \mathbb{R}^{N+1}$ be an allocation to trader t. Let $\alpha(y) \equiv \{\alpha_t(y)\}_t$. We shall say $\alpha(y)$ is *feasible for y* if

$$\sum_t \alpha_t(y) = \left(\sum_t \bar{x}_t, \sum_t \bar{B}_t \right). \tag{21}$$

We shall say that an allocation $\alpha(y)$ *cannot be Pareto dominated by a planner who knows y* if

$$\alpha(y) \equiv \{x_t(y), B_t(y)\}_t \text{ is feasible for } y; \tag{22}$$

If $\alpha(y) \equiv \{\hat{x}_t(y), \hat{B}_t(y)\}_t$ is feasible for y, there is some trader k such that $E[U_k(\bar{u} \cdot \hat{x}_k(y) + R\hat{B}_k(y)) \mid y] \leqslant E[U_k(\bar{u} \cdot x_k(y) + RB_k(y)) \mid y]$. (23)

Condition (23) states that it is not possible to find an allocation $\alpha(y)$ that will make all traders strictly "better off" than they were at $\alpha(y)$. There are two important points about "better off" in this context. First, each trader's utility of the bundle $(x_t(y), B_t(y))$ is evaluated conditional on all the economy's information. That is, (23) is very strong in that it says that an omniscient central planner, with far more information than any consumer, cannot make a Pareto improvement on $\alpha(y)$. Second, this is a notion of constrained Pareto optimality since the planner can only reallocate risk among consumers using existing securities.

The following theorem shows why it is reasonable to call markets where prices form a sufficient statistic "informationally efficient."

Theorem 2 *If $U_t(\cdot)$ is strictly monotone and $\tilde{P}$ in (2)–(4) is a sufficient statistic, then the associated allocation $\alpha(y) \equiv \{x_t(y_t, \tilde{P}(y)), B_t(y_t, \tilde{P}(y))\}_{i=1}^T$ cannot be Pareto dominated by a planner who knows y.*

Proof By lemma 1, if $\tilde{P}$ is a sufficient statistic, then there is an equilibrium in the artificial economy $\tilde{P}^a$ that is a sufficient statistic and has an associated allocation $\{x_t^a(y_t, \tilde{P}^a(y)), B_t^a(y_t, \tilde{P}^a(y))\}_t = \alpha(y)$ for all y. The artificial economy is an ordinary Arrow-Debreu economy in the commodities (x_t, B_t) indexed by y. That is, define for each y, $\bar{U}_t(x_t, B_t; y) \equiv E[U_t(x_t\bar{u} + B_tR) \mid y]$. For the economy indexed by y, an Arrow-Debreu economy is defined where traders have utility functions $\bar{U}_t$ and budget constraints as in (5). The competitive allocations for this economy are Pareto optimal for each y. For each y, Pareto optimality of $\alpha(y)$ in the artificial economy is equivalent to the statement that $\alpha(y)$ cannot be blocked by a planner who knows y. QED

The Classical Theorem of welfare economics says that when individuals, by each acting competitively and in their own best interests, reach equilibrium, it is as if an invisible hand had given them allocations that maximize social welfare. Theorem 2 is stronger. It states that individuals, by each acting competitively with their private information, attain allocations that are as if given by an invisible hand with *all* the economy's information. There is a sense in which this theorem is too strong. If information is costly, then individuals will have no incentive to collect information. See section 3.5 for further discussion of this point.

3.4 Implications for the Pricing of Capital Assets

Soon after the publication of Tobin's separation theorem, Sharpe [15] and others realized that if everyone is to hold the same portfolio of risky assets, then this must be the market portfolio. This is seen in (16), which gives the equilibrium condition for an economy where *all* traders observe y. Lemma 4 showed that for such an economy, all traders hold a vector of risky assets that is a scalar multiple of the aggregate endowment vector $\bar{X}$. Thus, from (16), we may write down the Capital Asset Pricing Model (CAPM):

$$E[\tilde{r}_j^a \mid y] - r_f = \beta_j^a\{E[\tilde{r}_m^a \mid y] - \tilde{r}_f\} \qquad \text{if} \quad j = 1, 2, \ldots, N, \tag{24}$$

where

$\tilde{r}_m^a \equiv (\bar{u} \cdot \bar{X} - \tilde{P}^a\bar{X})/\tilde{P}^a\bar{X}$ is the rate of return on the market portfolio $\bar{X}$,

$\tilde{r}_j^a \equiv (\bar{u}_j - \tilde{P}_j^a\, y))/\tilde{P}_j^a$ is the rate of return on asset j,

$\beta_j^a \equiv \mathrm{Cov}(\tilde{r}_j^a, \tilde{r}_m^a \mid y)/\mathrm{Var}(\tilde{r}_m^a \mid y)$, which is independent of the realization y of $\tilde{y}$ by the joint Normality of $(\bar{u}, \tilde{y})$, and

$r_f \equiv R - 1.$

The strong form of the "efficient markets" hypothesis states that (24) is an accurate description of the way returns are generated (see Fama [5]). Note that this states that returns are generated as if each trader in the market has observed all the economy's information. Our version of the strong form of the "efficient markets" hypothesis is that the market clearing price is a sufficient statistic in (2)–(4). Thus, by lemma 1, it follows that (24) implies

$$E[\tilde{r}_j \mid \tilde{P} = P] - r_f = \beta_j \{ E[\tilde{r}_m \mid \tilde{P} = P] - r_f \}, \tag{25}$$

where $\tilde{r}_j$ and $\tilde{r}_m$ are the same as before except that $\tilde{P}^a$ is replaced by informational equilibrium price $\tilde{P}$, and $\beta_j \equiv \mathrm{Cov}(\tilde{r}_j, \tilde{r}_m \mid \tilde{P} = P)/\mathrm{Var}(\tilde{r}_m \mid \tilde{P} = P)$.

Note that if the market is informationally efficient, then (24) and (25) are identical equations. However, (25) is much easier to test empirically than (24). This is because (24) contains $\tilde{y}$ while (25) contains $\tilde{P}$, which is observable at a low cost to the empirical worker testing the CAPM. Thus to estimate the "beta" of a security, a model based upon (25) should be used rather than the usual model

$$E\tilde{r}_j - r_f = \beta_j^* \{ E\tilde{r}_m - r_j \}, \tag{26}$$

where $\beta_j^* \equiv \mathrm{Cov}(\tilde{r}_j, \tilde{r}_m)/\mathrm{Var}\,\tilde{r}_m$. [Note that (25) does not imply (26) because $\beta_j \neq \beta_j^*$ if price contains information.]

It is important to note that the fact that prices convey information to traders *does not* imply that "technicians" (traders who look at *past* prices) can make money. The opposite is true. The definition of informational equilibrium in (2)–(4) requires that after the market clears at $P(y)$, the knowledge of the fact that the price was $P(y)$ will in no way change traders' demands. Traders who look at past prices for information waste their time, for the fact that prices last period were "high" may mean that expected returns are high, but the prices immediately rise to the point where this information is of no value. That is, the definition of equilibrium in (2)–(4) is exactly the equilibrium concept to use if you believe that technicians make no money. Note that this is the case irrespective of whether prices are sufficient statistics. (That is, we assume markets are "weakly" efficient in that this is what (2)–(4) means, and prove that under joint Normality, the market will be strongly efficient in the sense of Fama [5].)

3.5 Implications of Costly Information and Costly Trade

As noted previously, the theorems of this chapter are too strong to be true statements about the world. Suppose that the equilibrium price random variable is a sufficient statistic and (a) information is costly to individuals or (b) trade is costly. It is clear that if information is costly, then no competitive equilibrium exists that reveals information. To see this, suppose that an equilibrium exists that reveals information. Then some types of traders must be collecting information, say, a subset $t = 1, 2, \ldots, T_0$. In this case $(\tilde{y}_1, \tilde{y}_2, \ldots, \tilde{y}_{T_0}, \tilde{u})$ is jointly Normal since $(\tilde{y}, \tilde{u})$ is jointly Normal. Then under the assumptions of theorem 1, price is a sufficient statistic for the density $f(\tilde{y}_1, \tilde{y}_2, \ldots, \tilde{y}_{T_0}, u)$. That is, price perfectly aggregates the information contained in $(\tilde{y}_1, \tilde{y}_2, \ldots, \tilde{y}_{T_0})$. Thus, take any one of the informed traders who has paid for his information y_t. He funds $E[U_t \mid y_t, P] = E[U_t \mid P]$, so he gets no benefit from his information. Thus, each informed trader will decide not to collect information. Hence, the equilibrium price will reveal no information. It is very important to note that each trader assumes that the equilibrium price random variable will not be affected by his decision to buy information or assets. Suppose information has a cost with the property that when no trader is informed (i.e., the price is a constant function of y), it is profitable for each trader, taking the price random variable as unaffected by his action, to become informed. In this case the above argument shows that no competitive equilibrium exists. (It is not an equilibrium to have no traders informed, and it is not an equilibrium to have some traders informed.) For a more detailed analysis of this problem, see Grossman and Stiglitz [9].

When the equilibrium price is a sufficient statistic, all traders have homogeneous beliefs and hold the same portfolio of risky assets. All that is needed for trade is a market for shares of a mutual fund that holds the market portfolio. Suppose that it is cheaper to trade in shares of a mutual fund than to purchase all of the individual securities separately. In this case there will be very little trade in individual securities. If it is costly to maintain a competitive market, then there will not be enough trade to pay for the fixed operating cost. However, once a market closes, traders lose the information provided by the price of the security previously traded.

To formalize the above statements, consider the economy described in (2)–(4) with only the first $L < N$ markets open. Let $\bar{x}_{At} \in \mathbb{R}_+^L$ be trader t's endowment of the first L assets, while $\bar{x}_{Bt} \in R_+^{N-L}$ is his endowment of the other assets. An equilibrium for the economy with L open markets is a price random variable $\tilde{P}_L: \mathcal{Y} \to \mathbb{R}_+^L$ such that

if for $t = 1, 2, \ldots, T$ $x_{At}(y_t, P) \in \mathbb{R}^L$, $B_t(y_t, P) \in \mathbb{R}$ is a solution to $\max_{x_A, B} E[U_t(\bar{u} \cdot (x_{At}, \bar{x}_{Bt}) + RB) \mid y_t, P_L]$ subject to

$$P_L(y)x_A + B \leqslant P_L(y)\bar{x}_{At} + \bar{B}_t \equiv W_{At}, \tag{27}$$

then

$$(\forall y \in \mathscr{Y}) \quad \sum_{t=1}^{T} x_{At}(y_t, \tilde{P}_L(y)) = \overline{X}_A, \quad \sum_{t=1}^{T} B_t(y_t, \tilde{P}_L(y)) = \sum_{t=1}^{T} \overline{B}_t.^8 \tag{28}$$

Note that in the above economy each trader is stuck with his endowment of nontraded goods. Further, the above economy is identical in structure to the economy in (2)–(4) except that each trader gets an expected utility out of traded goods that depends on his information about untraded goods because (a) of wealth effects leading to different levels of risk aversion as $\tilde{u}_B \overline{x}_{Bt} = \sum_{j=L+1}^{N} \tilde{u}_j \overline{x}_{jt}$ varies and (b) $\tilde{u}_B$ and $\tilde{u}_A$ are correlated. Examples of assets that are not traded in organized competitive markets are human capital, some types of real estate, and small (noncorporate) businesses.

We can use lemma 1 for the above economy by defining an artificial economy where each trader observes all the information in the economy, i.e., y_t, P_t is replaced by y in (27). Denote the equilibrium price random variable by $\tilde{P}_L^a = \tilde{P}_L^a(y)$. By lemma 1 there is a solution to (27) that is a sufficient statistic if and only if there is a $\tilde{P}_L^a$ that is a sufficient statistic. As in lemma 3, $\tilde{P}_L^a(y)$ depends on y only through $m(y)$. To see this, note that each trader t has a demand that satisfies

$$x_{At}^a(m, P_L) = k_t^A(m, P_L)\Sigma_A^{-1}(m_A - RP_L^a) - \Sigma_A^{-1}\Sigma_{AB}\overline{x}_{Bt}, \tag{29}$$

where

$$\Sigma = \begin{pmatrix} \Sigma_A & \Sigma_{AB} \\ \Sigma_{BA} & \Sigma_B \end{pmatrix}, \qquad m = \begin{pmatrix} m_A \\ m_B \end{pmatrix},$$

and $k_t^A(m, P)$ is as in (14) except that $\overline{m}(x)$ is replaced by $RW_{0t} + m_B \overline{x}_{Bt} + (m_A - RP_L)x_{At}$ and $\overline{\sigma}(x)$ is replaced by $x_{At} \cdot \Sigma_{At} \cdot x_{At} + 2x_{At} \cdot \Sigma_{AB} \cdot \overline{x}_{Bt} + \overline{x}_{Bt} \cdot \Sigma_B \cdot \overline{x}_{Bt}$. Market clearing and (30) imply

$$P_L^a(y) = m_A(y) - \frac{\Sigma_A \overline{X}_A + \Sigma_{AB}\overline{X}_B}{k^A(m(y), P_L^a(y))}. \tag{30}$$

where

$$\overline{X} = \begin{pmatrix} \overline{X}_A \\ \overline{X}_B \end{pmatrix} \qquad \text{and} \qquad k^A(m, P_L) \equiv \Sigma_t k_t^a(m, P_L).$$

From (30) $P_L^a(y)$ reveals, at most, $m_A(y)$ and not $m(y)$. Further, unless traders' utility functions exhibit constant absolute risk aversion [so that $k_t^a(m, P)$ is a constant independent of m and P], traders will want to know $m(y)$. That is, unless $k_t^a(m, P)$ is a constant, the equilibrium in the artificial economy is not an equilibrium for the economy in (27) and (28).

There is another way to model the economy so that price is not a sufficient statistic. In contrast to the above, assume that traders *do* exhibit constant absolute risk aversion, but also assume that the total stock of nontraded assets, $\overline{X}_B$, is a random variable. Note that these assets are never traded, so there is no reason why each trader should know the total stock of, say, human capital, with certainty. Note that this is less plausible for traded securities in that the total stock of traded securities is much more likely to be known by each trader (this is because when traders purchase assets, they purchase a *share* of something and would thus know what share of the company they are getting).

If $\overline{X}_B$ is a realization of a random variable $\tilde{\overline{X}}_B$, then the equilibrium price will be a random variable with a distribution induced by the joint distribution of $\tilde{y}$ and $\tilde{\overline{X}}_B$.[9] Thus, denote a solution to (30) by $P_L^a(y, \overline{X}_B)$. It is clear that in general $P_L^a(y, \overline{X}_B)$ is not a sufficient statistic. That is, from (30), P_L^a reveals $m_A(y)$ + [a random variable]. If $\tilde{\overline{X}}_B$ and $\tilde{y}$ are uncorrelated, then P_L^a is certainly not a sufficient statistic for $\tilde{u}$, or even $\tilde{u}_A$. Since lemma 1 can clearly be applied here, if P_L^a is not a sufficient statistic, then there will not exist a solution to (2)–(4) that is a sufficient statistic.

The purpose of the above analysis was to argue that theorem 1 works because there are as many markets as the fundamental elements of uncertainty. If it is the case that trade or information is costly so that price cannot be a sufficient statistic, then some markets will become too thin and shut down. When some markets shut down, two things happen: (a) Traders observe a price that has lower dimensionality and thus reveals less information, and (b) a new source of uncertainty is added to the model due to the existence of stocks of nontraded goods, and this further reduces the informational content of the equilibrium price. Thus, when information and trade are costly, equilibrium must involve some markets that are too thin to operate competitively and an equilibrium price in competitive markets that is not exactly a sufficient statistic. The "amount of deviation from sufficiency" is determined by the underlying cost of information and trade.[10]

Appendix

We present some useful facts about conditional expectation and sufficient statistics. If $\tilde{X}$ and $\tilde{Y}$ are random variables and $F(\cdot)$ is a (measurable) function, then

$$E[\tilde{X} \mid F(\tilde{Y})] = E[E[\tilde{X}] \mid \tilde{Y}] \mid F(\tilde{Y})], \qquad (A1)$$

$$E[\tilde{X} \mid F(\tilde{Y})] = E[E[\tilde{X} \mid F(\tilde{Y})]\mid \tilde{Y}] \tag{A2}$$

(see Ash [2, p. 260]).

For our purposes the following definition of a sufficient statistic will be enough (there are more general definitions). Let $\tilde{Y}$ and $\tilde{u}$ be real random variables defined on a common probability space.[11] Let $f(Y \mid u)$ be a family of densities parametrized by u. We shall say that $t(Y)$ is a sufficient statistic if there exist two functions $g_1(Y)$ and $g_2(u, t(Y))$ such that $f(Y \mid u) \equiv g_1(Y) \cdot g_2(u, t(Y))$, for all (u, Y). If we are given a density on u, say, $r(u)$, such that the joint distribution of $(\tilde{Y}, \tilde{u})$ is generated by $f(Y \mid u)r(u)$, then it is easy to see that for any (measurable) real function $F(\cdot)$,

$$E[F(\tilde{u})\mid \tilde{Y} = Y] = E[F(\tilde{u})\mid t(\tilde{Y}) = t(Y)] \qquad \text{if } t \text{ a sufficient statistic.} \tag{A3}$$

The converse is also true. That is, if the density on $\tilde{u}$, $r(u)$ is everywhere positive and the statistic t has a density $q(t \mid u)$ [i.e., there exists a measure $v_3(\cdot)$ such that $\text{Prob}(t(Y) \in T \mid u) = \int_T q(t \mid u)\, dv_3(t)$ for all measurable sets T] and

$$E[F(\tilde{u})\mid \tilde{Y} = Y] = E[F(\tilde{u})\mid t(\tilde{Y}) = t(Y)] \qquad \text{for all } F(\cdot), \tag{A4}$$

then $t(\cdot)$ is a sufficient statistic. To see this, note that (A4) implies that the conditional density of $\tilde{u}$ given $\tilde{Y}$, $K_1(u \mid Y)$, is the same as the conditional density of $\tilde{u}$ given $t(\tilde{Y})$, $K_2(u \mid t)$. Thus, by Bayes's rule for all Y such that $\int r(u')f(Y \mid u')\, dv_2(u') > 0$ (and other Y may clearly be ignored),

$$K_1(u \mid Y) = \frac{r(u)f(Y \mid u)}{\int r(u')f(Y \mid u')\, dv_2(u')}$$

$$= K_2(u \mid t(Y))$$

$$= \frac{r(u)q(t(Y)\mid u)}{\int r(u')q(t(Y)\mid u)\, dv_2(u')}. \tag{A5}$$

Using the condition that $r(u) > 0$, we have

$$f(Y \mid u) = \frac{\int r(u')f(Y \mid u')\, dv_2(u')}{\int r(u')q(t(Y)\mid u')\, dv_2(u')} \cdot q(t(Y)\mid u). \tag{A6}$$

Thus we have provided a factorization of the density $f(Y \mid u)$ into two parts; the first part is independent of u and the second part depends on Y only through $t(Y)$. We have thus shown that

If $E[F(\tilde{u})\mid \tilde{Y} = Y] = E[F(\tilde{u})\mid t(\tilde{Y}) = t(Y)]$ for all $F(\cdot)$, then $t(\cdot)$ is a sufficient statistic. $\tag{A7}$

This is a slight generalization of the theorem by Raiffa and Schlaifer [14, p. 34], where it is shown that if (A4) holds for *all prior densities* $r(u)$ (this is called Bayesian sufficiency), then $t(\cdot)$ is a sufficient statistic.

In this chapter $(\tilde{u}, \tilde{Y})$ will be jointly Normal, so that we say that $t(Y)$ is a sufficient statistic if (A4) holds, or the factorization criterion is satisfied.

There is another concept of "sufficiency" in the literature, due to Blackwell [3].[12] Let $\tilde{s}$ be a random variable defined on the same probability space as $\tilde{Y}$ and $\tilde{u}$. The random variable $\tilde{s}$ is *Blackwell sufficient* for $\tilde{Y}$ if for *all* decision payoff functions $V(a, u)$, and all sets A

$$E\left[\max_{a \in A} E[V(a, \tilde{u})| \tilde{s}]\right] \geq E\left\{\max_{a \in A} E[V(a, \tilde{u})| \tilde{Y}]\right\}, \qquad (A8)$$

where a is an action and A is the set of all actions for the particular decision function $V(a, u)$. The idea of the definition is that the payoff to an action "a" depends upon the realization of a random variable $\tilde{u}$. Suppose a person can contract to see a realization of either $\tilde{s}$ or $\tilde{Y}$, but must choose the random variable *before* observing its realization. Then he will choose $\tilde{s}$ if and only if (A8) holds. (For example, knowledge of the weather helps decide which crop should be planted. There are two possible weather satellites that can be launched, one with realizations described by $\tilde{s}$ and the other described by $\tilde{Y}$. Obviously, the satellite must be launched before the information it will generate is known.)

There is a relationship between Blackwell sufficiency and the previously defined notion of a sufficient statistic. In particular:

If there exists a measurable function $g(\cdot)$ such that $\tilde{s} = g(\tilde{Y})$, then $\tilde{s}$ is Blackwell sufficient for $\tilde{Y}$ if and only if $g(\cdot)$ is a sufficient statistic. $\qquad$ (A9)

To see this, note that if $g(\cdot)$ is a sufficient statistic, $E[V(a, \tilde{u})| s] = E[V(a, \tilde{u})| g(Y)] = E[V(a, \tilde{u})| Y]$, and therefore (A8) holds with equality and $s = g(Y)$ is Blackwell sufficient for Y.

On the other hand, suppose that $s = g(Y)$ is Blackwell sufficient for Y. Then (A8) must hold with equality because by (A1), $E[V | g(Y)] = E[E[V | Y]| g(Y)]$. Hence

$$\max_a E[V | g(Y)] = \max_a E[E[V | Y]| g(Y)] \leq E\left\{\max_a E[V | Y]| g(Y)\right\}. \qquad (A10)$$

If we take unconditional expectations of both sides of this last inequality, we get

$$E\left[\max_a E[V \mid g(Y)]\right] \leqslant E\left\{E\left\{\max_a E[V \mid Y] \mid g(Y)\right\}\right\} = E\left\{\max_a E[V \mid Y]\right\}.$$

[The last equality follows from (A1) with $\tilde{X}$ replaced by $\max_a E[V \mid Y]$, $\tilde{Y}$ replaced with $g(Y)$, and $F(\tilde{Y})$ replaced by any function that is constant for all Y.] Thus from (A8) and the previous inequality

$$E\left\{\max_a E[V \mid S]\right\} = E\left\{\max_a E[V \mid Y]\right\}. \tag{A11}$$

However, since (A11) is obtained by taking the expectation of both sides of (A10), it follows that there cannot be strict inequality in (A10). Hence,

$$\max_a E[E[V \mid Y] \mid g(Y)] = E\left\{\max_a E[V \mid Y] \mid g(Y)\right\}. \tag{A12}$$

The same argument can be applied again since

$$E[V(a_0, \tilde{u}) \mid Y] \leqslant \max_a E[V(a, \tilde{u}) \mid Y] \quad \text{for any } a_0 \in A. \tag{A13}$$

Equation (A13) cannot be a strict inequality for any Y such that $g(Y)$ is constant, or (A12) would be violated. Thus for any realization s of $\tilde{s}$

$$E[V(a^*(s), \tilde{u}) \mid Y] = \max_a E[V(a, \tilde{u}) \mid Y] \quad \text{for all } Y \text{ such that } g(Y) = s, \tag{A14}$$

where $a^*(s)$ is the $a \in A$ that maximizes $E[E[V(a, \tilde{u}) \mid Y] \mid g(Y) = s]$. From (A14) it is clear that the distribution of $\tilde{u}$ given Y, say, $K(\tilde{u} \mid Y)$, must be constant for all Y such that $g(Y) = s$, for suppose there exist Y_1, Y_2 such that $g(Y_1) = g(Y_2) = s$ and $K(\tilde{u} \mid Y_1) \neq K(\tilde{u} \mid Y_2)$. Then it is clear that a function $V(a, \tilde{u})$ and a set A exist with the property that if a_i is the element of A that uniquely maximizes $E[V(a, \tilde{u}) \mid \tilde{Y} = Y_i]$ for $i = 1, 2$, then $a_1 \neq a_2$. This contradicts (A14), which states that $E[V(a, \tilde{u}) \mid Y]$ must have the same maximizer for all Y such that $g(Y) = s$. Hence $K(\tilde{u} \mid Y)$ depends on Y only through $g(Y)$. Hence by (A7), $\tilde{s} = g(\tilde{Y})$ is a sufficient statistic.

Notes

1. We shall assume that information and returns are jointly Normal. The standard assumption is that returns are Normal conditional on information. Thus our assumption is slightly stronger.

2. In (4), $(\forall y \in \mathcal{Y})$ could be replaced with "for all $y \in \mathcal{Y}$ except for a set A such that $v(\omega \in \Omega: \tilde{y}(\omega) \in A) = 0$." Note further that in (2) there may be many versions of the conditional expectation of U_t given $\tilde{y}_t$, $\tilde{P}$, differing from each other on sets of

measure zero; however, this in no way affects the analysis of the following sections. See Kreps [12] for further remarks on this problem.

3. Here, and elsewhere in the chapter, we shall use $P^a(y)$ to denote a realization of the random variable $\tilde{P}^a$.

4. An equilibrium for the artificial economy, $P^a(y)$, will exist under the above assumptions if $\tilde{x}_t \gg 0$ and $U_t(\cdot)$ is bounded for each trader t, and if a lower bound is put on short sales, so that traders' budget sets are compact. This is because under the above assumptions the economy is like the standard Arrow-Debreu economy with commodities $(x, B) \in \mathbb{R}^{N+1}$. We do not assume that there is a unique equilibrium price random variable, $P^a(y)$. We do assume throughout that price is generated by the same equilibrium price random variable for all y.

5. Danthine [4], in a different context, showed that price is a sufficient statistic in an example where all traders have the *same* coefficient of constant absolute risk aversion.

6. This result is in some ways similar to that of Jordan [10, pp. 11–12]. Therein he shows that if there is a complete set of contingent claims markets for all states of nature (including information states: a market for claims contingent on each $\omega \in \Omega$), then a Rational Expectations equilibrium will involve traders holding allocations that they would have held in an equilibrium for an economy where each agent had all the economy's information. We assume there are no markets for claims contingent on realizations of σ and, further, that there are markets only for particular composites of contingent claims on realizations of $\tilde{u}$. That is, by purchasing one share of asset t, a consumer gets $\tilde{u}_j(\omega)$ dollars in state ω. The consumer has no way of combining shares of assets so that he gets $\tilde{u}_j(\omega)$ dollars if the state is ω and zero dollars otherwise. Though the economy has far fewer than a complete set of markets, the fact that portfolio separation occurs implies that only two markets are necessary as pointed out in lemma 4. I would conjecture that theorem 1 is true whenever there is portfolio separation.

7. There may be other Rational Expectations equilibrium prices that are not sufficient statistics. See Grossman [7] for a uniqueness proof in the constant absolute risk aversion case.

8. The symbol $\tilde{u} \cdot (x_{At}, \tilde{x}_{Bt})$ means $\sum_{j=1}^{L} \tilde{u}_t x_{tt} + \sum_{j=L+1}^{N} \tilde{u}_j \tilde{x}_{jt}$.

9. That is, $\tilde{X}_B \colon \Omega \to \mathbb{R}^{N-L}_+$ is a random variable that represents uncertainty about aggregate endowments of B goods.

10. See Grossman and Stiglitz [9] for a model that shows how the cost of information determines endogenously the number of informed traders and the information content of the Rational Expectations equilibrium price.

11. The following definitions may help clarify the above notes. Let $\tilde{Y}$ be the identity mapping defined on a probability space $(W, \mathscr{W}, p_u)$, where $p_u(\cdot)$ is a measure on $\mathscr{W}$ indexed by a parameter u. A *parameter space* is a probability space $(U, \mathscr{U}, v)$. The "unknown" parameter u is an element of U. Define $\tilde{u}$ to be the

identity mapping on U. Then v is interpreted as the prior probability measure on the unknown parameter u. It is helpful to define a joint probability space ($W \times U$, $\mathcal{W} \times \mathcal{U}, p_u \times v) \equiv (\Omega, S, v)$, where $v(W_0 \times U_0) = \int_{U_0} p_u(W_0) \, dv(u)$, for $W_0 \times U_0 \in \mathcal{W} \times \mathcal{U}$. Thus, we think of the random variable $(\tilde{Y}, \tilde{u})$ as defined as the projection mappings on (Ω, S, v). We shall assume that each of the random variables has a density. That is, for some measure, v_1, $p_u(\tilde{Y} \in W_0) = \int_{W_0} \partial(Y \mid u) \, dv_1(Y)$ for all $u \in U$, so that $f(Y \mid u)$ is the density of $\tilde{Y}$. Similarly, assume there is a measure v_2 such that $v(U_0) = \int_{U_0} r(u) \, dv_2(u)$, so that $r(u)$ is the density of $\tilde{u}$.

12. I am grateful to Richard Kihlstrom for his aid with the following analysis.

References

1. K. J. Arrow, *Essays in the Theory of Risk-Bearing*, Markham, Chicago/North-Holland, Amsterdam, 1971.

2. R. B. Ash, *Real Analysis and Probability*, Academic Press, New York, 1972.

3. D. Blackwell, "Equivalent comparisons of experiments," *Ann. Math. Statist.* 24 (1953), 265–272.

4. J. Danthine, "Information, futures prices, and stabilizing speculation," *J. Econ. Theory* 17 (1978), 79–98.

5. E. Fama, "Efficient capital markets: A review of theory and empirical work," *J. Finance* 25 (1970), 383–417.

6. J. Green, "Information, Efficiency and Equilibrium," Discussion Paper No. 284, Harvard Institute of Economic Research, Harvard University, May 1973.

7. S. J. Grossman, Appendix in "On the Efficiency of Competitive Stock Markets where Traders Have Diverse Information," Technical Report No. 182, Institute for Mathematical Studies in the Social Sciences, Stanford University, September 1975.

8. S. J. Grossman, "On the efficiency of competitive stock markets where traders have diverse information," *J. Finance* 31 (1976), 573–585.

9. S. J. Grossman and J. E. Stiglitz, "On the impossibility of informationally efficient markets," Technical Report no. 259, Institute for Mathematical Studies in the Social Science, Stanford University, April 1978.

10. J. S. Jordan, "On the Predictability of Economic Events," Discussion Paper No. 329, Department of Economics, University of Pennsylvania, February 1976.

11. R. E. Kihlstrom and L. J. Mirman, "Information and market equilibrium," *Bell J. Econ.* 6 (1975), 357–376.

12. D. M. Kreps, "A note on fulfilled expectations equilibria," *J. Econ. Theory* 14 (1977).

13. R. E. Lucas, "Expectations and the neutrality of money," *J. Econ. Theory* 4 (1972), 103–124.

14. H. Raiffa and R. Schlaifer, "Applied Statistical Decision Theory," Division of Research, Graduate School of Business Administration, Harvard University, 1961.

15. W. F. Sharpe, "Capital asset prices: a theory of market equilibrium under conditions of risk," *J. Finance* (1964), 416–422.

16. J. Tobin, "Liquidity preference as behavior towards risk," *Rev. Econ. Stud.* 25 (1958), 65–86.

4

The Existence of Futures Markets, Noisy Rational Expectations, and Informational Externalities

4.1 Introduction

It is a fact that futures markets exist in some commodities and not others. Similarly, contingent commodity contracts of the type described by Debreu do not exist for all commodities in all states of the world. Any explanation of this phenomenon must be intimately connected with a theory of what functions these markets serve. The Keynes-Hicks theory of commodity futures markets is that they provide a mechanism by which risk averse speculators insure other risk averse traders who hold (positive or negative) stocks of a commodity subject to price fluctuation.[1]

We propose a new explanation of the role of futures markets as a place where information is exchanged, and where people who collect and analyze information about future states of the world can earn a return on their investment in information gathering. In particular, it is shown how the private and social incentives for the operation of a futures market depend on how much information spot prices alone can convey from "informed" to "uninformed" traders. (Firms that have information about future states of the world are called "informed," while firms that do not are called "uninformed.")

In equilibrium, without a futures market, informed firms will use their information about next period's price to make spot market purchases. The commodity purchase is stored in anticipation of a capital gain. Therefore, the trading activity of informed firms in the present spot market makes the spot price a function of their information. Uninformed traders can use the spot price as a statistic that reveals some of the informed traders' information. When the spot price reveals all of the informed traders' information, both types of traders have the same beliefs about next period's price. In this case there will be no incentive to trade based upon differences in beliefs about next period's price.

In general the spot price will *not* reveal all of the informed traders' information because there are many other factors ("noise") that determine the price along with the informed traders' information. This implies that in equilibrium with only a spot market, informed and uninformed traders will have different beliefs about next period's price. The difference in beliefs creates an incentive for futures trading in addition to the usual hedging incentive. When a futures market is introduced, uninformed firms will have the futures price as well as the spot price transmitting the informed firms' information to them. This is the informational role of futures markets.

The model has the following testable implications. The degree of predictability of a future spot price from only a current spot price determines the private incentives for futures trading in a commodity that has no futures market. For commodities with futures markets the volume of futures trading is directly related to how poorly current and futures prices predict the future spot price, relative to how well various exogenous variables predict the future spot price. "How well" refers to mean square prediction error conditional on available information, not biasedness of the predictions.

The model has relevance for Hirshleifer's [11] contention that there is probably over-investment in information collection. He argues that there are often large private gains from investment in information collection when there are little or no social gains. We show that when one takes into account the fact that *many* people will see private gains from investment in information, prices will reflect that information. Further, the text analyzes an extreme example where prices reflect all the information that informed traders collect, and other traders who invested nothing can get that information free by just observing market prices. This example is constructed so that there are social gains to collecting information about the intertemporal allocation of a crop, yet there are little or no private gains in equilibrium because all of the information will be reflected in market prices.

The model also suggests that we do not see markets for delivery of goods contingent on all states of the world because with so many prices revealing information, private incentives for investment in information about states of the world would be small. Hence "speculative capital" would not be attracted to many markets and they would thus be too "thin" to exist.

I use the concept of prices as statistics in a noisy rational expectations equilibrium context as has been done by Lucas [17] to study the neutrality of money. Green [5] has analyzed noisy and nonnoisy rational expectations equilibria in markets with informed and uninformed traders. Kihlstrom and Mirman [15] have established conditions under which equilibrium prices reveal the information of informed traders.

4.2   Information Transfers without Futures Markets

Consider a commodity that can be produced only at certain times during the year, though people desire to consume it throughout the year. Further, assume the commodity is storable. An obvious example is wheat. Let the market contain consumers of wheat whose demand for wheat each period is based only on that period's price of wheat. The market also contains firms that store wheat from one harvest to the next. These firms induce an intertemporal allocation of the harvest. For the sake of simplicity the following model assumes no carry-over from harvest to harvest and thus only analyzes the intertemporal allocation of a single harvest. Let

$$P_2 = D_2(I, w_2), \tag{1}$$

$$D_2(I, w_2) \equiv h_1 I + h_2 w_2, \tag{1a}$$

$$D_1(P_1) = Q - I, \tag{2}$$

$$D_1(P_1) \equiv h_3 + h_4 P_1, \tag{2a}$$

where the h_j are given real numbers satisfying $h_1 < 0$, $h_2 > 0$, and $h_4 < 0$. Equation (1) gives the period 2 demand for the consumption of "wheat." It is assumed that in period 2 there is no production, only consumption of the wheat carried over from period 1. The carry-over (inventories) of wheat is denoted by I. w_2 is the realization of a random variable, $\tilde{w}_2$. (Throughout this chapter, random variables will be denoted by a tilde.) Equation (1a) states that the period 2 demand curve has a linear form. The assumption that $h_2 > 0$ is a matter of convention, while $h_1 < 0$ is assumed because the demand curve is required to be downward sloping. Given I, $\tilde{P}_2$ is a random variable, the distribution of which depends on the distribution of $\tilde{w}_2$. Q is a given real number, the "harvest." It is the total amount of the commodity, the consumption of which is divided between period 1 and period 2. Thus, since I is the amount of "harvest" carried over for period 2 consumption, $Q - I$ is the amount of consumption in period 1. Equation (2) is the period 1 demand curve. It gives the price P_1, at which total period 1 consumption $Q - I$, will be demanded. Equation (2a) requires this demand curve to be linear, and $h_4 < 0$ is assumed to make the demand curve downward sloping.

We are interested in modeling the process by which information about the true distribution of $\tilde{w}_2$ is transferred by the competitive price system. For this purpose, let $\tilde{\theta}$ be a vector random variable such that $\tilde{w}_2$ and $\tilde{\theta}$ are jointly normally distributed. Then the conditional density of $\tilde{w}_2$ given $\tilde{\theta}$ is well-defined and is a normal density, which we write as $f(\tilde{w}_2 \mid \theta)$.

Informed traders know the true θ. Uninformed traders know the marginal density of θ, $\mu(\theta)$. $\mu(\theta)$ can be interpreted, from a Bayesian point of view, as a representation of prior beliefs about the true value of θ. Alternatively, $\mu(\theta)$ can be interpreted as the probability density of the law nature uses in choosing θ each period. Under either interpretation uninformed traders can make inferences about $\tilde{w}_2$ using $\int f(\tilde{w}_2 \mid \theta)\mu(\theta)\,d\theta$, while informed traders know a particular θ, say, $\tilde{\theta} = \theta_0$, and use $f(\tilde{w}_2 \mid \theta_0)$.

At the opening of the period one spot market, informed traders will have received a θ, and uninformed traders will use their prior, μ. Assume informed firms maximize profits from storage of wheat,

$$E\{[(\tilde{P}_2 - P_1)I - C(I)]\mid \theta\},\tag{3}$$

with respect to I. $C(\cdot)$ is a storage cost function, where for expositional convenience we assume the special form

$$C(I) \equiv \frac{cI^2}{2}\tag{3a}$$

with $c > 0$. Suppose that an optimal inventory policy occurs at $E[(\tilde{P}_2 - P_1)\mid \theta] = C'(I)$.[2] Thus the optimal policy can be denoted by

$$S\{E[(\tilde{P}_2 - P_1)\mid \theta]\} \equiv \frac{1}{c}(E[(\tilde{P}_2 - P_1)\mid \theta]).\tag{4}$$

We shall describe below the distribution under which the expectation in (4) is taken. Uninformed firms are not given θ, but only the period 1 spot price. They maximize

$$E\{(\tilde{P}_2 - P_1)I - C(I)\mid \tilde{P}_1 = P_1\},\tag{5}$$

with respect to I, to get an optimal inventory policy

$$S\{E[\tilde{P}_2 \mid P_1] - P_1\},\tag{6}$$

where $S(\cdot)$ is the same in (4) and (6) due to the fact that informed and uninformed firms have the same storage cost function. We assume this latter property in order to concentrate on information differences.

We define an equilibrium as a pair of functions (i.e., real valued random variables), $(\tilde{P}_1, \tilde{P}_2)$, with $\tilde{P}_1(\cdot) \equiv P_1^e(\theta)$, $\tilde{P}_2(\cdot) \equiv P_2^e(w_2, \theta)$ such that[3]

$$P_2^e(w_2, \theta) = D_2(I^e(\theta), w_2) \qquad \text{for all} \quad (\theta, w_2), \tag{7}$$

$$D_1[P_1^e(\theta)] = Q - I^e(\theta) \qquad \text{for all} \quad \theta, \tag{8}$$

$$I^e(\theta) \equiv S[E[\tilde{P}_2 \mid \tilde{P}_1 = P_1^e(\theta)] - P_1^e(\theta)] + S\{E[\tilde{P}_2 \mid \theta] - P_1^e(\theta)\}, \tag{9}$$

$$E[\tilde{P}_2 \mid \theta] = \int_{-\infty}^{\infty} P_2^e(w_2, \theta) f(w_2 \mid \theta) \, dw_2. \tag{10}$$

The idea of the definition in (7)–(10) is that when the informed firms learn θ, they can then calculate an expected equilibrium price using the probability density $f(w_2 \mid \theta)$ as in (10). Hence their demand for inventories will depend on which θ they get. Thus the equilibrium period 1 spot price will depend on θ [thus $\tilde{P}_1(\cdot) \equiv P_1^e(\theta)$]. The equilibrium spot price in period 2 will depend on the realization of $\tilde{w}_2$ and on how much inventories are carried over from period 1. But the size of the carry-over depends on θ through the actions of the informed firms. Hence the equilibrium price in period 2 will depend on the realization of $\tilde{w}_2$ and on the knowledge gained by the informed firms [thus

$$\tilde{P}_2(\cdot) = P_2^e(w_2, \theta)].$$

Since the equilibrium period 1 spot price depends on θ, uninformed firms can use $\tilde{P}_1$ as a *statistic* to get information about θ from the informed firms. Equation (7) requires that all the inventories carried over from period 1 be consumed at the price $P_2^e(w_2, \theta)$ when $\tilde{w}_2 = w_2$ and informed firms learn θ. Equation (8) requires that $P_1^e(\theta)$ clear the market in period 1, when informed firms learn θ and a price comes about such that consumers' desire for current consumption equals the difference between the "harvest" and the amount of "grain" that storage firms desire to store at price $P_1^e(\theta)$. This approach to Rational Expectations is examined in some simple models in Grossman [7].

Note that equation (9) involves the term $E[\tilde{P}_2 \mid \tilde{P}_1 = P_1^e(\theta)]$. This conditional expectation cannot be defined in an elementary way in general. However, if $P_1^e(\theta)$ is a linear function of θ, then since θ is normally distributed, $\tilde{P}_1$ will be normally distributed. Furthermore, if $P_2^e(w_2, \theta)$ is a linear function of (w_2, θ), then, since (w_2, θ) is multivariate normal, $\tilde{P}_2$ will be normally distributed. Thus if $P_1^e(\cdot)$, and $P_2^e(\cdot, \cdot)$ are linear functions, then $\tilde{P}_1$ and $\tilde{P}_2$ are jointly normally distributed. Then $E[\tilde{P}_2 \mid \tilde{P}_1 = P_1^e(\theta)]$ can be evaluated using elementary normal theory (see the appendix). Below we show that the linearity assumptions about demand and marginal cost functions implies the existence of linear price function. Equation (9) gives the total carry-over of inventories from period 1 to period 2. It is sum of informed and uninformed firms' inventory decisions. For notational simplicity, we have assumed that there is one informed and one uninformed firm.[4]

To see the importance of the above problem, assume for the moment that equilibrium exists and is unique (see theorem 2). Consider

$$E[\tilde{P}_2 \mid \theta] - E[\tilde{P}_2 \mid \tilde{P}_1 = P_1^e(\theta)] \equiv d(\theta). \tag{11}$$

$d(\theta)$ measures the difference in the expectations about next period's price between informed and uninformed firms. When $d(\theta) > 0$, informed firms anticipate a higher price than uninformed firms. Hence informed firms would like to take "long" positions (i.e., buy contracts for future delivery at the price $E[\tilde{P}_2 \mid \theta]$), while uninformed firms would like to be "short" (i.e., sell contracts for future delivery at a price $E[\tilde{P}_2 \mid \theta]$). That is, when spot prices leave informed and uninformed firms with different expectations in equilibrium, there seems to be an incentive for futures trading. Note that all firms are risk neutral, so there is no insurance motive for futures trading.

For the market described by (1)–(11), it will never be the case that $d(\theta) \neq 0$. We shall show below (theorem 1) that in equilibrium all the *relevant* information gathered by informed firms is disseminated by the period 1 spot price.

Theorem 1   *If* $(\tilde{P}_1, \tilde{P}_2)$ *is an equilibrium, [i.e.,* $\tilde{P}_1(\cdot) = P_1^e(\theta)$, *and* $\tilde{P}_2(\cdot) = P_2^e(w_2, \theta)$], *then*

$$E[\tilde{P}_2 \mid \theta] = E[\tilde{P}_2 \mid P_1^e(\theta)] \qquad \text{for all} \quad \theta. \tag{12}$$

Proof   From (8) and (9)

$$S\{E[\tilde{P}_2 \mid \theta] - P_1\} = Q - S\{E[\tilde{P}_2 \mid P_1] - P_1\} - D_1(P_1). \tag{13}$$

From (4) and (13)

$$E[\tilde{P}_2 \mid \theta] = P_1 + c[Q - S\{E[\tilde{P}_2 \mid P_1] - P_1\} - D_1(P_1)]. \tag{14}$$

The right-hand side of (14) is a function of P_1 only. Q is a nonstochastic positive number and $E[\tilde{P}_2 \mid P_1]$ is a function of P_1. Hence, $E[\tilde{P}_2 \mid \theta]$ is a function of $P_1^e(\theta)$. Thus[5]

$$E\{E[\tilde{P}_2 \mid \theta] \mid \tilde{P}_1 = P_1^e(\theta)\} = E[\tilde{P}_2 \mid \theta]. \tag{15}$$

(That is, (14) implies that if P_1 is known, then $E[\tilde{P}_2 \mid \theta]$ is known. Therefore $P_1^e(\theta)$ reveals $E[\tilde{P}_2 \mid \theta]$.)

Note that from the discussion in the appendix, i.e. (A5),

$$E\{E[\tilde{P}_2 \mid \theta] \mid \tilde{P}_1 = P_1^e(\theta)\} = E[\tilde{P}_2 \mid \tilde{P}_1 = P_1^e(\theta)]. \tag{16}$$

Equations (15) and (16) imply that $E[\tilde{P}_2 \mid \tilde{P}_1] = E[\tilde{P}_2 \mid \theta]$ in any equilibrium. QED

Theorem 2 *The linearity assumptions* (1a), (2a), *and quadratic storage costs imply that equilibrium exists and is unique; i.e.,* (7)–(10) *has a unique solution.*

Proof Theorem 1 showed that in any equilibrium both traders have information θ. Therefore equilibrium for the model in (7)–(10) will be the same as in a market where *all* traders have information θ. Below we calculate the unique equilibrium for such a market. Equations (1) and (2) imply

$$P_2 = D_2(Q - D_1(P_1), w_2). \tag{17}$$

Using (1a) and (1b), (17) becomes $P_2 = h_1[Q - (h_3 + h_4 P_1)] + h_2 w_2$. Thus

$$E[\tilde{P}_2 \mid \theta] = h_1[Q - (h_3 + h_4 P_1)] + h_2 E[\tilde{w}_2 \mid \theta]. \tag{18}$$

Theorem 1 implies that $E[\tilde{P}_2 \mid P_1]$ can be replaced by $E[\tilde{P}_2 \mid \theta]$ in (13). Since $S\{\cdot\}$ is a linear function, equations (13) and (18) are two linear equations in two variables: $E[\tilde{P}_2 \mid \theta]$ and P_1. The assumptions made about h_1, h_2, h_4 imply the existence of unique solutions of the form

$$P_1 = \pi_{10} + \pi_{11}Q + \pi_{12}E[\tilde{w}_2 \mid \theta], \tag{19}$$

$$E[\tilde{P}_2 \mid \theta] = \pi_{20} + \pi_{21}Q + \pi_{22}E[\tilde{w}_2 \mid \theta], \tag{20}$$

where the π_{ij} are functions of the h_j and the marginal cost of storage c. The assumptions that $h_1 < 0$, $h_2 > 0$, and $h_4 < 0$ imply that $\pi_{12} > 0$. The reader can verify that

$$\pi_{12} = \frac{-2h_2}{h_4(c - 2h_1) - 2},$$

which is positive. Hence, from (19) P_1 reveals $E[\tilde{w}_2 \mid \theta]$. Define

$$\tilde{P}_1^0(\theta) \equiv \pi_{10} + \pi_{11}Q + \pi_{12}E[\tilde{w}_2 \mid \theta] \tag{21}$$

and

$$\tilde{P}_2^0(w_2, \theta) \equiv D_2(Q - D_1[P_1^e(\theta)], \tilde{w}_2); \tag{22}$$

then (21) and (22) give equilibrium prices in the sense of (7)–(10). QED

Define the maximized profit functions for informed and uninformed firms as

$$\pi_a(\theta) = \max_I [\{E[\tilde{P}_2^0 \mid \theta] - P_1^0(\theta)\}I - C(I)],$$

$$\pi_b(P_1^0) = \max_I [\{E[\tilde{P}_2^0 \mid P_1^0] - P_1^0(\theta)\}I - C(I)].$$

Corollary 2.1 $\pi_a(\theta) \equiv \pi_b(P_1^0(\theta))$ *for all* θ.

Proof   Immediate from theorems 1 and 2.   QED

Hence the informed firms make no profits from their information; all of it leaks out to uninformed firms through the period 1 spot price. For example, when informed firms get a θ that leads them to expect a high period 2 spot price, they bid up the period 1 spot price in such a way that uninformed firms learn that informed firms anticipate a high price. In theorem 1, spot prices act like a xerographic machine, freely distributing the information of the informed firms to uninformed firms. Note that in (2) there is no noise in the period 1 spot market. Since we have assumed Q a known constant, when an uninformed firm "sees" a P_1, it can "know" total inventories I. Uninformed firms would like to know $E[\tilde{P}_2 \mid \theta]$. Since they "know" I, they "know" $S\{E[\tilde{P}_2 \mid \theta] - P_1^0\} + S\{E[\tilde{P}_2 \mid P_1^0] - P_1^0\}$. Since $S\{E[\tilde{P}_2 \mid P_1^0 - P_1^0\}$ is a function only of P_1^0, which uninformed firms observe, the uninformed firms can know $S\{E[\tilde{P}_2 \mid \theta] - P_1^0\}$ from their knowledge of I and $S\{E[\tilde{P}_2 \mid P_1^0] - P_1^0\}$ that is implied by their knowledge of P_1^0. But $S(\cdot)$ is an invertible function, so that $E[\tilde{P}_2 \mid \theta]$ can be known through the knowledge of P_1^0. As this verbal argument indicates, theorem 1 has nothing to do with the linearity assumptions about demand and marginal cost functions. As I show in Grossman [6], theorems 1 and 2 hold with strictly convex cost functions and downward sloping demand functions.

Note that nothing has been said about the invertibility of $P_1^0(\theta)$. In general, this function will not be invertible, so uninformed firms will be unable to learn θ from observing P_1^0.

However, θ is not of direct interest to the uninformed firms; $E[\tilde{P}_2^0 \mid \theta]$ is of interest to them, and this they always learn by observing $P_1^0(\theta)$. Note: Suppose θ is, for example, a vector of 10,000 independent normal, univariate, random variables, with 20,000 unknown parameters in their joint density function. Then $\theta \in R^{10,000}$, and it will not be the case such that there is a unique $\theta \in R^{10,000}$ and such that $P_1^0(\theta) = P_1$ (for a given number P_1), even though there is a unique $E[\tilde{P}_2^0 \mid \theta]$ associated with $P_1^0(\theta) = P_1$— and this is what is of economic relevance here. Thus the important work of Green [5] and Kihlstrom and Mirman [15], which has studied the problem of when market prices reveal all the information of informed traders in terms of the invertibility of $P_1^0(\theta)$, is not of strong relevance here. That is, though θ completely characterizes the distribution of $\tilde{w}_2$, the information relevant to uninformed firms' optimization problems need not always be θ.

The above model gives some insights about "informational externalities" as discussed in Hirshleifer [11], Stiglitz [20], and Green [5]. Note that in the model (1)–(2) there is clearly social value to learning about the distribution of $\tilde{w}_2$ because it can lead to a better intertemporal allocation of the "harvest" both in the ex-ante and ex-post senses discussed in Starr [19]. That is, if there were a social planner who could get the true θ for free, he would surely want it. This can be proved formally by putting (1)–(7) in a general equilibrium context; or more directly, the result follows from Starr's analysis, which indicates that in general, the appropriate intertemporal distribution of goods depends on the probability distribution of states of the world when there is production (which is what storage corresponds to here). Hirshleifer suggests, by example, that there will be an over-investment in collecting information because there can be a private incentive to learn about the distribution of $\tilde{w}_2$ even in cases where there is no social value to knowing the distribution, which is the case in a pure exchange economy with identical individuals. He suggests that even in an economy with production, the private incentives to collect information are greater than the social value of the information. Green's work suggests that the price system corrects some of that externality in the pure exchange economy because if many people invest in information, that information will be reflected in market prices, and if completely disseminated by market prices, the private incentive for investment in information that is socially valueless (in the sense of Hirshleifer) is much reduced.

Corollary 2.1 shows that here, where there is social value to learning θ, there is no private incentive to invest in learning about θ. As Stiglitz [20] has noted, Hirshleifer ignores the fact that when there are private incentives for one individual who takes prices as given to invest in information, there will be incentives for many individuals to so invest. We have shown that when this occurs, all the information would be revealed to traders who invested nothing in learning about θ, but get the relevant information free by observing P_1^0. Thus this model has properties that are just the opposite of those discussed by Hirshleifer. When one takes into account the cost of investment in information on prices, the private value of investment is below the social value.

The model in (1)–(10) captures the idea that spot prices transmit information from informed to uninformed traders. It is a nonnoisy model in that all information is transferred. A natural source of noise is to have random factors affecting supply and demand in period 1. The next section shows the importance of a futures market with noise present in the system.

4.3   An Informational Role for Futures Markets

Consider the new system

$$P_2 = D_2(I, w_2),$$ (23)

$$D_1(P_1) = w_1 - I.$$ (24)

In equation (24) we replace the certain "harvest," Q, with the realization of a real valued random variable $\tilde{w}_1$. $\tilde{w}_1$ represents random factors in the "harvest" (or in the demand for current consumption). We may assume that the joint distribution of $(\tilde{w}_1, \tilde{w}_2)$ is unknown, and uninformed firms devote resources to learn it. However, in "equilibrium" informed firms will be able to infer the realization of $\tilde{w}_1$ from P_1. That is, suppose there is a random variable $\tilde{\alpha}$, of which informed firms learn the realization α. Suppose $\tilde{\alpha}$ is correlated with $(\tilde{w}_1, \tilde{w}_2)$. Then informed firms, after observing α, make an inventory decision that will depend on α and P_1, which is all that they observe. Denote the decision by $I_a(\alpha, P_1)$. The uninformed firms will make inventory decisions based only on P_1. Denote their decision by $I_b(P_1)$. Hence an equilibrium period 1 price must solve

$$D_1(P_1) = w_1 - I_a(\alpha, P_1) - I_b(P_1).$$ (25)

If we denote the solution to (25) by $\hat{P}_1(\alpha, w_1)$, then it is clear that if the informed firm is given $\hat{P}_1(\alpha, w_1) = P_1$, and a particular α, then it can infer exactly the realization of $\tilde{w}_1$. Thus the conditional distribution of $\tilde{w}_1$ given α and P_1 satifies

$$\text{Prob}[\tilde{w}_1 = D_1(P_1) + I_a(\alpha, P_1) + I_b(P_1) | \hat{P}_1(\alpha, w_1) = P_1, \alpha] = 1.$$

Thus w_1 is revealed to informed firms in equilibrium. Since w_1 is revealed to informed firms in equilibrium, we may assume in defining a particular equilibrium that informed firms know the realization of $\tilde{w}_1$, and devote no resources to the study of its distribution. Thus, assume as in section 4.2 that informed firms observe $\tilde{\theta}$ that is correlated with $\tilde{w}_2$, and then solve

$$\max_I [(E[\tilde{P}_2 \mid w_1, \theta] - P_1)I - C(I)]$$

to get an inventory supply function

$$S_u(w_1, \theta, P_1) \equiv S(E[\tilde{P}_2 \mid w_1, \theta] - P_1), \tag{26}$$

where $S(\cdot)$ is as in (4). The symbol $E[\tilde{P}_2 \mid w_1, \theta]$ will be defined below. Similarly, uninformed firms

$$\max_I [(E[\tilde{P}_2 \mid P_1] - P_1)I - C(I)]$$

to get an inventory supply function

$$S_b(P_1) \equiv S[E[\tilde{P}_2 \mid P_1] - P_1]. \tag{27}$$

Define an equilibrium as a pair of mappings $(\tilde{P}_2, \tilde{P}_1)$ such that

$$\tilde{P}_1(\cdot) \equiv P_1^e(w_1, \theta), \qquad \tilde{P}_2(\cdot) \equiv P_2^e(w_1, w_2, \theta)$$

and

$$P_2^e(w_1, w_2, \theta) = D_2[I^e(w_1, \theta), w_2] \qquad \text{for all} \quad w_1, w_2, \text{ and } \theta, \tag{28}$$

$$D_1[P_1^e(w_1, \theta)] = w_1 - I^e(w_1, \theta), \tag{29}$$

$$I^e(w_1, \theta) \equiv S\{E[\tilde{P}_2 \mid \tilde{P}_1 = P_1^e(w_1, \theta)] - P_1^e(w_1, \theta)\}$$

$$+ S\{E[\tilde{P}_2 \mid \theta, w_1] - P_1^e(\theta, w_1)\}, \tag{30}$$

where

$$E[\tilde{P}_2 \mid \theta, w_1] \equiv \int_{-\infty}^{\infty} P_2^e(w_1, w_2, \theta) f(w_2 \mid \theta) \, dw_2. \tag{31}$$

To facilitate comparisons with the previous section we assume that $\tilde{w}_1$ is normally distributed independent of $\tilde{w}_2$ and $\tilde{\theta}$, with density function $m(w_1)$.

As in the previous section we are concerned with equilibrium differences in beliefs about P_2. That is, how much information does $P_1^e(w_1, \theta)$ reveal about $E[\tilde{P}_2 \mid \theta, w_1]$? Note that (29) and (30) can be written as

$$D_1(P_1) + S\{E[\tilde{P}_2 \mid P_1] - P_1\} = w_1 - S\{E[\tilde{P}_2 \mid \theta, w_1] - P_1\}. \tag{32}$$

The left-hand side of (32) is a function of P_1. Thus P_1 reveals the left-hand side of (32) to uninformed firms. Therefore, by (32), P_1 reveals $w_1 - S\{E[\tilde{P}_2 \mid \theta, w_1] - P_1\}$ to uninformed firms. But since w_1 is unknown to uninformed firms, P_1 cannot, in general, reveal $E[\tilde{P}_2 \mid \theta, w_1]$ to them. To discover exactly what P_1 reveals it is convenient to use the linearity assumptions in (1a)–(3a) to rewrite (32) as

$$S\{E[\tilde{P}_2 \mid P_1] - P_1\} + \frac{(c - h_1)D_1(P_1) - P_1}{c} = y_1, \tag{33}$$

where

$$y_1 \equiv \frac{(c - h_1)}{c} w_1 - \frac{h_2}{c} E[\tilde{w}_2 \mid \theta]. \tag{34}$$

In deriving (33) we have used the fact that

$$E[\tilde{P}_2 \mid \theta, w_1] = h_1(w_1 - D_1(P_1)) + h_2 E[\tilde{w}_2 \mid \theta]. \tag{35}$$

From equation (33) it can be seen that P_1 reveals y_1. y_1 is a linear combination of w_1 and $E[\tilde{w}_2 \mid \theta]$. Uninformed firms are interested in $E[\tilde{P}_2 \mid \theta, w_1]$. To know this they must know $h_1 w_1 + h_2 E[\tilde{w}_2 \mid \theta]$ by (35). But y_1 *reveals the wrong linear combination* of w_1 and $E[\tilde{w}_2 \mid \theta]$ by (34), since $c > 0$. The following theorem characterizes the equilibrium more exactly.

Theorem 3   *Suppose $P_1(y_1)$ is the solution to*

$$S\{E[\tilde{P}_2 \mid \tilde{y}_1 = y_1] - P_1\} + \frac{(c - h_1)D_1(P_1) - P_1}{c} = y_1 \tag{36}$$

for P_1 as a function of y_1. Let

$$P_1^e(w_1, \theta) \equiv P_1\left(\frac{(c - h_1)w_1 - h_2 E[\tilde{w}_2 \mid \theta]}{c}\right), \tag{37}$$

and

$$P_2^e(w_1, w_2, \theta) \equiv D_2(w_1 - D_1(P_1^e(w_1, \theta)), w_2); \tag{38}$$

then $P_1^e(\cdot)$, $P_2^e(\cdot)$ is an equilibrium, i.e., satisfies (28)–(31).

Proof   First note that, for each y_1, (36) has exactly one solution $P_1(y_1)$. This follows from the linearity assumptions (1a)–(3a) and $h_1 < 0$ and $h_4 < 0$. The solution is

$$P_1(y_1) = \frac{cy_1 - E[\tilde{y}_2 \mid y_1] - (c - 2h_1)h_3}{h_4(c - 2h_1) - 2}, \tag{39}$$

where

$$\tilde{y}_2 \equiv h_1 \tilde{w}_1 + h_2 E[\tilde{w}_2 \mid \theta]. \tag{40}$$

(Note from (35) that $\tilde{y}_2$ is the part of $E[\tilde{P}_2 \mid \theta, w_1]$ that uninformed firms want to learn.) From elementary normal distribution theory (see appendix),

$$E[\tilde{y}_2 \mid y_1] = E\tilde{y}_2 + \frac{\text{Cov}(\tilde{y}_1, \tilde{y}_2)}{\text{Var}\,\tilde{y}_1}(y_1 - E\tilde{y}_1). \tag{41}$$

From (34), (40) and the independence of w_1 and $E[\tilde{w}_2 \mid \theta]$,

$$\sigma_{12} \equiv \text{Cov}(\tilde{y}_1, \tilde{y}_2) = \frac{(c - h_1)}{c} h_1 \,\text{Var}\,\tilde{w}_1 - \frac{h_2^2}{c} \text{Var}(E[\tilde{w}_2 \mid \theta]). \tag{42}$$

Since $c > 0$, $h_1 < 0$ and variances are positive, $\sigma_{12} < 0$.

This implies that $E[\tilde{y}_2 \mid y_1]$ is a strictly decreasing function of y_1. It follows that $P_1(y_1)$ in (39) is invertible. This implies that, for all y_1,

$$E[\tilde{P}_2 \mid \tilde{y}_1 = y_1] = E[\tilde{P}_2 \mid P_1(\tilde{y}_1) = P_1(y_1)].$$

Therefore, in (36) $E[\tilde{P}_2 \mid \tilde{y}_1 = y_1]$ can be replaced by $E[\tilde{P}_2 \mid P_1(\tilde{y}_1) = P_1]$. This makes (36) and (33) identical. $P_2^e(\cdot)$ is defined by (38) in such a way that if P_1^e clears the period 1 market, then P_2^e must clear the period 2 market. Since $P_1(y_1)$ clears the period 1 market and $P_1^e(w_1, \theta)$ is the value of $P_1(y_1)$ when $y_1 = ((c - h_1)w_1/c) - (h_2/c)E[\tilde{w}_2 \mid \theta]$ [and y_1 always equals this by definition in (34)], $P_1^e(\cdot)$, $P_2^e(\cdot)$ is an equilibrium.   QED

It is important to note the following:

Theorem 4   *Equilibrium is unique.*

Proof   We first show that equilibrium is unique in the class of all functions $P_1(\theta, w_1)$ that are functions of (θ, w_1) only through $y_1 \equiv ((c - h_1)w_1/c) - (h_2/c)E[\tilde{w}_2 \mid \theta]$. Suppose $\hat{P}_1(y_1)$ and $P_1^0(y_1)$ solve (33) with $\hat{P}_2 \equiv D_2(w_1 - D_1(\hat{P}_1), w_2)$ and $P_2^0 \equiv D_2(w_1 - D_1(P_1^0), w_2)$. Then $E[\tilde{P}_2 \mid \hat{P}_1(\tilde{y}_1) = \hat{P}_1(y_1)] = E[\tilde{P}_2 \mid \tilde{y}_1 = y_1]$, since P_1 reveals the value of $\tilde{y}_1$ by (33) [i.e., the left-hand side of (33) is some function of P_1, say $H(P_1)$, so (33) states $H(P_1) = y_1$], and trivially, y_1 reveals the value of P_1 since $P_1 = \hat{P}_1(y_1)$. Thus $\tilde{y}_1$ and $\hat{P}_1$ are the same statistics; for the identical reasons $E[P_2^0 \mid P_1^0(\tilde{y}_1) = P_1^0(y_1)] = E[P_2^0 \mid \tilde{y}_1 = y_1]$. This implies that $\hat{P}_1(y_1)$ and $P_1^0(y_1)$ are both solutions of (35). But (36) has only one solution. (Note that

$$E[\tilde{P}_2 \mid \tilde{y}_1] = E[\tilde{P}_2 \mid P_1(\tilde{y}_1) = P_1]$$

$$= E[D_2(w_1 - D_1(P_1), w_2) \mid P_1(\tilde{y}_1) = P_1]$$

$$= E[P_2^e \mid P_1(\tilde{y}_1) = P_1] = E[P_2^e \mid \tilde{y}_1 = y_1].$$

Suppose $P_1(\theta, w_1)$ is an equilibrium that contains more information than y_1 so that there is *no* function $H(\cdot)$ such that $P_1(\theta, w_1) = H(y_1)$ for all θ, w_1. We show that this is impossible. Let

$$G(P_1) \equiv E[\tilde{y}_2 \mid P_1(\theta, w_1) = P_1] - [(2h_1 - c)h_4 + 2]P_1 - (2h_1 - c)h_3.$$

Since any equilibrium must satisfy (33), it can be shown that, for all (θ, w_1),

$$G(P_1(\theta, w_1)) = cy_1,$$

using (35), (39), and $E\{E[\tilde{P}_2 \mid \theta, w_1] \mid P_1\} = E[\tilde{P}_2 \mid P_1]$. If $G(P_1)$ is invertible, then $P_1(\theta, w_1)$ and y_1 are equivalent statistics, but we have assumed that $P_1(\theta, w_1)$ contains more information than y_1. Thus $G(P_1)$ is not invertible, and there are at least two different functions $P_1^a(y_1)$ and $P_1^b(y_1)$ such that for all y_1,

$$G(P_1^a(y_1)) = cy_1 \qquad \text{and} \qquad G(P_1^b(y_1)) = cy_1.$$

Clearly P_1^a and P_1^b contain less information than $P_1(\theta, w_1)$. Therefore

$$E\{E[\tilde{y}_2 \mid P_1(\theta, w_1)] \mid P_1^a\} = E[\tilde{y}_2 \mid P_1^a]$$

similarly for P_1^b. Taking expectations of both sides of $G(P_1^a) = cy_1$ conditional on P_1^a yields

$$E[\tilde{y}_2 \mid P_1^a] - [(2h_1 - c)h_4 + 2]P_1^a - (2h_1 - c)h_3 = cy_1,$$

where we have used $E[\tilde{y}_1 \mid P_1^a] = y_1$ because $G(P_1^a) = cy_1$. Therefore $P_1^a(y_1)$ is an equilibrium and similarly for $P_1^b(y_1)$. This contradicts the previous result that there is a unique equilibrium price function of y_1. QED

Since the equilibrium spot price does not reveal $E[\tilde{P}_2 \mid \theta, w_1]$ to uninformed firms, there will be equilibrium differences in beliefs about $\tilde{P}_2$. Let

$$D(w_1, \theta) \equiv E[\tilde{P}_2 \mid \theta, w_1] - E[\tilde{P}_2 \mid \tilde{P}_1 = P_1^e(w_1, \theta)]. \tag{44}$$

We now calculate this equilibrium difference in beliefs.

$$E[\tilde{P}_2 \mid P_1] = E\{E[\tilde{P}_2 \mid \theta, w_1] \mid P_1\} = E[\tilde{y}_2 \mid P_1] - h_1 D_1(P_1). \tag{45}$$

The second equality follows from (35) and (40), while the first follows from the fact that P_1 is a function of (w_1, θ). Using (35), (40), (43), and (45), we can write (44) as

$$D(w_1, \theta) = \tilde{y}_2 - E[\tilde{y}_2 \mid y_1].$$

If we take $E[D(w_1, \theta)]$ as a measure of the average difference in belief between the traders, then this will always be zero by definition.

$E[D(w_1, \theta)]^2$ is a more reasonable measure of differences in belief because it cumulates the absolute value of the difference:

$$E\{[D(w_1, \theta)]^2 | y_1\} = \text{Var}[D(w_1, \theta)| y_1] + \{E[D(w_1, \theta)| y_1]\}^2.$$

So

$$E\{[D(w_1, \theta)]^2 | y_1\} = \text{Var}[\tilde{y}_2 | y_1] + 0. \tag{46}$$

The right-hand side of (46) does not depend on y_1, because $\tilde{y}_1$, $\tilde{y}_2$ are jointly normal. Therefore

$$E[D(w_1, \theta)]^2 = \text{Var}[\tilde{y}_2 | y_1]. \tag{47}$$

The left-hand side of (47) is zero (almost everywhere) if and only if $D(w_1, \theta)$ is zero (almost everywhere). Hence the difference in belief is zero (almost everywhere) if and only if $\text{Var}[\tilde{y}_2 | y_1]$ is zero (almost everywhere). Referring to (34) and (40), this can occur only if $\tilde{w}_1$ or $E[\tilde{w}_1 | \theta]$ has a degenerate distribution (since $c > 0$ and $\tilde{\theta}$ and $\tilde{w}_1$ are assumed independent). It is exactly in this sense that $\tilde{w}_1$ is noise. We have just proved

Corollary 4.1 *If $E[\tilde{w}_2 | \theta]$ is not a degenerate function of θ, (i.e., if θ contains information), then $D(w_1, \theta) = 0$ (almost everywhere) if and only if w_1 is degenerate.*

Hence, given that $\tilde{w}_1$ does not have a degenerate distribution, $D(\theta, w_1)$ will not be zero everywhere. In equilibrium, with no futures market, informed firms will have different expectations about next period's price than uninformed firms. Thus one type will desire to be "long" (buy contracts for future delivery at $E[\tilde{P}_2 | \theta, w_1]$), while another will desire to be "short" (sell contracts for future delivery at $E[\tilde{P}_2 | \theta, w_1]$). Further, the informed firms will make more money (in an appropriate expected value sense) than the uninformed firms.

Let

$$\pi_a(w_1, \theta) \equiv \max_I \{(E[\tilde{P}_2 | \theta, w_1] - P_1^e(w_1, \theta))I - C(I)\}.$$

If $P_1^e(w_1, \theta) = P_1$, let

$$\pi_b(P_1) = \pi_b(P_1^e(w_1, \theta))$$

$$\equiv \max_I \{(E[\tilde{P}_2 | \tilde{P}_1 = P_1^e(w_1, \theta)] - P_1^e(w_1, \theta))I - C(I)\}.$$

Let

$g(P_1) \equiv E[\tilde{P}_2 \mid \tilde{P}_1 = P_1]$ and $R(w_1, \theta) \equiv E[\tilde{P}_2 \mid \theta, w_1]$,

and note that, by (A5) in the appendix,

$g(P_1) = E[R(w_1, \theta) \mid \tilde{P}_1 = P_1]$.

Theorem 5 $E[\pi_a(\tilde{w}_1, \tilde{\theta})] \geqq E[\pi_b(P_1^e(\tilde{w}_1, \tilde{\theta}))]$; *the inequality is strict if $\tilde{w}_1$ is not degenerate and θ contains information.*

Proof Let $S(\cdot)$ denote the optimal inventory. Then

$\pi_a(w_1, \theta) = R(w_1, \theta) - P_1)S(R(w_1, \theta) - P_1) - C[S(R(w_1, \theta) - P_1)]$.

As $S(R(w_1, \theta) - P_1)$ is the optimal investment policy for type a firms,

$$\pi_a(w_1, \theta) \geqq (R(w_1, \theta) - P_1)S(g(P_1) - P_1) - C[S(g(P_1) - P_1)]; \tag{48}$$

thus

$$E[\pi_a(w_1, \theta) \mid P_1] \geqq (g(P_1) - P_1)S\{g(P_1) - P_1\} - C[S\{g(P_1) - P_1\}]. \tag{49}$$

But the right-hand side of (49) is just $\pi_b(P_1)$. Take expectations of both sides of (49), use $E\{E[\pi_a \mid P_1]\} = E\pi_a$, and find $E\pi_a \geqq E\pi_b$. If θ contains information and $\tilde{w}_1$ is not degenerate, then $D(w_1, \theta) \neq 0$ on some set, say, B, of positive measure. Therefore on B, $g(P_1) \neq R(w_1, \theta)$, and thus $S\{g(P_1) - P_1\} \neq S\{R(w_1, \theta) - P_1\}$. Since the optimal investment policy is unique, (48) holds as a strict inequality on B.   QED

In considering how much to invest in information before the period 1 spot market opens, firms are interested in knowing how much better off they will be by being informed than by not being informed. Theorem 5 shows that with noise in the price system informed firms can earn a return on their information. That is, if a lifetime subscription to a news-letter that reveals θ costs $E\pi_a - E\pi_b$ dollars, then the above market will be in equilibrium with both informed and uninformed firms participating. The nonnoisy equilibrium of the last section would have broken down if information were costly. However, a noisy price system does not symmetrize peoples' beliefs. Therefore there is an incentive for futures trading. However, it will be shown in the next section that the introduction of a futures market removes the noise from the price system.[6]

The following corollary is suggestive of the empirical content of the hypothesis that futures markets are important as disseminators of information.

Corollary 5.1 *Under the assumption of quadratic storage costs,*

$$E\pi_a - E\pi_b = \frac{1}{2c}\text{Var}[R(\tilde{w}_1, \tilde{\theta})| P_1] = \frac{1}{2c}\text{Var}[R(\tilde{w}_1, \tilde{\theta})] \tag{50a}$$

and

$$E\pi_a - E\pi_b = \frac{1}{2c}\text{Var}[D(w_1, \theta)] \equiv \frac{1}{2c}E[D(w_1, \theta)]^2. \tag{50b}$$

Proof As $C(I) = cI^2/2$, $\pi_a(w_1, \theta) = (1/2c)[R(w_1, \theta) - P_1]^2$ and $\pi_b(P_1) = (1/2c)[g(P_1) - P_1]^2$, whence

$$\pi_a(w_1, \theta) - \pi_b(P_1)$$

$$= \frac{1}{2c}\{[R(w_1, \theta)]^2 - (g(P_1))^2 - 2P_1 R(w_1, \theta) + 2P_1 g(P_1)\}.$$

As $g(P_1) \equiv E[R(\tilde{w}_1, \theta)| P_1]$, (57) implies

$$E[\pi_a(\tilde{w}_1, \tilde{\theta}) - \pi_b(\tilde{P}_1)| P_1] = (1/2c)(E[(R(\tilde{w}_1, \tilde{\theta}))^2| P_1] - (g(P_1))^2,$$

whence $E[\pi_a(w_1, \theta)| P_1] - \pi_b(P_1) = (1/2c)\text{Var}[R(\tilde{w}_1, \tilde{\theta})| P_1]$. But $\tilde{R}$ and $\tilde{P}_1$ are jointly normal so this last equality is unconditionally true. (50b) follows from (44), $\text{Var}\{E[\tilde{P}_2 | P_1]| P_1\} = 0$, and $E[D(w_1, \theta)] = 0$.   QED

Theorem 5 says that the incentive to invest in information is positively related to "how well" the spot price predicts the true (in the sense of the knowledge of informed firms) expected future price. As, $R(w_1, \theta) = E[\tilde{P}_2|$ all information in the system], $\text{Var}[R(\tilde{w}_1, \tilde{\theta})| P_1]$ refers to how well the period 1 spot price predicts the average period 2 spot price, from the point of view of uninformed firms. If we (as econometricians) regress P_2 on P_1, from a time series for a particular commodity, and look at the sample standard deviations of the residuals (i.e., the standard error of the estimate in the regression $P_{2t} = \alpha_0 + \alpha_1 P_{1t} + u_t$), this is an estimate of $\sqrt{(\text{Var}[R(\tilde{w}_1, \tilde{\theta})| P_1])}$. When this is large for one commodity and small for another commodity, we would anticipate a smaller private incentive for futures trading and for information collecting in the case of the commodity with the smaller estimated $\text{Var}[R(\tilde{w}_1, \tilde{\theta})| P_1]$.

The reason for believing that the potential size of futures trading relates to the difference in profits between informed and uninformed firms is that the size of the profit difference, $E\pi_a - E\pi_b$, is directly related to the "size of the expectations difference," on average $E[D(w_1, \theta)]^2$, by (50b), which is related to how much noise is in the price system. However, when an explicit futures market is put in, the model $E[\tilde{P}_2 \mid P_1]$ is no longer the relevant predictor for uninformed firms as there is another statistic, the price of futures contracts, that will contain information. In the next section we shall show how this reduces the profit difference between the traders (and hence the incentive to gather information) while at the same time it reduces the noisiness of the price system.

4.4   Explicit Introduction of Futures Market into the Model

Let x represent a promise, made in period 1, to purchase x units of a commodity in period 2, at a price P_f. If x is negative, then it is to be interpreted as a promise to deliver x units in period 2. Define

$$\pi = (P_2 - P_1)I - C(I) + (P_2 - P_f)x. \tag{51}$$

Let informed firms choose x and I to maximize

$$\pi_a(\theta, w_1, I, x) = E[\pi \mid \theta, w_1]. \tag{52}$$

Similarly, let uninformed firms choose x and I to maximize

$$\pi_b(P_1, P_f, I, x) = E[\pi \mid P_1, P_f]. \tag{53}$$

Let the demand functions for period 1 and period 2 consumption be, as before,

$$P_2 = D_2(I, w_2) \tag{54}$$

and

$$D_1(P_1) = w_1 - I. \tag{55}$$

For reasons that will be clear presently, it is convenient to define equilibrium in terms of prices and allocations. If

$$\tilde{P}_1(\cdot) \equiv P_1^0(w_1, \theta), \qquad \tilde{P}_2(\cdot) \equiv P_2^0(w_1, w_2, \theta), \qquad \tilde{P}_f(\cdot) \equiv P_f^0(w_1, \theta),$$

$$\tilde{I}_a(\cdot) \equiv I_a^0(w_1, \theta), \qquad \tilde{I}_b(\cdot) \equiv I_b^0(P_1^0, P_f^0), \qquad \tilde{x}(\cdot) \equiv x^0(w_1, \theta),$$

define $\{\tilde{P}_1, \tilde{P}_2, \tilde{P}_f, \tilde{I}_a, \tilde{I}_b, \tilde{x}\}$ to be an equilibrium when for each (θ, w_1, w_2)

$$\tilde{\pi}_a(\theta, w_1, I_a^0, x^0) \geq \tilde{\pi}_a(\theta, w_1, I, x) \qquad \text{for all} \quad I \geq 0, \quad x \in \mathcal{R}, \tag{56}$$

$$\tilde{\pi}_b(\theta, w_1, I_b^0, -x^0) \geq \tilde{\pi}_b(\theta, w_1, I, x) \qquad \text{for all} \quad I \geq 0, \quad x \in \mathcal{R}, \tag{57}$$

$$D_1(P_1^0) = w_1 - I_a^0 - I_b^0, \tag{58}$$

$$P_2^0 = D_2(I_a^0 + I_b^0, w_2), \tag{59}$$

where in (56)–(59), the symbol P_2^0 means $P_2^0(w_1, w_2, \theta)$, and similarly for P_1^0, I_a^0, x^0. $\tilde{\pi}_a$ and $\tilde{\pi}_b$ refer to (51)–(53), except that in (51) P_2 is replaced by $\tilde{P}_2$, P_1 is replaced by $\tilde{P}_1$, and P_f is replaced by $\tilde{P}_f$.

Equation (56) requires that (I_a^0, x^0) be an optimal choice for the informed firms under the price system $(\tilde{P}_1, \tilde{P}_2, \tilde{P}_f)$; (57) requires that $(I_b^0, -x^0)$ be optimal and that net futures contracts be zero ("promises to deliver" must equal "promises to purchase" in equilibrium). Equations (58) and (59) require market clearing in period 1 and 2 spot markets.

Theorem 6, below, shows that in equilibrium with a futures market, all information is transferred from informed to uninformed traders. Thus, the futures markets removes the noise from the system introduced in section 4.3.

Theorem 6   Let $\tilde{P}_1(w_1, \theta)$ be the solution to

$$\int_{-\infty}^{+\infty} D_2(w_1 - D_1(P_1), w_2) f(w_2 \mid \theta) \, dw_2 - P_1 = C'\left[\frac{w_1 - D_1(P_1)}{2}\right] \quad (60)$$

for P_1 in terms of (w_1, θ). (This exists by the linearity assumptions.) Define

$$\hat{P}_f(w_1, \theta) \equiv \int_{-\infty}^{+\infty} D_2(w_1 - D_1(\hat{P}_1(w_1, \theta)), w_2) f(w_2 \mid \theta) \, dw_2, \quad (61)$$

$$\hat{P}_2(w_1, w_2, \theta) \equiv D_2[w_1 - D_1(\hat{P}_1[w_1, \theta]), w_2], \quad (62)$$

$$\hat{I}_a(w_1, \theta) = \frac{w_1 - D_1(\hat{P}_1(w_1, \theta))}{2}, \quad (63)$$

$$\hat{I}_b(\hat{P}_1, \hat{P}_f) \equiv [C']^{-1}(\hat{P}_f - \hat{P}_1) = \frac{w_1 - D_1(\hat{P}_1)}{2}. \quad (64)$$

$([C']^{-1}(a)$ is the unique number b such that $C'(b) = a)$

$\hat{x}(w_1, \theta)$ is an arbitrary real number; $\qquad\qquad\qquad\qquad\qquad\qquad\quad (65)$

then $\{\hat{P}_1, \hat{P}_2, \hat{P}_f, \hat{I}_a, \hat{I}_b, \hat{x}\}$ is an equilibrium.

Proof   Note that $\hat{P}_f = E[\hat{P}_2 \mid w_1, \theta]$ [from (61) and (62)], so from (51) and (52) any real x is optimal for an informed firm. Hence I_a is optimal for an informed firm if and only if $E[\hat{P}_2 \mid w_1, \theta] - \hat{P}_1 = C'(I_a)$, which is what (60) and (63) imply.

Note that $E[\hat{P}_2 \mid \hat{P}_1 = P_1(w_1, \theta), \hat{P}_f = \hat{P}_f(w_1, \theta)] = E[\hat{P}_2 \mid w_1, \theta]$. This follows from $\hat{P}_f - \hat{P}_1 = C'(I_b)$ [which follows from the definitions (60)–(64)], as $\hat{P}_f = E[\hat{P}_2 \mid w_1, \theta]$ and I_b is a function of $\hat{P}_1$ and $\hat{P}_f$ alone. It then follows that any real x is optimal for the uninformed firm as $\{E[\hat{P}_2 \mid P_1, P_f] - \hat{P}_f\} \cdot x$ = 0 for all x. Hence $\hat{I}_b$ is optimal for an uninformed firm if and only if $E[\hat{P}_2 \mid P_1, P_f] - \hat{P}_1 = C'(I_b)$. Thus $\hat{I}_b$ is optimal. The two spot markets are cleared by $\hat{P}_1$ and $\hat{P}_2$ by definitions (60) and (62).   QED

Corollary 6.1 $E[\hat{P}_2 \mid \hat{P}_1 = \hat{P}_1(w_1, \theta), \ \hat{P}_f = \hat{P}_f(w_1, \theta)] = E[\hat{P}_2 \mid w_1, \theta]$ *for all* (w_1, θ).

Corollary 6.2 $\text{Var}[E[\hat{P}_2 \mid w_1, \theta] \mid \hat{P}_1, \hat{P}_f] = 0.$

Proof $\text{Var}[E[\hat{P}_2 \mid w_1, \theta] \mid \hat{P}_1, \hat{P}_f] = \text{Var}\{E[\hat{P}_2 \mid \hat{P}_1, \hat{P}_f] \mid \hat{P}_1, \hat{P}_f\} = 0.$ QED

Corollary 6.3 $\pi_a(\theta, w_1, \hat{I}_a, \hat{x}) = \pi_b(\hat{P}_1, \hat{P}_f, \hat{I}_b, -\hat{x})$ *for all* (w_1, θ).

Thus, in equilibrium with futures trading, all information is transferred from informed to uninformed traders. Corollary 6.3 illustrates the problematical nature of having many markets in terms of the decreasing private appropriability of the social gains from investment in information. Corollary 2.1 showed that with no noise the private gain from free information is zero, and would be negative if learning about θ cost money. Theorem 5 showed that with noise and no futures market, informed firms make money on their information. Corollary 6.1 shows that the introduction of a futures market nullifies the ability of the noise, $\tilde{w}_1$, to maintain a return for informed firms on their information when it is free. When information is costly, informed firms would make less money than firms that get information only from prices. This is an extreme example designed to indicate how, when prices are statistics, there can be a divergence between the private gains and social benefits of investment in information. If we add more noise (see below), then $\tilde{P}_1$ and $\tilde{P}_f$ will not reveal all the information of the informed traders, and some investment in information will occur.

The above scenario, where we start with a little noise, add a market, and then require more noise to support the informed firms' interest in the market suggests the following observation. Why do we not have markets for delivery of commodities contingent on all possible states of the world? This is because with a price contingent on every possible random event, there could be very little investment in information in equilibrium. Since with no noise (and there cannot be noise as there is a price for *each* random event), all the information collected by an informed trader would be revealed by an extraordinarily refined price system. In the language of those who run futures markets: There could not be enough "speculative capital" attracted to an organized market with so many prices. Sandor [18] reports a lack of speculative capital in the trading of similar wheat futures contracts: "Gulf Wheat" and "Wheat." Our model interprets the lack of "speculative" interest in these commodity futures as due to the greater difficulty in appropriating private gains from investment in information in studying the random factors that determine the price of "Gulf Wheat" and (the composite commodity) "Wheat." This is due to the fact that there are too many prices revealing information from those who "speculate," (i.e., are informed) to traders who are not investing in being informed.

As noted in the proof of theorem 6, $\hat{P}_f = E[\hat{P}_2 \mid w_1, \theta]$ and the number of futures contracts traded is indeterminate in equilibrium. These two facts are obviously related. That the price of futures is an unbiased predictor of the future spot price is an empirically controversial issue. It is supported by Dusak [4] and Telser [21], but disputed by Cootner [3]. However, for the purpose of testing my model, corollary 6.2 is the important implication. This will be examined below in a model where the number of equilibrium futures contracts is determinate, and unbiasedness of $\hat{P}_f$ is no longer a necessary implication of the model.

Note that throughout the chapter, no mention has been made of "risk aversion." We have tried to push the information aspect as far as it will go without requiring assumptions about risk preference. This leads to a difficulty in theorem 6: The size of futures contracts is indeterminate in equilibrium [see equation (56)], though the equilibrium requires the existence of a futures market. Some mechanism is needed to make the net profit from holding a futures contract nonlinear in x. A natural method is suggested in the classical literature (cf. Keynes [13] and Arrow [1]): Endow traders with "risk aversion." We choose the following type of "risk aversion" because of its illustrative simplicity in this context. Let π be a normal random variable. Lintner [16] has used the following von Neumann–Morgenstern utility function in portfolio analysis:

$$U_a(\pi) = -e^{-a\pi}, \tag{66}$$

where $a > 0$. This utility function exhibits constant absolute risk aversion. Let

$$V_a(\tilde{\pi}) = E\tilde{\pi} - \frac{a}{2}\mathrm{Var}(\tilde{\pi}). \tag{67}$$

When $\tilde{\pi}$ is normal, U_a is a von Neumann–Morgenstern representation of the preference ordering on $\tilde{\pi}$ described by V_a.

$$(EU_a(\tilde{\pi}) = -\exp\{-aE\tilde{\pi} + (a^2/2)\operatorname{Var}(\tilde{\pi})\}$$

$$= -\exp\{-a[E\tilde{\pi} - (a/2)\operatorname{Var}(\tilde{\pi})]\}.$$

Thus $V_a(\tilde{\pi})$ is a monotone increasing function of $EU_a(\tilde{\pi})$.) We shall assume that firms maximize (67).

We shall introduce noise into the system by assuming that uninformed firms (i.e., type "b" firms) do not know the risk aversion parameter of the type "a" firms' utility function. Informed firms know (w_1, θ, a) each period. Let $Z = (w_1, \theta, a)$; then informed firms choose x_a^d, I_a^d to maximize

$$V_a(\tilde{\pi}) = E[\tilde{\pi} \mid Z] - \frac{a}{2}\operatorname{Var}[\tilde{\pi} \mid Z].$$

The equilibrium period 1 prices, $\tilde{P}_1$ and $\tilde{P}_f$, are functions only of Z, and not of $\tilde{w}_2$. Thus, from (51)

$$\operatorname{Var}(\tilde{\pi} \mid Z) = (x_a + I_a)^2 \operatorname{Var}(\tilde{P}_2 \mid Z).$$

Therefore necessary conditions for a maximum of $V_a(\tilde{\pi})$ are

$$E[\tilde{P}_2 \mid Z] - P_1 - C'(I_a^s) - a(x_a^d + I_a^s)\operatorname{Var}[\tilde{P}_2 \mid Z] = 0, \tag{68}$$

$$E[\tilde{P}_2 \mid Z] - P_f - a(x_a^d + I_a^s)\operatorname{Var}[\tilde{P}_2 \mid Z] = 0. \tag{69}$$

Equations (68) and (69) imply that

$$P_f - P_1 = C'(I_a^s). \tag{70}$$

Equation (69) implies

$$\frac{E[\tilde{P}_2 \mid Z] - P_f}{a\operatorname{Var}[\tilde{P}_2 \mid Z]} - I_a^s = x_a^d. \tag{71}$$

Similarly, if the uninformed firms have preferences given by $V_b(\tilde{\pi}) = E\tilde{\pi} - (b/2)\operatorname{Var}(\tilde{\pi})$, their optimal positions are given by

$$P_f - P_1 = C'(I_b^s), \tag{72}$$

$$\frac{E[\tilde{P}_2 \mid P_1, P_f] - P_f}{b\operatorname{Var}[\tilde{P}_2 \mid P_1, P_f]} - I_b^s = x_b^d. \tag{73}$$

An equilibrium is defined as a triplet of random variables $(\tilde{P}_1, \tilde{P}_2, \tilde{P}_f)$, with $\tilde{P}_1(\cdot) = \tilde{P}_1(Z)$, $\tilde{P}_f(\cdot) = \tilde{P}_f(Z)$, $\tilde{P}_2(\cdot) = \tilde{P}_2(Z, w_2)$ such that

$$x_a^d + x_b^d = 0, \tag{74}$$

$$I_a^s + I_b^s \equiv I^e(z) \tag{75}$$

$$D_1(\tilde{P}_1(z)) = w_1 - I^e(z), \ P_2(Z, w_2) = D_2(I^e(Z), w_2), \tag{76}$$

where in (70) and (71) $E[\tilde{P}_2 \mid P_1, P_f]$ means $E[\tilde{P}_2 \mid \tilde{P}_1(Z) = P_1, \ \tilde{P}_f(Z) = P_f]$, and similarly for $\text{Var}[\tilde{P}_2 \mid P_1, P_f]$. Denote the solutions to (74)–(76) by x_a^e, x_b^e, I_a^e, I_b^e.

Theorem 7   *Suppose that* $|x_a^e| < I_a^e$, *and* $\text{Var}[D_2(I^e, \tilde{w}_2)|Z] > 0$; *then*

$$\frac{x_a^e}{I_a^e} = \frac{-x_b^e}{I_b^e} = \frac{1 - \delta}{1 + \delta}, \tag{77}$$

where

$$\delta \equiv \frac{a}{b} \ \frac{\text{Var}[\tilde{P}_2 \mid Z]}{\text{Var}[\tilde{P}_2 \mid P_1, P_f]} \cdot \frac{E[\tilde{P}_2 \mid P_1, P_f] - P_f}{E[\tilde{P}_2 \mid Z] - P_f}. \tag{78}$$

Proof   Equations (70) and (72) imply that $I_a^e = I_b^e$. From (69), $|x_a^e| < I_a^e$ implies that $E[\tilde{P}_2 \mid Z] - P_f > 0$. Equation (77) follows immediately from (71), (73), and (74).   QED

Theorem 7 indicates that the volume of futures trading depends on a risk factor and an information factor. Suppose the price system $\tilde{P}_1$, $\tilde{P}_f$ reveals enough of the information about Z so that $\text{Var}[\tilde{P}_2 \mid Z] = \text{Var}[\tilde{P}_2 \mid P_1, P_f]$ and $E[\tilde{P}_2 \mid P_1, P_f] = E[\tilde{P}_2 \mid Z]$. Then $\delta = a/b$ and the volume of open contracts depends only on differences in risk preferences. If $a = b$, then $\delta = 1$ and there is no futures trading. However, if $a = b$, and all information is not revealed by the price system, then there will be futures trading based upon differences in information. The amount of trading depends upon how well the informed firms' information predicts P_2 versus how well the price system $(\tilde{P}_1, \tilde{P}_f)$ predicts P_2. This is observable by finding empirical proxies for $\text{Var}[\tilde{P}_2 \mid Z]$ and $E[\tilde{P}_2 \mid Z]$ and comparing them with $\text{Var}[\tilde{P}_2 \mid P_1, P_f]$ and $E[\tilde{P}_2 \mid P_1, P_f]$, which can be found from a regression of P_2 on P_1 and P_f. That is, the predictability of P_2 from various exogenous variables such as weather forecasts, crop forecasts, etc., could be compared with the predictability of P_2 from P_1 and P_f, from a time series of P_2, P_1, P_f and exogenous variables that are proxies for Z.

An interesting special case occurs when the period 2 demand function, (54), has the form

$$P_2 = D_2(I) + w_2. \tag{79}$$

Lemma 7.1 *Suppose period 2 demand is given by (79); then*

$$E[(X_a^e)^2 \mid P_1, P_f] = k_1 \operatorname{Var}[E[\tilde{P}_2 \mid Z] \mid P_1, P_f] + \frac{k_2}{4}(I^e)^2, \tag{80}$$

where

$$k_1 \equiv [a \operatorname{Var}(\tilde{w}_2 \mid Z) + b \operatorname{Var}(\tilde{w}_2 \mid P_1, P_f)]^{-2},$$

$$k_2 \equiv \left[\frac{a \operatorname{Var}(\tilde{w}_2 \mid Z) - b \operatorname{Var}(\tilde{w}_2 \mid P_1, P_f)}{a \operatorname{Var}(\tilde{w}_2 \mid Z) + b \operatorname{Var}(\tilde{w}_2 \mid P_1, P_f)} \right]^2.$$

If $E[\tilde{P}_2 \mid Z], P_1, P_f$ are jointly normal, then

$$E[(x_a^e)^2] = k_1 \operatorname{Var}[E[\tilde{P}_2 \mid Z] \mid P_1, P_f] + k_2 E(I^e)^2. \tag{81}$$

Proof Note that I^e is a function only of P_1 and P_f, by (70), (72), and (75). Thus $\operatorname{Var}[\tilde{P}_2 \mid P_1, P_f] = \operatorname{Var}(\tilde{w}_2 \mid P_1, P_f)$ and $\operatorname{Var}(\tilde{P}_2 \mid Z) = \operatorname{Var}(\tilde{w}_2 \mid Z)$. Using this, (71), (73), and (74) yield

$$x_a^e = \sqrt{k_1}(E[\tilde{P}_2 \mid Z] - E[\tilde{P}_2 \mid P_1, P_f]) + \sqrt{k_2}\frac{I^2}{2}, \tag{82}$$

where k_1 and k_2 are given above and we have used the fact that $I_a^s = I_b^s$. Note that $E[E[\tilde{P}_2 \mid Z]P_1, P_f] = E[\tilde{P}_2 \mid P_1, P_f]$, since P_1 and P_f are just functions of Z. Hence

$$E\{E[\tilde{P}_2 \mid Z] - E[\tilde{P}_2 \mid P_1, P_f]\mid P_1, P_f\} = 0. \tag{83a}$$

Therefore,

$$\operatorname{Var}[E[\tilde{P}_2 \mid Z] \mid P_1, P_f] = E\{(E[\tilde{P}_2 \mid Z] - E[\tilde{P}_2 \mid P_1, P_f])^2 \mid P_1, P_f\}^2. \tag{83b}$$

If both sides of (82) are squared, then (80) follows directly using (83). Equation (81) follows from the property of normal distributions (see appendix), which implies $\operatorname{Var}[E[\tilde{P}_2 \mid Z] \mid P_1, P_f]$ does not depend on P_1 and P_f. QED

A useful measure of the average volume of futures trading is $E[x_a^e]^2$. We cannot use $E[x_a^e]$, since there can be a lot of futures trading with x_a^e sometimes negative (meaning informed traders are "short") and sometimes positive in such a way that $E[x_a^e] = 0$. Lemma 7.2 shows how the average volume of futures trading is explained by an information factor and a hedging factor. If all information is transferred by the price system, $(\tilde{P}_1, \tilde{P}_f)$, then $E[\tilde{P}_2 \mid Z] = E[\tilde{P}_2 \mid P_1, P_f]$ and thus $\operatorname{Var}[E[\tilde{P}_2 \mid Z] \mid P_1, P_f] = 0$. Therefore, from (81), [or (82)] the determinant of trade is the hedging motive. In the above case increases in hedged stocks lead to more trade by an amount that depends on k_2. The size of k_2 depends only on the differential risk averseness of the two traders, as

$$\text{Var}(\tilde{w}_2 \mid Z) = \text{Var}(\tilde{w}_2 \mid P_1, P_f).$$

On the other hand, when the price system is noisy,

$$\text{Var}[E[\tilde{P}_2 \mid Z] \mid P_1, P_f] > 0$$

and trade can be large even if $a = b$ or $I^e = 0$.

When $I^e = 0$, trade takes place only due to differences in beliefs. Equation (81) is important because it suggests a method for judging the size of the latter effect. If data are collected on size of open contracts and hedged stocks, then (81) states that the intercept of a linear regression of $(x_a^e)^2$ on $(I^e)^2$ could be used to measure the "difference in beliefs" effect, while the slope coefficient would measure the hedging effect. Grossman [6] contains a detailed discussion of how lemma 6.2, theorem 7, and lemma 7.1 can be used to develop tests of the model.

4.5   Summary

It is important to make distinct the *Positive* and *Normative* implications of our results. *Positively*, the models suggests that whenever there are profits from competitive firms learning inside information without futures markets, then there will be a tendency for futures markets to develop. That is, informed firms will profit from their information if and only if some of that information is *not* transmitted to uninformed firms by equilibrium spot prices. When some information remains untransmitted, informed and uninformed firms have different expectations about the future spot price. Hence informed traders can make speculative profits by futures trading. The model suggests that the size of these profits is positively related to how well (in the sense of the size of the variance of residuals) current spot prices can predict future spot prices relative to how well various exogenous variables can predict future spot prices. The model in section 4.4 predicts that the volume of futures trading depends on how well the current spot and futures prices predict the future spot price relative to how well exogenous variables predict the future spot price.

Normatively, there are two points: (i) Without a futures market there is social value in having firms study the distribution of w_2 in that this leads to a better intertemporal allocation of the harvest. However, the equilibrium price system will reveal some of the information of the informed firms to the uninformed firms. By examining an extreme case, where all the relevant information is revealed via the price system, it is clear that there are informational externalities that make the private gain from collecting information less than the social gain. (ii) In going from a competitive equilibrium without a futures market to one with a futures market there is the benefit from insurance that is usually discussed in the literature on contingent and future commodity markets. There is further benefit in that the spreading of correct information from informed to uninformed firms leads to an improved intertemporal allocation of the harvest. But there is social harm from the creation of the futures market in that the divergence between the social and private value of information collection becomes greater with a futures market than without one, as more information is freely distributed by prices when there are more prices. (Throughout, transactions costs have been ignored. An accurate accounting of the net social benefit to futures trading should incorporate these costs. This is beyond the scope of the present analysis.)

In future work, we shall examine the above problem from a general equilibrium point of view for two reasons. First, it will be possible to derive formally the welfare effects of having more markets that reveal more information. Second, when there are many goods in the economy informed firms can make money on their information by buying stocks of close substitutes and complements of the good they have information about. Thus there will be many new prices and many new potential noise sources. We feel the methods of this chapter could be used to derive a *sufficient set of markets* that would be stable in terms of not revealing so much information that "speculative capital" is driven from the markets forcing some to close; the price system would contain just enough noise exactly to cover the cost of information collection.

Appendix

Here we collect some facts on conditional expectations used in the text.

If $\tilde{X}$ and $\tilde{Y}$ are jointly normally distributed, then

$$E[\tilde{X} \mid \tilde{Y} = Y] = E\tilde{X} + \frac{\text{Cov}(\tilde{X}, \tilde{Y})}{\text{Var}(\tilde{Y})} \{Y - E\tilde{Y}\}, \tag{A1}$$

$$\text{Var}[\tilde{X} \mid \tilde{Y} = Y] = \text{Var}(\tilde{X}) - \frac{[\text{Cov}(\tilde{X}, \tilde{Y})]^2}{\text{Var}(\tilde{Y})} \tag{A2}$$

(see Hoel [12, p. 200]). From (A1) note that $E[\tilde{X} \mid Y]$ is a function of Y. If the expectation of both sides of (A1) is taken, we see that

$$E\{E[\tilde{X} \mid \tilde{Y} = Y]\} = E\tilde{X}. \tag{A3}$$

Note that $\text{Var}[\tilde{X} \mid \tilde{Y} = Y]$ is not a function of Y, as $\text{Var}(\tilde{X})$, $\text{Cov}(\tilde{X}, \tilde{Y})$, and $\text{Var}(\tilde{Y})$ are just parameters of the joint distribution of $\tilde{X}$ and $\tilde{Y}$. Two other relevant properties of conditional expectation are

$$E\{E[\tilde{Y} \mid F(\tilde{X})] \mid \tilde{X}\} = E[\tilde{Y} \mid F(\tilde{X})], \tag{A4}$$

and

$$E\{E[\tilde{Y} \mid \tilde{X}] \mid F(\tilde{X})\} = E[\tilde{Y} \mid F(\tilde{X})], \tag{A5}$$

where $F(\cdot)$ is a given function on the range of $\tilde{X}$ (see Ash [2, p. 260]). An intuitive explanation of (A4) and (A5) derives from the fact that $\tilde{X}$ has more information than $F(\tilde{X})$. Successive conditioning cannot add information. Therefore the outcome of successive conditioning using different random variables is the conditional expectation of $\tilde{Y}$ given the least informative random variable.

Notes

1. Hardy [10] has suggested that futures markets are casinos, and speculators are not risk averse. Arrow [1] has discussed the role of contingent income contracts as a method of bearing risk. There is controversy in the empirical literature as to the adequacy of the above theories (see, for example, Telser [21], Cootner [3], and Dusak [4]).

2. Throughout the chapter we ignore nonnegativity constraints on prices and inventories. By choosing the parameters in (1a) and (2a) appropriately we can make the probability of negative prices or inventories arbitrarily small. See Grossman [6] for the much more complicated analysis where these constraints are taken into account, and normality of $\tilde{\theta}$ and $\tilde{w}_2$ is not assumed.

3. Throughout the chapter we ignore all measure theoretic technicalities. For example, in (8) below, "for all θ" means for almost all θ with respect to the measure induced by $\mu(\theta)$ on the range of $\tilde{\theta}$. See Grossman [6] for an explicit measure theoretic statement of the underlying probability spaces and a rigorous approach to the conditional expectations employed later in the text. Here, as all random variables are jointly normal these technicalities are not important.

4. If there were n_u uninformed firms and n_I informed firms, then (9) would read

$$I^e = n_I S\{E[\tilde{P}_2 \mid P_1] - P_1\} + n_u S\{E[\tilde{P}_2 \mid \theta - P_1\}.$$

The analysis would be unchanged as long as $n_I > 0$ and both n_I and n_u are taken as exogenous constants.

5. Let $Y \equiv E[\tilde{P}_2 \mid \theta]$, $X \equiv P_1^e(\theta)$. By (14) there is a function, say, $h(\cdot)$, such that $Y = h(X)$. Equation (15) uses the fact that $E[\tilde{Y} \mid X] = E[h(X) \mid X] = h(X) = Y$.

6. We have said nothing about how much is invested in learning θ, and why some firms invest to become informed and others do not. Presumably, some people are more skilled and/or enjoy trying to learn θ more than others. In Grossman [8] I analyzed an explicit problem where resources could be devoted to experimentation that would yield information about θ. Kihlstrom [14] has analyzed, from a Bayesian point of view, the demand for information about product quality, without explicit consideration of Bayesian experimental design. Grossman, Kihlstrom, and Mirman [9] consider the investment in information from the point of view of Bayesian experimental design. These considerations will be used in future work to determine an equilibrium investment in information. Herein we concentrate only on the private and social benefits to investment in information and their relationship to the existence of futures markets. All the results in this chapter hold no matter how θ is generated, since given whatever informed firms pay for θ they bring that θ to the period 1 spot market, and the price must clear the market. That is, when the period 1 spot market opens, the cost of θ is a "sunk" cost and can be ignored.

References

[1] Arrow, K. J. "The Role of Secutiries in the Optimal Allocation of Risk-Bearing," *Review of Economic Studies*, 31, 1 (January 1964), 91–96.

[2] Ash, R. B. *Real Analysis and Probability* (New York: Academic Press, 1972).

[3] Cootner, P. "Returns to Speculators: Telser versus Keynes," *Journal of Political Economy*, 68, 4 (August 1960), 396–404.

[4] Dusak, K. "Futures Trading and Investor Returns: An Investigation of Commodity Market Risk Premiums." *Journal of Political Economy*, 81, 6 (November/ December 1973), 1387–1406.

[5] Green, J. R. "Information, Efficiency and Equilibrium" (Duscussion Paper No. 284, Harvard Institute of Economic Research, March 1973).

[6] Grossman, S. J. "The Existence of Futures Markets, Noisy Rational Expectations and Informational Externalities" (from Ph.D. dissertation, University of Chicago, Department of Economics, 1975).

[7] Grossman, S. J. "Rational Expectations and the Econometric Modeling of Markets Subject to Uncertainty: A Bayesian Approach," *Journal of Econometrics*, 3 (1975), 255–272.

[8] Grossman, S. J. "Equilibrium under Uncertainty, and Bayesian Adaptive Control Theory," in *Adaptive Economic Models*, Day, R. and Groves, T. (eds.) (Academic Press, 1975).

[9] Grossman, S. J., Kihlstrom, R., and Mirman, L. "A Bayesian Approach to the Production of Information and Learning by Doing," *Review of Economic Studies* (this issue).

[10] Hardy, C. O. *Risk and Risk Bearing* (Chicago: University of Chicago Press, 1940).

[11] Hirshleifer, J. "The Private and Social Value of Information and the Reward to Inventive Activity," *American Economic Review*, 61, 4 (May 1971), 561—574.

[12] Hoel, P. G. *Introduction to Mathematical Statistics* (New York: John Wiley and Sons, Inc., 1962).

[13] Keynes, J. M. *A Treatise on Money*, Vol. II (London: Macmillan & Co, 1930).

[14] Kihlstrom. R. "A Bayesian Model of Demand for Information about Product Quality," *International Economic Review*, 15, 1 (February 1974), 99—118.

[15] Kihlstrom, R. and Mirman, L. J. "Information and Market Equilibrium," *Bell Journal of Economics and Management Science* (Spring 1975).

[16] Lintner, J. "The Aggregation of Investors Diverse Judgment and Preferences in Purely Competitive Securities Markets," *Journal of Financial and Quantitative Analysis*, 4, 4 (December 1969), 347—400.

[17] Lucas, R. E. "Expectations and the Neutrality of Money," *Journal of Economic Theory*, 4, 2 (April 1972), 103—124.

[18] Sandor, R. "Internal Research Memorandum" (Department of Economic Research and Planning, The Chicago Board of Trade, May 1974).

[19] Starr, R. "Optimal Production and Allocation under Uncertainty," *Quarterly Journal of Economics*, 87, 1 (February 1973), 81—95.

[20] Stiglitz, J. "Perfect and Imperfect Capital Markets" (paper presented to the Dallas meetings of the Econometric Society, December 1971).

[21] Telser, L. "Futures Trading and the Storage of Cotton and Wheat," *Journal of Political Economy*, 66, 3 (June 1958), 233—255.

5   On the Impossibility of Informationally Efficient Markets

If competitive equilibrium is defined as a situation in which prices are such that all arbitrage profits are eliminated, is it possible that a competitive economy can always be in equilibrium? Clearly not, for then those who arbitrage make no (private) return from their (privately) costly activity. Hence the assumptions that all markets, including that for information, are always in equilibrium and always perfectly arbitraged are inconsistent when arbitrage is costly.

We propose here a model in which there is an equilibrium degree of disequilibrium: Prices reflect the information of informed individuals (arbitrageurs) but only partially, so that those who expend resources to obtain information do receive compensation. How informative the price system is depends on the number of individuals who are informed; but the number of individuals who are informed is itself an endogenous variable in the model.

The model is the simplest one in which prices perform a well-articulated role in conveying information from the informed to the uninformed. When informed individuals observe information that the return to a security is going to be high, they bid its price up, and conversely when they observe information that the return is going to be low. Thus the price system makes publicly available the information obtained by informed individuals to the uniformed. In general, however, it does this imperfectly; this is perhaps lucky, for were it to do it perfectly, an equilibrium would not exist.

In the introduction, we shall discuss the general methodology and present some conjectures concerning certain properties of the equilibrium. The remaining analytic sections of the chapter are devoted to analyzing in detail an important example of our general model, in which our conjectures concerning the nature of the equilibrium can be shown to be correct. We conclude with a discussion of the implications of our approach and results, with particular emphasis on the relationship of our results to the literature on "efficient capital markets."

5.1   The Model

Our model can be viewed as an extension of the noisy rational expectations model introduced by Robert Lucas and applied to the study of information flows between traders by Jerry Green (1973), Grossman (1975, 1976, 1978), and Richard Kihlstrom and Leonard Mirman. There are two assets: a safe asset yielding a return R and a risky asset, the return to which, u, varies randomly from period to period. The variable u consists of two parts,

$$u = \theta + \varepsilon, \tag{1}$$

where θ is observable at a cost c, and ε is unobservable.[1] Both θ and ε are random variables. There are two types of individuals, those who observe θ (informed traders) and those who observe only price (uninformed traders). In our simple model, all individuals are, *ex ante*, identical; whether they are informed or uninformed just depends on whether they have spent c to obtain information. Informed traders' demands will depend on θ and the price of the risky asset P. Uninformed traders' demands will depend only on P, but we shall assume that they have rational expectations; they learn the relationship between the distribution of return and the price, and use this in deriving their demand for the risky assets. If x denotes the supply of the risky asset, an equilibrium when a given percentage, λ, of traders are informed, is thus a price function $P_\lambda(\theta, x)$ such that, when demands are formulated in the way described, demand equals supply. We assume that uninformed traders do not observe x. Uninformed traders are prevented from learning θ via observations of $P_\lambda(\theta, x)$ because they cannot distinguish variations in price due to changes in the informed trader's information from variations in price due to changes in aggregate supply. Clearly, $P_\lambda(\theta, x)$ reveals some of the informed trader's information to the uninformed traders.

We can calculate the expected utility of the informed and the expected utility of the uninformed. If the former is greater than the latter (taking account of the cost of information), some individuals switch from being uninformed to being informed (and conversely). An overall equilibrium requires the two to have the same expected utility. As more individuals become informed, the expected utility of the informed falls relative to the uninformed for two reasons:

a. The price system becomes more informative because variations in θ have a greater effect on aggregate demand and thus on price when more traders observe θ. Thus, more of the information of the informed is available to the uninformed. Moreover, the informed gain more from trade with the uninformed than do the uninformed. The informed, on average, buy securities when they are "underpriced" and sell them when they are "overpriced" (relative to what they would have been if information were equalized).[2] As the price system becomes more informative, the difference in their information—and hence the magnitude by which the informed can gain relative to the uninformed—is reduced.

b. Even if the above effect did not occur, the increase in the ratio of informed to uninformed means that the relative gains of the informed, on a per capita basis, in trading with the uninformed will be smaller.

We summarize the above characterization of the equilibrium of the economy in the following two conjectures:

Conjecture 1   The more individuals who are informed, the more informative is the price system.

Conjecture 2   The more individuals who are informed, the lower the ratio of expected utility of the informed to the uninformed.

(Conjecture 1 obviously requires a definition of "more informative"; this is given in the next section and in note 7.)

The equilibrium number of informed and uninformed individuals in the economy will depend on a number of critical parameters: the cost of information, how informative the price system is (how much noise there is to interfere with the information conveyed by the price system), and how informative the information obtained by an informed individual is.

Conjecture 3   The higher the cost of information, the smaller will be the equilibrium percentage of individuals who are informed.

Conjecture 4   If the quality of the informed trader's information increases, the more their demands will vary with their information and thus the more prices will vary with θ. Hence, the price system becomes more informative. The equilibrium proportion of informed to uninformed may be either increased or decreased, because even though the value of being informed has increased due to the increased quality of θ, the value of being uninformed has also increased because the price system becomes more informative.

Conjecture 5   The greater the magnitude of noise, the less informative will the price system be, and hence the lower the expected utility of uninformed individuals. Hence, in equilibrium the greater the magnitude of noise, the larger the proportion of informed individuals.

Conjecture 6   In the limit, when there is no noise, prices convey all information, and there is no incentive to purchase information. Hence, the only possible equilibrium is one with no information. But if everyone is uninformed, it clearly pays some individual to become informed.[3] Thus, there does not exist a competitive equilibrium.[4]

Trade among individuals occurs either because tastes (risk aversions) differ, endowments differ, or beliefs differ. This paper focuses on the last of these three. An interesting feature of the equilibrium is that beliefs may be precisely identical in either one of two situations: when all individuals are informed or when all individuals are uninformed. This gives rise to

Conjecture 7   That, other things being equal, markets will be thinner under those conditions in which the percentage of individuals who are informed (λ) is either near zero or near unity. For example, markets will be thin when there is very little noise in the system (so λ is near zero), or when costs of information are very low (so λ is near unity).

In the last few paragraphs, we have provided a number of conjectures describing the nature of the equilibrium when prices convey information. Unfortunately, we have not been able to obtain a general proof of any of these propositions. What we have been able to do is to analyze in detail an interesting example, entailing constant absolute risk-aversion utility functions and normally distributed random variables. In this example, the equilibrium price distribution can actually be calculated, and all of the conjectures provided above can be verified. The next sections are devoted to solving for the equilibrium in this particular example.[5]

5.2   Constant Absolute Risk-Aversion Model

A.   The Securities

The ith trader is assumed to be endowed with stocks of two types of securities: $\overline{M}_i$, the riskless asset, and $\overline{X}_i$, a risky asset. Let P be the current price of risky assets and set the price of risk free assets equal to unity. The ith trader's budget constraint is

$$PX_i + M_i = W_{0i} \equiv \overline{M}_i + P\overline{X}_i. \tag{2}$$

Each unit of the risk free asset pays R "dollars" at the end of the period, while each unit of the risky asset pays u dollars. If at the end of the period, the ith trader holds a portfolio (M_i, X_i), his wealth will be

$$W_{1i} = RM_i + uX_i. \tag{3}$$

B.   Individual's Utility Maximization

Each individual has a utility function $V_i(W_{1i})$. For simplicity, we assume all individuals have the same utility function and so drop the subscripts i. Moreover, we assume the utility function is exponential, i.e.,

$$V(W_{1i}) = -e^{-aW_{1i}}, \qquad a > 0,$$

where a is the coefficient of absolute risk aversion. Each trader desires to maximize expected utility, using whatever information is available to him, and to decide on what information to acquire on the basis of the consequences to his expected utility.

Assume that in equation (1) θ and ε have a multivariate normal distribution, with

$$E\varepsilon = 0, \tag{4}$$

$$E\theta\varepsilon = 0, \tag{5}$$

$$\mathrm{Var}(u^*|\theta) = \mathrm{Var}\,\varepsilon^* \equiv \sigma_\varepsilon^2 > 0 \tag{6}$$

since θ and ε are uncorrelated. Throughout this chapter we shall put a $*$ above a symbol to emphasize that it is a random variable. Since W_{1i} is a linear function of ε, for a given portfolio allocation, and a linear function of a normally distributed random variable is normally distributed, it follows that W_{1i} is normal conditional or θ. Then, using (2) and (3), the expected utility of the *informed* trader with information θ can be written

$$E(V(W_{1i}^*|\theta)$$

$$= -\exp\left(-a\left\{E[W_{1i}^*|\theta] - \frac{a}{2}\mathrm{Var}[W_{1i}^*|\theta]\right\}\right)$$

$$= -\exp\left(-a\left[RW_{0i} + X_I\{E(u^*|\theta) - RP\} - \frac{a}{2}X_I^2\,\mathrm{Var}(u^*|\theta)\right]\right)$$

$$= -\exp\left(-a\left[RW_{0i} + X_I(\theta - RP) - \frac{a}{2}X_I^2\sigma_\varepsilon^2\right]\right), \tag{7}$$

where X_I is an informed individual's demand for the risky security. Maximizing (7) with respect to X_I yields a demand function for risky assets:

$$X_I(P, \theta) = \frac{\theta - RP}{a\sigma_\varepsilon^2}. \tag{8}$$

The right-hand side of (8) shows the familiar result that with constant absolute risk aversion, a trader's demand does not depend on wealth; hence the subscript i is not on the left-hand side of (8).

We now derive the demand function for the uninformed. Let us assume the only source of "noise" is the per capita supply of the risky security x.

Let $P^*(\cdot)$ be some particular price function of (θ, x) such that u^* and P^* are jointly normally distributed. (We shall prove that this exists below.)

Then, we can write for the uninformed individual

$$E(V(W_{1i}^*)|P^*) = -\exp\left[-a\left\{E[W_{1i}^*|P^*] - \frac{a}{2}\text{Var}[W_{1i}^*|P^*]\right\}\right]$$

$$= -\exp\left[-a\left\{RW_{0i} + X_U(E[u^*|P^*] - RP)\right.\right.$$

$$\left.\left. - \frac{a}{2}X_U^2\,\text{Var}[u^*|P^*]\right\}\right]. \tag{7'}$$

The demands of the uninformed will thus be a function of the price function P^* and the actual price P:

$$X_U(P; P^*) = \frac{E[u^*|P^*(\theta, x) = P] - RP}{a\,\text{Var}[u^*|P^*(\theta, x) = P]}. \tag{8'}$$

C. Equilibrium Price Distribution

If λ is some particular fraction of traders who decide to become informed, then define an equilibrium price system as a function of (θ, x), $P_\lambda(\theta, x)$, such that for all (θ, x) per capita demands for the risky assets equal supplies:

$$\lambda X_I(P_\lambda(\theta, x), \theta) + (1 - \lambda)X_U(P_\lambda(\theta, x); P_\lambda^*) = x. \tag{9}$$

The function $P_\lambda(\theta, x)$ is a statistical equilibrium in the following sense. If over time uninformed traders observe many realizations of (u^*, P_λ^*), then they learn the joint distribution of (u^*, P_λ^*). After all learning about the joint distribution of (u^*, P_λ^*) ceases, all traders will make allocations and form expectations such that this joint distribution persists over time. This follows from (8), (8′), and (9), where the market-clearing price that comes about is the one that takes into account the fact that uninformed traders have learned that it contains information.

We shall now prove that there exists an equilibrium price distribution such that P^* and u^* are jointly normal. Moreover, we shall be able to characterize the price distribution. We define

$$w_\lambda(\theta, x) = \theta - \frac{a\sigma_\varepsilon^2}{\lambda}(x - Ex^*) \tag{10a}$$

for $\lambda > 0$, and define $w_0(\theta, x)$ as the number

$$w_0(\theta, x) = x \qquad \text{for all } (\theta, x), \tag{10b}$$

where w_λ is just the random variable θ, plus noise.[6] The magnitude of the noise is inversely proportional to the proportion of informed traders, but is proportional to the variance of ε. We shall prove that the equilibrium price is just a linear function of w_λ. Thus, if $\lambda > 0$, the price system conveys information about θ, but it does so imperfectly.

D.   Existence of Equilibrium and a Characterization Theorem

Theorem 1   *If $(\theta^*, \varepsilon^*, x^*)$ has a nondegenerate joint normal distribution such that θ^*, ε^*, and x^* are mutually independent, then there exists a solution to (9) that has the form $P_\lambda(\theta, x) = \alpha_1 + \alpha_2 w_\lambda(\theta, x)$, where α_1 and α_2 are real numbers that may depend on λ, such that $\alpha_2 > 0$. (If $\lambda = 0$, the price contains no information about θ.) The exact form of $P_\lambda(\theta, x)$ is given in equation (A10) in appendix B. The proof of this theorem is also in appendix B.*

The importance of theorem 1 rests in the simple characterization of the information in the equilibrium price system: P_λ^* is informationally equivalent to w_λ^*. From (10) w_λ^* is a "mean-preserving spread" of θ; i.e., $E[w_\lambda^*|\theta] = \theta$ and

$$\text{Var}[w_\lambda^*|\theta] = \frac{a^2\sigma_\varepsilon^4}{\lambda^2}\text{Var}\, x^*. \tag{11}$$

For each replication of the economy, θ is the information that uninformed traders would like to know. But the noise x^* prevents w_λ^* from revealing θ. How well-informed uninformed traders can become from observing P_λ^* (equivalent w_λ^*) is measured by $\text{Var}[w_\lambda^*|\theta]$. When $\text{Var}[w_\lambda^*|\theta]$ is zero, w_λ^* and θ are perfectly correlated. Hence when uninformed firms observe w_λ^*, this is equivalent to observing θ. On the other hand, when $\text{Var}[w_\lambda^*|\theta]$ is very large, there are "many" realizations of w_λ^* that are associated with a given θ. In this case the observation of a particular w_λ^* tells very little about the actual θ which generated it.[7]

From equation (11) it is clear that large noise (high $\text{Var}\, x^*$) leads to an imprecise price system. The other factor that determines the precision of the price system $(a^2 \sigma_\varepsilon^4 / \lambda^2)$ is more subtle. When a is small (the individual is not very risk averse) or σ_ε^2 is small (the information is very precise), an informed trader will have a demand for risky assets that is very responsive to changes in θ. Further, the larger λ is, the more responsive is the total demand of informed traders. Thus small $(a^2 \sigma_\varepsilon^4 / \lambda^2)$ means that the aggregate demand of informed traders is very responsive to θ. For a fixed amount of noise (i.e., fixed $\text{Var}\, x^*$) the larger are the movements in aggregate demand that are due to movements in θ, the more will price movements be due to movements in θ. That is, x^* becomes less important relative to θ in determining price movements. Therefore, for small $(a^2 \sigma_\varepsilon^4 / \lambda^2)$ uninformed traders are able to know confidently that price is, for example, unusually high due to θ being high. In this way information from informed traders is transferred to uninformed traders.

E. Equilibrium in the Information Market

What we have characterized so far is the equilibrium price distribution for given λ. We now define an *overall* equilibrium to be a pair (λ, P_λ^*) such that the expected utility of the informed is equal to that of the uninformed if $0 < \lambda < 1$; $\lambda = 0$ if the expected utility of the informed is less than that of the uninformed at P_0^*; $\lambda = 1$ if the expected utility of the informed is greater than the uninformed at P_1^*. Let

$$W_{Ii}^\lambda \equiv R(W_{0i} - c) + [u - RP_\lambda(\theta, x)]X_I(P_\lambda(\theta, x), \theta), \qquad (12a)$$

$$W_{U1}^\lambda \equiv RW_{0i} + [u - RP_\lambda(\theta, x)]X_U(P_\lambda(\theta, x); P_\lambda^*), \qquad (12b)$$

where c is the cost of observing a realization of θ^*. Equation (12a) gives the end of period wealth of a trader if he decides to become informed, while (12b) gives his wealth if he decides to be uninformed. Note that end of period wealth is random due to the randomness of W_{0i}, u, θ, and x.

In evaluating the expected utility of W_{Ii}^λ, we do not assume that a trader knows which realization of θ^* he gets to observe if he pays c dollars. A trader pays c dollars and then gets to observe some realization of θ^*. The overall expected utility of W_{Ii}^λ averages over all possible θ^*, ε^*, x^*, and W_{0i}. The variable W_{0i} is random for two reasons. First, from (2) it depends on $P_\lambda(\theta, x)$, which is random as (θ, x) is random. Second, in what follows we will assume that $\overline{X}_i$ is random.

We shall show below that $EV(W_{Ii}^\lambda)/EV(W_{Ui}^\lambda)$ is independent of i, but is a function of λ, a, c, and σ_ε^2. More precisely, in appendix B we prove

Theorem 2   *Under the assumptions of theorem 1, and if $\overline{X}_i$ is independent of (u^*, θ^*, x^*), then*

$$\frac{EV(W_{Ii}^\lambda)}{EV(W_{Ui}^\lambda)} = e^{ac} \sqrt{\frac{\text{Var}(u^*|\theta)}{\text{Var}(u^*|w_\lambda)}}. \tag{13}$$

F.   Existence of Overall Equilibrium

Theorem 2 is useful, both in proving the uniqueness of overall equilibrium and in analyzing comparative statics. Overall equilibrium, it will be recalled, requires that for $0 < \lambda < 1$, $EV(W_{Ii}^\lambda)/EV(W_{Ui}^\lambda) = 1$. But from (13)

$$\frac{EV(W_{Ii}^\lambda)}{EV(W_{Ui}^\lambda)} = e^{ac} \sqrt{\frac{\text{Var}(u^*|\theta)}{\text{Var}(u^*|w_\lambda)}} \equiv \gamma(\lambda). \tag{14}$$

Hence overall equilibrium simply requires, for $0 < \lambda < 1$,

$$\gamma(\lambda) = 1. \tag{15}$$

More precisely, we now prove

Theorem 3   *If $0 \leqslant \lambda \leqslant 1$, $\gamma(\lambda) = 1$, and P_λ^* is given by (A10) in appendix B, then (λ, P_λ^*) is an overall equilibrium. If $\gamma(1) < 1$, then $(1, P_1^*)$ is an overall equilibrium. If $\gamma(0) > 1$, then $(0, P_0^*)$ is an overall equilibrium. For all price equilibria P_λ that are monotone functions of w_λ, there exists a unique overall equilibrium (λ, P_λ^*).*

Proof   The first three sentences follow immediately from the definition of overall equilibrium given above equation (12), and theorems 1 and 2. Uniqueness follows from the monotonicity of $\gamma(\cdot)$ which follows from (A11) and (14). The last two sentences in the statement of the theorem follow immediately.   QED

In the process of proving theorem 3, we have noted

Corollary 1 $\gamma(\lambda)$ *is a strictly monotone increasing function of λ.*

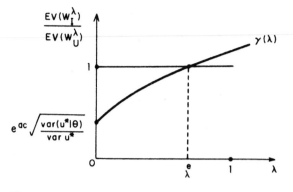

Figure 5.1

This looks paradoxical; we expect the ratio of informed to uninformed expected utility to be a decreasing function of λ. But, *we have defined utility as negative*. Therefore as λ rises, the expected utility of informed traders does go down relative to uninformed traders.

Note that the function $\gamma(0) = e^{ac}(\text{Var}(u^*|\theta)/\text{Var}\,u^*)^{1/2}$. Figure 5.1 illustrates the determination of the equilibrium λ. The figure assumes that $\gamma(0) < 1 < \gamma(1)$.

G.   Characterization of Equilibrium

We wish to provide some further characterization of the equilibrium. Let us define

$$m = \left(\frac{a\sigma_\varepsilon^2}{\lambda}\right)^2 \frac{\sigma_x^2}{\sigma_\theta^2}, \tag{16a}$$

$$n = \frac{\sigma_\theta^2}{\sigma_\varepsilon^2}. \tag{16b}$$

Note that m is inversely related to the informativeness of the price system since the squared correlation coefficient between P_λ^* and θ^*, ρ_θ^2 is given by

$$\rho_\theta^2 = \frac{1}{1 + m}. \tag{17}$$

Similarly, n is directly related to the quality of the informed trader's information because $n/(1 + n)$ is the squared correlation coefficient between θ^* and u^*.

Equations (14) and (15) show that the cost of information, c, determines the equilibrium ratio of information quality between informed and uninformed traders $(\text{Var}(u^*|\theta))/\text{Var}(u^*|w_\lambda)$. From (1), (A11) of appendix A, and (16), this can be written as

$$\frac{\text{Var}(u^*|\theta)}{\text{Var}(u^*|w_\lambda)} = \frac{1+m}{1+m+nm} = \left(1 + \frac{nm}{1+m}\right)^{-1}. \tag{18}$$

Substituting (18) into (14) and using (15), we obtain, for $0 < \lambda < 1$, in equilibrium

$$m = \frac{e^{2ac} - 1}{1 + n - e^{2ac}}, \tag{19a}$$

or

$$1 - \rho_\theta^2 = \frac{e^{2ac} - 1}{n}. \tag{19b}$$

Note that (19) holds for $\gamma(0) < 1 < \gamma(1)$, since these conditions insure that the equilibrium λ is between zero and one. Equation (19b) shows that the equilibrium informativeness of the price system is determined completely by the cost of information c, the quality of the informed trader's information n, and the degree of risk aversion a.

H.   Comparative Statics

From equation (19b), we immediately obtain some basic comparative statics results:

1. An increase in the quality of information (n) increases the informativeness of the price system.

2. A decrease in the cost of information increases the informativeness of the price system.

3. A decrease in risk aversion leads informed individuals to take larger positions, and this increases the informativeness of the price system.

Further, all other changes in parameters, such that n, a, and c remain constant, do not change the equilibrium degree of informativeness of the price system; other changes lead only to particular changes in λ of a magnitude to exactly offset them. For example:

4. An increase in noise (σ_x^2) increases the proportion of informed traders. At any given λ, an increase in noise reduces the informativeness of the price system; but it increases the returns to information and leads more

individuals to become informed; the remarkable result obtained above establishes that *the two effects exactly offset each other* so that the equilibrium informativeness of the price system is unchanged. This can be illustrated diagrammatically if we note from (16a) that for a given λ, an increase in σ_x^2 raises m, which from (18) lowers $(\mathrm{Var}(u^*|\theta))/\mathrm{Var}(u^*|w_\lambda)$. Thus from (14) a rise in σ_x^2 leads to a vertical downward shift of the $\gamma(\lambda)$ curve in figure 5.1, and thus a higher value of λ^e.

5. Similarly an increase in σ_ε^2 for a constant n (equivalent to an increase in the variance of u since n is constant) leads to an increased proportion of individuals becoming informed—and indeed again just enough to offset the increased variance, so that the degree of *informativeness* of the price system remains unchanged. This can also be seen from figure 5.1 if (16) is used to note that an increase in σ_ε^2 with n held constant by raising σ_θ^2 leads to an increase in m for a given λ. From (18) and (14) this leads to a vertical downward shift of the $\gamma(\lambda)$ curve and thus a higher value of λ^e.

6. It is more difficult to determine what happens if, say, σ_θ^2 increases, keeping σ_u^2 constant (implying a fall in σ_ε^2)—that is, *the information obtained is more informative*. This leads to an increase in n, which from (19b) implies that the equilibrium informativeness of the price system rises. From (16) it is clear that m and nm both fall when σ_θ^2 rises (keeping $\sigma_u^2 = \sigma_\theta^2 + \sigma_\varepsilon^2$ constant). This implies that the $\gamma(\lambda)$ curve may shift up or down depending on the precise values of c, a, and n.[8] This ambiguity arises because an improvement in the precision of informed traders' information, with the cost of the information fixed, increases the benefit of being informed. However, some of the improved information is transmitted, via a more informative price system, to the uninformed; this increases the benefits of being uninformed. If n is small, both the price system m is not very informative *and* the marginal value of information to informed traders is high. Thus the *relative* benefits of being informed rises when n rises, implying that the equilibrium λ rises. Conversely when n is large the price system is very informative and the marginal value of information is low to informed traders so the relative benefits of being uninformed rises.

7. From (14) it is clear that an increase in the cost of information c shifts the $\gamma(\lambda)$ curve up and thus decreases the percentage of informed traders.

The above results are summarized in the following theorem.

Theorem 4   *For equilibrium λ such that $0 < \lambda < 1$:*

A. *The equilibrium informativeness of the price system, ρ_θ^2, rises if n rises, c falls, or a falls.*

B. *The equilibrium informativeness of the price system is unchanged if σ_x^2 changes, or if σ_u^2 changes with n fixed.*

C. *The equilibrium percentage of informed traders will rise if σ_x^2 rises, σ_u^2 rises for a fixed n, or c falls.*

D. *If $\bar{n}$ satisfies $(e^{2ac} - 1)/(\bar{n} - (e^{2ac} - 1)) = \bar{n}/(\bar{n} + 1)$, then $n \overset{(<)}{>} \bar{n}$ implies that λ falls (rises) due to an increase in n.*

Proof Parts A–C are proved in the above remarks. Part D is proved in note 8. QED

I. Price Cannot Fully Reflect Costly Information

We now consider certain limiting cases, for $\gamma(0) \leqslant 1 \leqslant \gamma(1)$, and show that equilibrium does not exist if $c > 0$ and price is fully informative.

1. As the cost of information goes to zero, the price system becomes more informative, but at a positive value of c, say, $\hat{c}$, all traders are informed. From (14) and (15) $\hat{c}$ satisfies

$$e^{a\hat{c}} \sqrt{\frac{\mathrm{Var}(u^*|\theta)}{\mathrm{Var}(u^*|w_1)}} = 1.$$

2. From (19a) as the precision of the informed trader's information n goes to infinity, i.e., $\sigma_\varepsilon^2 \to 0$ and $\sigma_\theta^2 \to \sigma_u^2$, σ_u^2 held fixed, the price system becomes perfectly informative. Moreover, the percentage of informed traders goes to zero! This can be seen from (18) and (15). That is, as $\sigma_\varepsilon^2 \to 0$, $nm/(1 + m)$ must stay constant for equilibrium to be maintained. But from (19b) and (17), m falls as σ_ε^2 goes to zero. Therefore nm must fall, but nm must not go to zero or else $nm/(1 + m)$ would not be constant. From (16) $nm = (a/\lambda)^2 \sigma_\varepsilon^2 \sigma_x^2$, and thus λ must go to zero to prevent nm from going to zero as $\sigma_\varepsilon^2 \to 0$.

3. From (16a) and (19a) it is clear that as noise σ_x^2 goes to zero, the percentage of informed traders goes to zero. Further, since (19a) implies that m does not change as σ_x^2 changes, the informativeness of the price system is unchanged as $\sigma_x^2 \to 0$.

Assume that c is small enough so that it is worthwhile for a trader to become informed when no other trader is informed. Then if $\sigma_x^2 = 0$ or $\sigma_\varepsilon^2 = 0$, there exists no competitive equilibrium. To see this, note that equilibrium requires either that the ratio of expected utility of the informed to the uninformed be equal to unity, or that if the ratio is larger than unity, no one be informed. We shall show that when no one is informed, it is less than unity so that $\lambda = 0$ cannot be an equilibrium; but when $\lambda > 0$, it is greater than unity. That is, if $\sigma_x^2 = 0$ or $\sigma_\varepsilon^2 = 0$, the ratio of expected utilities is not a continuous function of λ at $\lambda = 0$.

This follows immediately from observing that at $\lambda = 0$, $\mathrm{Var}(u^*|w_0) = \mathrm{Var}\, u^*$, and thus by (14)

$$\frac{EV(W_{Ii}^0)}{EV(W_{Ui}^0)} = e^{ac}\sqrt{\frac{\sigma_\varepsilon^2}{\sigma_\varepsilon^2 + \sigma_\theta^2}}$$

$$= e^{ac}\sqrt{\frac{1}{1+n}},\tag{20}$$

while if $\lambda > 0$, by (18)

$$\frac{EV(W_{Ii}^\lambda)}{EV(W_{Ui}^\lambda)} = e^{ac}\sqrt{\frac{1}{1 + n\dfrac{m}{m+1}}}.$$

But if $\sigma_x^2 = 0$ or $\sigma_\varepsilon^2 = 0$, then $m = 0$, $nm = 0$ for $\lambda > 0$, and hence

$$\frac{EV(W_{Ii}^\lambda)}{EV(W_{Ui}^\lambda)} = e^{ac}.\tag{21}$$

It immediately follows that

Theorem 5   (a) *If there is no noise ($\sigma_x^2 = 0$), an overall equilibrium does not exist if (and only if) $e^{ac} < \sqrt{1+n}$.* (b) *If information is perfect ($\sigma_\varepsilon^2 = 0$, $n = \infty$), there never exists an equilibrium.*

Proof   (a) If $e^{ac} < \sqrt{1+n}$, then by (20) and (21), $\gamma(\lambda)$ is discontinuous at $\lambda = 0$; $\lambda = 0$ is not an equilibrium since by (20) $\gamma(0) < 1$; $\lambda > 0$ is not an equilibrium since by (21) $\gamma(\lambda) > 1$. (b) If $\sigma_\varepsilon^2 = 0$ and $\sigma_\theta^2 = \sigma_u^2$ so that information is perfect, then for $\lambda > 0$, $nm = 0$ by (16) and hence $\gamma(\lambda) > 1$ by (21). From (20) $\gamma(0) = 0 < 1$.   QED

If there is no noise and some traders become informed, then *all* their information is transmitted to the uninformed by the price system. Hence each informed trader acting as a price taker thinks the informativeness of the price system will be unchanged if he becomes uninformed, so $\lambda > 0$ is not an equilibrium. On the other hand, if no traders are informed, then each uninformed trader learns nothing from the price system, and thus he has a desire to become informed (if $e^{ac} < (1 + n)^{1/2}$). Similarly if the informed traders get perfect information, then their demands are very sensitive to their information, so that the market-clearing price becomes very sensitive to their information and thus reveals θ to the uninformed. Hence all traders desire to be uninformed. But if all traders are uninformed, each trader can eliminate the risk of his portfolio by the purchase of information, so each trader desires to be informed.

In the next section we show that the nonexistence of competitive equilibrium can be thought of as the breakdown of competitive markets due to lack of trade. That is, we shall show that as σ_x^2 gets very small, trade goes to zero and markets serve no function. Thus competitive markets close for lack of trade "before" equilibrium ceases to exist at $\sigma_x^2 = 0$.

5.3 On the Thinness of Speculative Markets

In general, trade takes place because traders differ in endowments, preferences, or beliefs. Grossman (1975, 1977, 1978) has argued that differences in preferences are not a major factor in explaining the magnitude of trade in speculative markets. For this reason the model in section 5.2 gave all traders the same risk preferences (note that none of the results in section 5.2 are affected by letting traders have different coefficients of absolute risk aversion). In this section we assume that trade requires differences in endowments or beliefs and dispense with differences in risk preference as an explanatory variable.[9]

There is clearly some fixed cost in operating a competitive market. If traders have to bear this cost, then trade in the market must be beneficial. Suppose traders have the same endowments and beliefs. Competitive equilibrium will leave them with allocations that are identical with their initial endowments. Hence, if it is costly to enter such a competitive market, no trader would ever enter. We shall show below that in an important class of situations, there is continuity in the amount of net trade. That is, when initial endowments are the same and peoples' beliefs differ *slightly*, then the competitive equilibrium allocation that an individual gets will be only *slightly* different from his initial endowment. Hence, there will only be a slight benefit to entering the competitive market. This could, for sufficiently high operating costs, be outweighed by the cost of entering the market.

The amount of trade occurring at any date is a random variable—a function of θ and x. It is easy to show that it is a normally distributed random variable. Since one of the primary determinants of the size of markets is differences in beliefs, one might have conjectured that markets will be thin, in some sense, if almost all traders are either informed or uninformed. This is not, however, obvious, since the amount of trade by any single trader may be a function of λ as well, and a few active traders can do the job of many small traders. In our model, there is a sense, however, in which our conjecture is correct.

We first calculate the magnitude of trades as a function of the exogenous parameters, θ and x. Let $h \equiv \sigma_\varepsilon^2$, $\bar{x} = Ex^*$, and $\bar{\theta} \equiv E\theta^*$. (The actual trades will depend on the distribution of random endowments across all of the traders, but these we shall net out.) Per capita net trade is [10]

$$X_I - x = (1 - \lambda)\left[\left(nm + \frac{ah}{\lambda}\right)(x - \bar{x})\right.$$

$$\left. + [(m + 1)n - 1](\theta - \bar{\theta}) + \bar{x}nm \right]$$

$$+ [1 + m + \lambda nm]. \tag{22}$$

Thus, the mean of total informed trade is

$$E\lambda(X_I - x) = \frac{(1 - \lambda)\lambda m\bar{x}}{1 + m + \lambda nm}, \tag{23}$$

and its variance is

$$\sigma_\theta^2(1 - \lambda)^2\lambda^2\left[[(m + 1)n - 1]^2 \right.$$

$$\left. + \left(nm + \frac{a\sigma_\varepsilon^2}{\lambda}\right)^2 \frac{\sigma_x^2}{\sigma_\theta^2} \right] + (1 + m + \lambda nm)^2 n^2. \tag{24}$$

In the last section we considered limiting values of the exogenous variables with the property that $\lambda \to 0$. The following theorem will show that the mean and variance of trade go to zero as $\lambda \to 0$. That is, the distribution of $\lambda(X_I - x)$ becomes degenerate at zero as $\lambda \to 0$. This is not trivial because as $\lambda \to 0$ due to $n \to \infty$ (very precise information), the informed trader's demand $X_I(P, \theta)$ goes to infinity at most prices because the risky asset becomes riskless with perfect information.

Theorem 6   (a) *For sufficiently large or small c, the mean and variance of trade is zero.* (b) *As the precision of informed traders' information n goes to infinity, the mean and variance of trade go to zero.*

Proof (a) From remark (1) in section 5.2.I, $\lambda = 1$ if $c \leqslant \hat{c}$, which from (23) and (24) implies trade is degenerate at zero. From (14), for c sufficiently large, say, c^0, $\gamma(0) = 1$, so the equilibrium $\lambda = 0$. As c goes to c^0 from below $\lambda \to 0$, and from (14), (15), and (18) $\lim_{c \uparrow c^0}(1 + nm/(1 + m))^{-1/2} = e^{-ac^0}$. Hence $\lim_{c \uparrow c^0}(nm/1 + m)$ is a finite positive number. Thus from (22) mean trade goes to zero as $c \uparrow c^0$. If the numerator and the denominator of (24) are divided by $(1 + m)^2$, then again using the fact that $m/1 + m$ has a finite limit gives the result that as $c \uparrow c^0$, $\lambda \to 0$, and variance of trade goes to zero.

(b) By (14), (15), and (18), $nm/(1 + m)$ is constant as $n \to \infty$. Further, from remark (2) of section 5.2.I, $\lambda \to 0$ as $n \to \infty$. Hence from (23) and (24), the mean and variance of trade go to zero.

(c) From remark (3) in section 5.2.I, m is constant and λ goes to zero as $\sigma_x^2 \to 0$. Therefore mean trade goes to zero. In (24), note that $(nm + a\sigma_\varepsilon^2/\lambda)^2\sigma_x^2/\sigma_\theta^2 = (nm\sigma_x/\sigma_\theta + (m)^{1/2})^2$ by (16a). Hence the variance of trade goes to zero as $\sigma_x^2 \to 0$.   QED

Note further that $\lambda(X_I - x) + (1 - \lambda)(X_U - x) = 0$ implies that no trade will take place as $\lambda \to 1$. Thus, the result that competitive equilibrium is incompatible with informationally efficient markets should be interpreted as meaning that speculative markets where prices reveal a lot of information will be very thin because it will be composed of individuals with very similar beliefs.

5.4   On the Possibility of Perfect Markets

In section 5.2 we showed that the price system reveals the signal w_λ^* to traders, where

$$w_\lambda \equiv \theta - \frac{a\sigma_\varepsilon^2}{\lambda}(x - Ex^*).$$

Thus, for given information of informed traders θ, the price system reveals a noisy version of θ. The noise is $(a\sigma_\varepsilon^2/\lambda)(x - Ex^*)$. Uninformed traders learn θ to within a random variable with mean zero and variance $(a\sigma_\varepsilon^2/\lambda)^2 \operatorname{Var} x^*$, where σ_ε^2 is the precision of informed traders' information, $\operatorname{Var} x^*$ is the amount of endowment uncertainty, λ is the fraction of informed traders, and a is the degree of absolute risk aversion. Thus, in general, the price system does not reveal all the information about "the true value" of the risky asset. (θ is the true value of the risky asset in that it reflects the best available information about the asset's worth.)

The only way informed traders can earn a return on their activity of information gathering, is if they can use their information to take positions in the market that are "better" than the positions of uninformed traders. "Efficient Markets" theorists have claimed that "at any time prices fully reflect all available information" (see Eugene Fama 1970, p. 383). If this were so, then informed traders could not earn a return on their information.

We showed that when the efficient markets hypothesis is true and information is costly, competitive markets break down. This is because when $\sigma_\varepsilon^2 = 0$ or $\text{Var}\, x^* = 0$, then w_λ and thus the price reflect all the information. When this happens, each informed trader, because he is in a competitive market, feels that he could stop paying for information and do as well as a trader who pays nothing for information. But all informed traders feel this way. Hence having any positive fraction informed is not an equilibrium. Having no one informed is also not an equilibrium, because then each trader, taking the price as given, feels that there are profits to be made from becoming informed.

Efficient Markets theorists seem to be aware that costless information is a *sufficient* condition for prices to fully reflect all available information (see Fama, 1970, p. 387); they are not aware that it is a *necessary* condition. But this is a *reducto ad absurdum*, since price systems and competitive markets are important only when information is costly (see Fredrick Hayek, 1945, p. 452).

We are attempting to redefine the Efficient Markets notion, not destroy it. We have shown that when information is very inexpensive, or when informed traders get very precise information, then equilibrium exists and the market price will reveal most of the informed traders' information. However, it was argued in section 5.3 that such markets are likely to be thin because traders have almost homogeneous beliefs.

There is a further conflict. As Grossman (1975, 1977) showed, whenever there are differences in beliefs that are not completely arbitraged, there is an incentive to create a market. (Grossman, 1977, analyzed a model of a storable commodity whose spot price did not reveal all information because of the presence of noise. Thus traders were left with differences in beliefs about the future price of the commodity. This led to the opening of a futures market. But then uninformed traders had two prices revealing information to them, implying the elimination of noise.) But, because differences in beliefs are themselves endogenous, arising out of expenditure on information and the informativeness of the price system, the creation of markets eliminates the differences of beliefs that gave rise to them, and thus causes those markets to disappear. If the creation of markets were costless, as is conventionally assumed in equilibrium analyses, equilibrium would never exist. For instance, in our model, were we to introduce an additional security, say, a security that paid

$$z = \begin{cases} 1 & \text{if} \quad u > E\theta^* \\ 0 & \text{if} \quad u \leqslant E\theta^*, \end{cases}$$

then the demand y for this security by the informed would depend on its price, say, q on p and on θ, while the uninformed demand depends only on p and q:

$$\lambda y_I(q, p, \theta) + (1 - \lambda)y_u(q, p) = 0$$

is the condition that demand equals (supply is zero for a pure security). Under weak assumptions, q and p would convey all the information concerning θ. Thus, the market would be "noiseless" and no equilibrium could exist.

Thus, we could argue, as soon as the assumptions of the conventional perfect capital markets model are modified to allow even a slight amount of information imperfection and a slight cost of information, that the traditional theory becomes untenable. There *cannot* be as many securities as states of nature. For if there were, competitive equilibrium would not exist.

It is only because of costly transactions and the fact that this leads to there being a limited number of markets that competitive equilibrium can be established.

We have argued that because information is costly, prices cannot perfectly reflect the information which is available, since if it did, those who spent resources to obtain it would receive no compensation. There is a fundamental conflict between the efficiency with which markets spread information and the incentives to acquire information. However, we have said nothing regarding the social benefits of information, nor whether it is socially optimal to have "informationally efficient markets." We hope to examine the welfare properties of the equilibrium allocations herein in future work.

Appendix A

Here we collect some facts on conditional expectations used in the text. If X^* and Y^* are jointly normally distributed, then

$$E[X^* | Y^* = Y] = EX^* + \frac{\text{Cov}(X^*, Y^*)}{\text{Var}(Y^*)} \{Y - EY^*\}, \tag{A1}$$

$$\text{Var}[X^* | Y^* = Y] = \text{Var}(X^*) - \frac{[\text{Cov}(X^*, Y^*)]^2}{\text{Var}(Y^*)}. \tag{A2}$$

(See Paul Hoel, 1962, p. 200.) From (A1) note that $E[X^* | Y^*]$ is a function of Y. If the expectation of both sides of (A1) is taken, we see that

$$E\{E[X^* | Y^* = Y]\} = EX^* \tag{A3}$$

Note that $\text{Var}[X^* | Y^* = Y]$ is not a function of Y, as $\text{Var}(X^*)$, $\text{Cov}(X^*, Y^*)$, and $\text{Var}(Y^*)$ are just parameters of the joint distribution of X^* and Y^*.

Two other relevant properties of conditional expectation are

$$E\{E[Y^* | F(X^*)] | X^*\} = E[Y^* | F(X^*)], \tag{A4}$$

$$E\{E[Y^* | X] | F(X^*)\} = E[Y^* | F(X^*)], \tag{A5}$$

where $F(\cdot)$ is a given function on the range of X^* (see Robert Ash, 1972, p. 260).

Appendix B

Proof of theorem 1   (a) Suppose $\lambda = 0$; then (9) becomes

$$X_U(P_0(\theta, x), P_0^*) = x. \tag{A6}$$

Define

$$P_0(\theta, x) \equiv \frac{E\theta^* - ax\sigma_u^2}{R}, \tag{A7}$$

where σ_u^2 is the variance of u. Note that $P_0(\theta^*, x^*)$ is uncorrelated with u^*, as x^* is uncorrelated with u^*. Hence

$$E[u^* | P_0^* = P_0(\theta, x)] = Eu^* = E\theta^*,$$

$$\text{Var}[u^* | P_0^* = P_0(\theta, x)] = \text{Var}[u^*]. \tag{A8}$$

Substitution of (A8) in (8) yields

$$X_U(P_0^*, P_0(\theta, x)) = \frac{E\theta^* - RP_0(\theta, x)}{a \, \text{Var} \, u}. \tag{A9}$$

Substitution of (A7) in the right-hand side of (A9) yields $X_U(P_0^*(\theta, x), P_0^*) = x$, which was to be shown.

(b) Suppose $0 < \lambda \leqslant 1$. Let

$$P_\lambda(\theta, x) = \frac{\dfrac{\lambda w_\lambda}{a\sigma_\varepsilon^2} + \dfrac{(1-\lambda)E[u^*|w_\lambda]}{a\,\mathrm{Var}[u^*|w_\lambda]} - Ex^*}{R\left[\dfrac{\lambda}{a\sigma_\varepsilon^2} + \dfrac{(1-\lambda)}{a\,\mathrm{Var}[u^*|w_\lambda]}\right]}. \tag{A10}$$

Note that from equations (1), (10), (A1), and (A2),

$$E(u^*|w_\lambda) = E\theta^* + \frac{\sigma_\theta^2}{\mathrm{Var}\,w_\lambda}\cdot(w_\lambda - E\theta^*), \tag{A11a}$$

$$\mathrm{Var}(u^*|w_\lambda) = \sigma_\theta^2 + \sigma_\varepsilon^2 - \frac{\sigma_\theta^2}{\mathrm{Var}\,w_\lambda}, \tag{A11b}$$

$$\mathrm{Var}\,w_\lambda = \sigma_\theta^2 + \left(\frac{a\sigma_\varepsilon^2}{\lambda}\right)^2 \mathrm{Var}\,x^*. \tag{A11c}$$

Since $P_\lambda(\theta, x)$ is a linear function of w_λ, it is immediate that $E(u^*|w_\lambda) \equiv E(u^*|P_\lambda)$, $\mathrm{Var}(u^*|w_\lambda) = \mathrm{Var}(u^*|P_\lambda)$, etc. To see that P_λ^* is an equilibrium, we must show that the following equation holds as an identity in (θ, x), for $P_\lambda(\cdot)$ defined by (A10):

$$\lambda \cdot \frac{\theta - RP_\lambda}{a\sigma_\varepsilon^2} + (1-\lambda)\frac{E[u^*|w_\lambda] - RP_\lambda}{a\,\mathrm{Var}[u^*|w_\lambda]} = x. \tag{A12}$$

It is immediate from (10) that (A12) holds as an identity in θ and x.

Proof of theorem 2 (a) *Calculation of the expected utility of the informed.* Using the fact that W_{Ii}^λ is normally distributed conditional on $(\bar{X}_i, \theta, x)$,

$$E[V(W_{Ii}^\lambda)|\bar{X}_i, \theta, x] = \exp\left[-a\left\{E\left[W_{Ii}^\lambda|\bar{X}_i, \theta, x\right]\right.\right.$$
$$\left.\left. - \frac{a}{2}\mathrm{Var}[W_{Ii}^\lambda|\bar{X}_i, \theta, x]\right\}\right]. \tag{A13}$$

Using (8), (12), and the fact that (θ, x) determines a particular P,

$$E[W_{Ii}^\lambda|\bar{X}_i, \theta, x] = R(W_{0i} - c) + \frac{(E[u^*|\theta] - RP_\lambda)^2}{a\sigma_\varepsilon^2}, \tag{A14a}$$

$$\mathrm{Var}[W_{Ii}^\lambda|\bar{X}_i, \theta, x] = \frac{(E[u^*|\theta] - RP_\lambda)^2}{a^2\sigma_\varepsilon^2}. \tag{A14b}$$

Substitution of (A14) into (A13) yields

$$E[V(W_{Ii}^\lambda)|\overline{X}_i, \theta, x] = -\exp\Bigg[-aR(W_{0i} - c)$$

$$-\frac{1}{2\sigma_\varepsilon^2}(E[u^*|\theta] - RP_\lambda)^2\Bigg]. \tag{A15}$$

Note that, as $P_\lambda^*(\cdot) = P_\lambda(\theta, x)$,

$$E(E[V(W_{Ii}^\lambda)|\overline{X}_i, \theta, x]|P_\lambda, \overline{X}_i) = E[V(W_{Ii}^\lambda)|P_\lambda, \overline{X}_i] \tag{A16}$$

[see (A5)]. Note that since W_{0i} is nonstochastic conditional on $(P_\lambda, \overline{X}_i)$, equation (A15) implies

$$E[V(W_{Ii}^\lambda)|P_\lambda, \overline{X}_i] = -\exp[-aR(W_{0i}^\lambda - c)]$$

$$\cdot E\Bigg[\bigg\{\exp\Big[-\frac{1}{2\sigma_\varepsilon^2}(E[u|\theta] - RP_\lambda)^2\Big]\bigg\}|P_\lambda, \overline{X}_i\Bigg]. \tag{A17}$$

Note that by theorem 1, conditioning on w_λ^* is equivalent to conditioning on P_λ^*. Define

$$h_\lambda \equiv \mathrm{Var}(E[u^*|\theta]|w_\lambda) = \mathrm{Var}(\theta|w_\lambda), \quad h_0 \equiv \sigma_\varepsilon^2 \equiv h, \tag{A18}$$

$$Z \equiv \frac{E[u^*|\theta] - RP_\lambda}{\sqrt{h_\lambda}}. \tag{A19}$$

Using (3) and (A18), equation (A17) can be written as

$$E[V(W_{Ii}^\lambda)|P_\lambda, \overline{X}_i] = e^{ac}V(RW_{0i})E\Bigg[\exp\Big[-\frac{h_\lambda}{2\sigma_\varepsilon^2}Z^2\Big]|w_\lambda\Bigg] \tag{A20}$$

since $\overline{X}_i$ and w_λ are independent. Conditional on w_λ, P_λ is nonstochastic and $E[u^*|\theta]$ is normal. Hence conditional on w_λ, $(Z^*)^2$ has a noncentral chi-square distribution (see C. Rao, 1965, p. 181). Then for $t > 0$ the moment generating function for $(Z^*)^2$ can be written

$$E[e^{-tZ^2}|w_\lambda] = \frac{1}{\sqrt{1 + 2t}}\exp\Bigg[\frac{-(E[Z|w_\lambda])^2 t}{1 + 2t}\Bigg]. \tag{A21}$$

Note that $E[u^*|\theta] = E[u^*|\theta, x]$. Hence

$$E[E[u^*|\theta]|w_\lambda] = E[u^*|w_\lambda] = E\theta^* + \frac{\sigma_\theta^2}{\mathrm{Var}\, w_\lambda}(w_\lambda - E\theta^*) \tag{A22}$$

since w_λ is just a function of (θ, x). Therefore

$$E[Z^*|w_\lambda] = \frac{E[u^*|w_\lambda] - RP_\lambda}{\sqrt{h_\lambda}}.$$ (A23)

Since $u = \theta + \varepsilon$,

$$\text{Var}(u^*|w_\lambda) = \sigma_\varepsilon^2 + \text{Var}(\theta^*|w_\lambda) = \sigma_r^2 + h_\lambda.$$ (A24)

The nondegeneracy assumptions on $(x^*, \varepsilon^*, u^*)$ imply $h_\lambda > 0$. Set $t = (h_\lambda/2\sigma_\varepsilon^2)$; and evaluate (A21) using (A23) and (A24):

$$E\left[\exp\left[-\frac{h_\lambda}{2\sigma_\varepsilon^2}Z^2\right]\Big|w_\lambda\right] = \sqrt{\frac{\text{Var}(u^*|\theta)}{\text{Var}(u^*|w_\lambda)}}$$

$$\cdot \exp\left(\frac{-(E(u^*|w_\lambda) - RP_\lambda)^2}{2\,\text{Var}(u^*|w_\lambda)}\right).$$ (A25)

This permits the evaluation of (A20).

(b) *Calculation of expected utility of the uninformed.* Equations (8), (5), and the normality of W_{Ui}^λ conditional on w_λ can be used to show, by calculations parallel to (A13)–(A25), that

$$E[V(W_{Ui}^\lambda)|w_\lambda, \bar{X}_i] = V(RW_{0i})\exp\left(\frac{-(E(u^*|w_\lambda) - RP_\lambda)^2}{2\,\text{Var}(u^*|w_\lambda)}\right).$$ (A26)

Hence

$$E[V(W_{Ii}^\lambda)|w_\lambda, \bar{X}_i] - E[V(W_{Ui}^\lambda)|w_\lambda, \bar{X}_i] = \left(e^{ac}\sqrt{\frac{\text{Var}(u^*|\theta)}{\text{Var}(u^*|w_\lambda)}} - 1\right)$$

$$\cdot E[V(W_{Ui}^\lambda)|w_\lambda, \bar{X}_i].$$ (A27)

Taking expectations of both sides of (A27) yields

$$E[V(W_{Ii}^\lambda)] - E[V(W_{Ui}^\lambda)] = \left(e^{ac}\sqrt{\frac{\text{Var}(u^*|\theta)}{\text{Var}(u^*|w_\lambda)}} - 1\right)EV(W_{Ui}^\lambda).$$ (A28)

Equation (13) follows immediately from (A28).

Notes

1. An alternative interpretation is that θ is a "measurement" of u with error. The mathematics of this alternative interpretation differ slightly, but the results are identical.

2. The framework described herein does not explicitly model the effect of variations in supply, i.e., x on commodity storage. The effect of futures markets and

storage capabilities on the informativeness of the price system was studied by Grossman (1975, 1977).

3. That is, with no one informed, an individual can only get information by paying c dollars, since no information is revealed by the price system. By paying c dollars an individual will be able to predict better than the market when it is optimal to hold the risky asset as opposed to the risk-free asset. Thus his expected utility will be higher than an uninformed person gross of information costs. Thus for c sufficiently low all uninformed people will desire to be informed.

4. See Grossman (1975, 1977) for a formal example of this phenomenon in futures markets. See Stiglitz (1971, 1974) for a general discussion of information and the possibility of nonexistence of equilibrium in capital markets.

5. The informational equilibria discussed here may not, in general, exist. See Green (1977). Of course, for the utility function we choose equilibrium does exist.

6. If $y' = y + Z$, and $E[Z|y] = 0$, then y' is just y plus noise.

7. Formally, w_λ^* is an experiment in the sense of Blackwell which gives information about θ. It is easy to show that, ceteris paribus, the smaller $\text{Var}(w_\lambda^*|\theta)$, the more "informative" (or sufficient) in the sense of Blackwell, is the experiment; see Grossman, Kihlstrom, and Mirman (1977, p. 539).

8. From (14) and (18) it is clear that λ rises if and only if $\text{Var}(u^*|\theta) \div \text{Var}(u^*|w_\lambda)$ falls due to the rise in σ_θ^2 for a given λ. This occurs if and only if $nm/(1 + m)$ rises. Using (16) to differentiate $nm/(1 + m)$ with respect to σ_ε^2 subject to the constraint that $d\sigma_u^2 = 0$ (i.e., $d\sigma_\theta^2 = -d\sigma_\varepsilon^2$), we find that the sign of

$$\frac{d}{d\sigma_\theta^2}\left(\frac{nm}{1+m}\right) = \text{sgn}\left[m\left(\frac{n+1}{n}\right) - 1\right]$$

$$= \text{sgn}\left[\left(\frac{\gamma}{n-\gamma}\right)\left(\frac{n+1}{n}\right) - 1\right],$$

where $\gamma \equiv e^{2ac} - 1$ and the last equality follows from equation (19a). Thus for n very large the derivative is negative so that λ falls due to an increase in the precision of the informed trader's information. Similarly if n is sufficiently small, the derivative is positive and thus λ rises.

9. In the model described in section 5.2 it was assumed that an individual's endowment $\bar{X}_i$ is independent of the market's per capita endowment x^*. This was done primarily so there would not be useful information in an individual's endowment about the total market endowment. Such information would be useful in equilibrium because an individual observes $P_\lambda(\theta, x)$. If due to observing $\bar{X}_i$, he knows something about x, then by observing $P_\lambda(\theta, x)$, $\bar{X}_i$ is valuable in making inferences about θ. To take this into account is possible, but would add undue complication to a model already overburdened with computations.

10. Calculation of distribution of net trades

$$\frac{\lambda}{ah}(\theta - RP_\lambda) + \frac{(1 - \lambda)[(\bar{\theta} - RP_\lambda)(1 + m)n + \theta - \bar{\theta} - (ah/\lambda)(x - \bar{x})]}{ah(1 + m + nm)n} = x,$$

or

$$\frac{(\theta - RP_\lambda)}{ah}\left(\lambda + \frac{(1 - \lambda)(1 + m)}{1 + m + nm}\right)$$

$$= \left(\frac{\theta - RP_\lambda}{ah}\right)\left(\frac{1 + m + \lambda nm}{1 + m + nm}\right)$$

$$= x + \frac{(1 - \lambda)([(m + 1)n - 1](\theta - \bar{\theta}) + (ah/\lambda)(x - \bar{x}))}{ah(1 + m + \lambda nm)n},$$

or

$$X_I = \frac{1 + m + nm}{1 + m + \lambda nm}$$

$$\cdot \left[x + \frac{(1 - \lambda)([(m + 1) - 1](\theta - \bar{\theta}) + (ah/\lambda)(x - \bar{x}))}{ah(1 + m + nm)n}\right],$$

$$X_I - x = \frac{(1 - \lambda)[(nm + (ah/\lambda))(x - \bar{x}) + [(m + 1) - 1](\theta - \bar{\theta}) + \bar{x}nm}{(1 + m + \lambda nm)n}.$$

References

Robert B. Ash, *Real Analysis and Probability*, New York 1972.

E. Fama, "Efficient Capital Markets: A Review of Theory and Empirical Work," *J. Finance*, May 1970, 25, 383–417.

J. R. Green, "Information, Efficiency and Equilibrium," disc. paper no. 284, Harvard Inst. Econ. Res., Mar. 1973.

J. R. Green, "The Non-Existence of Informational Equilibria," *Rev. Econ. Stud.*, Oct. 1977, 44, 451–464.

S. Grossman, "Essays on Rational Expectations," unpublished doctoral dissertation, Univ. Chicago 1975.

S. Grossman, "On the Efficiency of Competitive Stock Markets Where Traders Have Diverse Information," *J. Finance*, May 1976, 31, 573–585.

S. Grossman, "The Existence of Futures Markets, Noisy Rational Expectations and Informational Externalities," *Rev. Econ. Stud.*, Oct. 1977, 64, 431–449.

S. Grossman, "Further Results on the Informational Efficiency of Competitive Stock Markets," *J. Econ. Theory*, June 1978, 18, 81–101.

S. Grossman, R. Kihlstrom, and L. Mirman, "A Bayesian Approach to the Production of Information and Learning by Doing," *Rev. Econ. Stud.*, Oct. 1977, *64*, 533–547.

F. H. Hayek, "The Use of Knowledge in Society," *Amer. Econ. Rev.*, Sept. 1945, *35*, 519–530.

Paul G. Hoel, *Introduction to Mathematical Statistics*, New York 1962.

R. Kihlstrom and L. Mirman, "Information and Market Equilibrium," *Bell. J. Econ.*, Spring 1975, *6*, 357–376.

R. E. Lucas, Jr., "Expectations and the Neutrality of Money," *J. Econ. Theory*, Apr. 1972, *4*, 103–124.

C. Rao, *Linear Statistical Inference and Its Applications*, New York 1965.

J. E. Stiglitz, "Perfect and Imperfect Capital Markets," paper presented to the Econometric Society, New Orleans 1971.

J. E. Stiglitz, "Information and Capital Markets," mimeo., Oxford Univ. 1974.

6

An Analysis of the Implications for Stock and Futures Price Volatility of Program Trading and Dynamic Hedging Strategies

6.1 Introduction

The introduction of futures and options markets in stock indexes is strongly associated with the use of program trading strategies. Such strategies are used for spot/futures arbitrage, market timing, and portfolio insurance. It is this last use of program trading strategies that raises fascinating theoretical questions, the answers to which may have practical importance for understanding the impact of such strategies on the volatility of stock and futures prices.

Recent advances in financial theory have created an understanding of the environments in which a real security can be synthesized by a dynamic trading strategy in a risk-free asset and other securities.[1] The proliferation of new securities has been made possible, in part, by this theoretical work. The issuer of a new security can price the security based on the issuer's ability to synthesize the returns stream of the new security using a dynamic trading strategy in existing securities, futures, and options. This use of dynamic trading strategies has been extended even further by eliminating the "new" security altogether and just selling the dynamic hedging strategy directly. Portfolio insurance is the best example of the latter phenomenon.

In this chapter I contend that there is a crucial distinction between a synthetic security and a real security. In particular, the notion that a real security is redundant when it can be synthesized by a dynamic trading strategy ignores the informational role of real securities markets.[2] The

An earlier version of this chapter was prepared for the Conference on the Impact of Stock Index Futures Trading at the Center for the Study of Futures Markets, Columbia University, June 8, 1987. Helpful comments were received from Fischer Black and Frank Edwards, but they are not responsible for any errors or opinions contained here.

prices of real securities convey important information to market participants, and this information will not be conveyed if the real security is replaced by synthetic trading strategies. In particular, the replacement of a real security by synthetic strategies may in itself cause enough uncertainty about the price volatility of the underlying security that the real security is no longer redundant.

Portfolio insurance provides a good example of the difference between a synthetic security and a real security. One form of portfolio insurance uses a trading strategy in risk-free securities ("cash") and index futures to synthesize a European put on the underlying portfolio. If a put was traded on a securities market, then the price of the put would reveal important information about the desire of people to sell stock consequent to adverse future price moves.[3] For example, if everyone in the economy would like to get out of stocks before the price falls by more than 25%, then the price of such a put option would be very high. If only a few holders of stocks desired such protection, then the put option's market price would be low. The put's price thus reveals information *now* about the fraction of people with plans to get out of (or into) stocks in the *future*. The put's price reveals the extent to which the strategies of people can cohere in the future. Showing people the true cost of their plans may discourage people from attempting to purchase too much insurance in exactly those circumstances when the dynamic hedging strategy would raise stock price volatility.[4]

All of the above informational consequences of trading in a real security are absent if the real security is replaced by dynamic hedging strategies alone. How does a purchaser of a given strategy (such as a synthetic put) know the cost of insurance? Surely the cost depends on how many other people are planning to carry out similar stock selling and purchasing plans in the future. What mechanism exists to aggregate across people the information about future trading plans that will determine the cost and benefit of the current insurance strategy? Indeed, users of portfolio insurance strategies typically accept the assumption of the Black-Scholes model that the price of the underlying stock is independent of the amount of money protected by synthetic puts. This assumption is clearly false. If everyone follows the synthetic put strategy and attempts to sell stocks after a price falls, then the stock price will jump down (violating the price continuity assumption), and they will fail to achieve their desired hedge.

The marketing of *strategies* rather than *securities* has far-reaching implications for the volatility of the underlying stock and futures markets. There is no market force or price information that ensures that *strategies* can be implemented or informs the user of the total cost of implementation. In contrast, the purchaser of a *security* knows the cost of his purchase. For the economy as a whole, the price of the *security* reflects the cost of implementing the dynamic hedging strategy to which it may be equivalent. More important, the existence of a traded security will aggregate information (regarding future trading plans), that is currently dispersed among investors and, hence, provide valuable information about the cost of implementing the strategy.

The current price of a traded security also reveals information to people who can currently plan to take liquidity-providing positions in the future to offset the position changes implied by portfolio insurance strategies. For example, when a put option price is high, this reveals information that stock price volatility is high. Market makers, market timers, and other liquidity providers are thus informed that the future holds good opportunities for them. This leads them to make more capital available in the future to be used to take advantage of the stock price volatility. Of course, this will have the effect of reducing the actual volatility since a lot of capital will be present to invest in order to take advantage of excessive price moves.

In the absence of a real traded put option (of the appropriate striking price and maturity), there will be less information about the future price volatility associated with current dynamic hedging strategies.[5] There will thus be less information transmitted to those people who could make capital available to liquidity providers. It will therefore be more difficult for the market to absorb the trades implied by the dynamic hedging strategies. In effect, the stocks' future price volatility can rise because of a current lack of information about the extent to which dynamic hedging strategies are in place.

These points are elaborated in this paper as follows. Section 6.2 presents a schematic model of the impact of portfolio insurance on the stock and futures markets. Section 6.3 discusses the strategies used by investors who use synthetic hedging strategies and by market timers whose capital commitments can offset the effects of portfolio insurance. Section 6.4 developes a model of market equilibrium in a context where the number of users of dynamic hedging strategies is not known to all market participants. Section 6.5 discusses index arbitrage and futures trading. Section 6.6 discusses potential adaptations that may be useful to organized exchanges if the growth in the use of synthetic securities raises the information requirements necessary to maintain stable markets in the underlying securities.

6.2   The Organization of the Model

The purpose of this and the next two sections is to provide a schematic model of the informational consequences of trading strategies that are designed to create synthetic securities. We wish to elaborate the idea that market timers must commit capital before they know the extent of usage and the future price impact of the implementation of these strategies. This incomplete information will lessen their effectiveness in reducing the price volatility that can be caused when large portfolio insurance induced trades take place.

One purpose of the model to be developed below is to show that as the importance of portfolio insurance grows the price impact problem will also grow unless there is some mechanism by which the market can be informed in advance of the trades. The current market impact issues are minuscule relative to what would occur if 50% of all pension fund asset managers were to choose strategies designed to protect themselves against a loss on their stock portfolios. In order to minimize the market impact of such strategies, those who could provide substantial amounts of liquidity to the market would have to be informed substantially in advance so that they could choose not to commit their capital to other activities. In what follows, the time interval between date 1 and date 2 represents the amount of time that market timers and other liquidity providers would have to avoid committing their capital to other activities so that this capital can support the purchase or sale of securities in response to temporary price moves caused by the execution of portfolio insurance strategies.

It may help the reader to have a real example of the phenomenon under study. Such an example is the use of "sunshine trading" strategies in Stock Index Futures by the brokers for portfolio insurers (see Kidder, Peabody & Co., 1986). A broker using the sunshine trading technique announces to the brokerage and investment community that after a fixed period of time large orders will be brought to the trading floor and auctioned off at the best price. The purpose of preannounced trading is to give the investment community time to bring "market-timing capital" or the orders of customers who want the other side of the trade to the exchange trading floor so that the execution of a large order will not cause an adverse price move.[6]

The simplest model that can bring out the distinction between real securities and synthetic securities has three trading dates.

At date 1.   Some fraction f of security holders choose a dynamic hedging strategy. At the same time, market makers, market timers, and other liquidity providers (whom I shall henceforth group together under the title of market timers) decide how much capital to set aside for their attempts to profit from temporary price movements.

At date 2. News arrives about the underlying worth of the stock portfolio. This triggers trades based on the date 1 portfolio dynamic hedging strategy. The price change caused by the execution of the trades will depend on the amount of capital set aside at date 2 for market-timing activity. It may be helpful to imagine that there are two possible prices at date 2, P_{2g} and P_{2b}, depending on whether good or bad news about fundamentals arrives at date 2. The (market-clearing) prices at which trades can be executed will depend on f, as well as market-timing capital (denoted by M), available at date 2. I denote this dependence by writing $P_{2g} = P_{2g}(f, M)$ and $P_{2b} = P_{2b}(f, M)$.

At date 3. The stock price returns to its normal level, which reflects the underlying fundamental value of holding the stock portfolio. The normal level at date 3 depends on information about fundamentals, which arrives at date 3. It may be helpful to imagine that there are two possible prices at date 3, P_{3g} and P_{3b}, depending on whether good or bad news about fundamental arrives at date 3. Of course, the news about fundamentals that arrived at date 2 will be relevant for determining the level of possible date 3 prices, and I capture this by writing $P_{3g} = P_{3g}(2g)$ if good news at date 3 was preceded by good news at date 2, or $P_{3b} = P_{3b}(2g)$ if bad news at date 3 was preceded by good news at date 2, and similarly for other combinations of date 2 and date 3 news.

Since I am focusing on the informational consequences of the substitution of synthetic securities for real securities, I assume that f is uncertain, that is, a random variable. A summary of the resolution of uncertainty follows:

Date 1. A realization f occurs that is not public information.

Date 2. News about fundamentals arrives publicly prior to trade. The dynamic hedging strategy chosen at date 1 is implemented.

Date 3. News about fundamentals arrives publicly prior to trade. Price is determined fully by fundamentals.[7]

For expositional simplicity, at this stage in the analysis I ignore transaction costs and the distinction between futures and spot transactions in the underlying stock portfolio. The purpose of the model is to show how incomplete information at date 1 about the fraction f of portfolio managers using synthetic option strategies can leave market timers unprepared at date 2 to offset the trades of portfolio hedgers and that this causes the date 2 stock price to be more volatile than it would have been had real put options been traded at date 1.[8] I begin by explaining the behavior of each of the types of traders and then analyze how the behavior determines market clearing prices.

6.3   Trading Strategies Utilized

A.   Market Makers, Market Timers, and Other Liquidity Suppliers

At date 1, members of this group must decide how much capital to commit to activities that would leave their capital unavailable for market timing at date 2. That is, at date 1 capital can be committed or invested in activities for which it would be either very costly or impossible to withdraw the funds and use them to capitalize market-making transactions at date 2. For example, if a pension fund invests some of its capital in mortgages, or physical structures, then it will be very costly for it to sell them at short notice and use its capital to take advantage of a market-timing opportunity. Similarly, an investment bank may commit its capital to financing various activities other than market timing. These date 1 commitments of capital to activities for which there is a large cost of withdrawal at date 2 will lessen the funds available for date 2 market-timing activities.

How much capital will firms make available for market-timing activities? Clearly, this depends on the date 1–expected reward from taking market-timing positions at date 2. I now argue that this date 1–expected reward will be higher the larger the volatility of date 2–expected stock returns around the normal expected return. For example, if market timers at date 1 knew for certain that the expected return at date 2 for holding the stock from date 2 to date 3 would equal the normal return for holding the risk associated with the stock fundamentals, then they would have no particular incentive at date 1 to commit capital to date 2 market-timing activities.

The above point can be clarified by reference to the situation where there is either good or bad news about fundamentals. Suppose that at date 2 the two possible prices in the absence of parties using portfolio insurance would be P^*_{2g} and P^*_{2b}. These numbers have the property that portfolio owners would be willing to hold their existing stock levels, anticipating a random return of P_3/P^*_{2b}, computed from the bad news of date 2 to date 3, or P_3/P^*_{2g}, computed from the good news at date 2 to date 3.[9] Suppose that the implementation of dynamic hedging strategies will cause the date 2 price to be lower than P_{2b}^* in the bad news state and higher than P_{2g}^* in the good news state. Since, by assumption, date 3 is a point where prices are driven by fundamentals, this implies that the expected return as of the date 2 good news state (for holding the stock until date 3) will be lower than the normal expected return and the expected return in the date 2 bad news state will be higher than the normal expected return. In the date 2 bad news state, the market timers will make a net expected reward by increasing their stock holding, and in the date 2 good news state, they will make an expected reward by decreasing their holdings (possibly taking a short position).

The above argument shows that the market-timing rewards will be high the larger P_{2g} is above P_{2g}^*, and the smaller P_{2b} is below P_{2b}^*. This is precisely the statement that the larger the excess volatility is in the date 2 prices, the larger the expectation will be as of date 1 that rewards can be made from market-timing activity at date 2. Thus, given that there is a real opportunity cost of committing funds for market-timing activities, a higher date 2 excess price volatility will bring forth more market-timing capital. This supply curve for market-timing capital will be denoted by $M(V)$, where V is the excess volatility of date 2 prices as anticipated at date 1. Note that by definition M includes the possibility of leverage. That is, M gives the absolute value of the dollar size of the position that the market timer can take at date 2.

The above notion of "volatility" is a little obscure because of the 3-period model. In the 3-period model, the stock price at date 2, P_{2b}, falls relative to its normal level, P_{2b}^*, and this causes the expected return between date 2 and date 3 to rise. It is the fact that expected returns at date 2 move inversely with P_2 that creates a supply of market-timing capital. This notion of volatility, namely, that the execution of portfolio insurance orders will be associated with price reversals, is elaborated in the appendix.

It is now possible to describe the trading activity of market timers at date 2. The fraction of $M(V)$ that is invested will depend on P_2/P_2^*. When that ratio is small (and less than one) a larger proportion of $M(V)$ will be invested but, by definition, never more than 100%. Similarly, when P_2/P_2^* is large (and larger than one) up to $M(V)$ dollars worth of the stocks will be sold.[10]

When market-clearing prices at date 2 are generated, it will be shown that the market timers' trading strategy serves a stabilizing function. If at date 1 the market timers know that there is going to be date 2 volatility, they will commit capital to be used at date 2 to buy stocks when the price is lower than its normal level and to sell stocks when the price is above its normal level. This argument relies crucially on the hypothesis that market timers know the date 2 volatility at date 1. We shall see that if volatility is generated by the use of synthetic securities, then this volatility will be larger the larger the fraction is of portfolio managers (f) at date 1 who commit to a dynamic hedging strategy. To the extent that market timers do not know f at the time they choose M, they will find it difficult to forecast volatility.

In the absence of perfect information about volatility, market timers will choose an M that is optimal for some average level of volatility, denoted by M_a. In situations where the volatility V is high, M_a will be less than $M(V)$. In situations where V is low, M_a will be higher than $M(V)$. Therefore, the stabilizing role of market timers will be impeded by imperfect information about the determinants of price volatility.

B.   Buy and Hold Portfolio Managers

These parties do not follow dynamic hedging strategies. In particular, their risk preferences are such that, at prices P^*_{2g} and P^*_{2b}, they would keep their portfolio unchanged at date 2 in response to the date 2 news about fundamentals. In particular, when $f = 0$, the whole market is composed of people with these risk preferences, and P^*_2 gives the price at which the expected returns from holding stock are such that a buy and hold strategy (from date 1 to date 3) is optimal.

I am making a slightly artificial distinction between market timers and those following passive investment strategies. In general, if P_2 is less than P^*_2, then investors who planned to have a passive strategy as of date 1 may find a high expected return to increasing their investment in risky assets. Thus, this group may also serve a market-timing function. However, it is my assumption that their response to temporary price moves is much smaller than market timers. This is because their portfolio objective specifies a particular fraction of *portfolio value* to be invested in the risky asset, and a fall in price gives them a lower portfolio value. Thus, even in the face of higher expected returns per unit risk, these investors need not increase significantly their holdings of risky assets due to the fall in their portfolio value when P_2 is less then P^*_2.

C.   Users of Synthetic Securities, Portfolio Insurers

An investor uses a dynamic trading strategy in market contexts where the securities that would generate his desired pattern of returns across states of nature are unavailable.[11] This is a statement about the risk preferences and information of the investor, the risk preferences and information of the other market participants, and the number of explicit securities marketed. Trivially, if all investors were identical, they would all choose buy and hold strategies in the market index portfolio. However, if investors are sufficiently diverse, the only situation in which market equilibrium will involve all traders choosing buy and hold strategies at date 1 in *real* securities is when the market is explicitly complete, that is, for every state s_3 there exists a portfolio of securities that, when held to date 3, gives $1 if and only if state s_3 occurs (or equivalently, European options at all possible striking prices are marketed, where some of the striking prices may have to depend on the history that leads up to the final payoff if investors desire path-dependent final payoffs).

Our securities and futures markets allow an investor to achieve a middle ground between the above extremes. Investors may well be sufficiently diverse that a buy and hold strategy in a stock index is not optimal for everyone; however, markets are not sufficiently complete that a buy and hold strategy in a risk-free security and an option (with the investor's desired striking price) is marketed. Under the assumption of the Black-Scholes model that prices move continuously, the investor may still be able to achieve the same outcome (or close to it) by using a dynamic trading strategy to *synthesize* the desired security.[12]

Consider the following very simple example. Suppose that the stock price is $10 at date 1, and at date 2 it either rises or falls from its date 1 level by 10%. Suppose further that at date 3 the stock price can either rise or fall from its date 2 level by 10%. Thus, there are three possible date 3 prices: $8.1, $9.9, and $12.1. Let the investor start with 100 shares and assume that the risk-free interest rate is 0%. Suppose that the investor's preferences are such that he wants to get the highest expected date 3 wealth subject to the constraints that (a) *his date 3 wealth is no lower than $900*, and (b) *he is allowed to invest no more than his total wealth in the risky asset.*[13] If the expected return on the stock is higher than that of the risk-free asset, then it can be shown that the optimal trading strategy for the investor is (i) to invest all of his date 1 wealth in the risky asset (i.e., buy 100 shares at date 1); (ii) if the price at date 2 is $9, to sell all 100 shares and invests in the risk-free asset; and (iii) if the price at date 2 is $11, simply to hold on to his 100 shares.

Notice that the above strategy makes the holdings of the risky asset very volatile. A high expected return is achieved (subject to the constraint that the portfolio have a terminal value no lower than $900) by a high initial investment in risky assets supported by a *plan* to sell off all stocks at date 2 if the price falls. This is an extreme form of portfolio insurance. A plan that did not involve the sale of all stocks at date 2 in the event of a price fall would require a smaller initial investment in the risky asset and have lower expected returns.

The strategy also has the property that the final payoff to the strategy is path dependent (i.e., the strategy has a different payoff when the price reaches $9.9 at date 3 by first reaching $9 at date 2 than would be the case if $9.9 is reached from $11 at date 2). For some reason many portfolio insurers avoid the use of such path-dependent strategies even though they yield a higher expected return for the same level of insurance.[14]

A strategy used by many portfolio insurers is a path-independent one where a dynamic trading strategy is chosen that replicates the payoff that would derive from investing an amount of $S in the stock and buying a put with a striking price of $900.[15] The value for S is found by noting that the cost of the put plus the investment in the stock S must equal the date 1 value of the portfolio, which in the above example is $1,000. This strategy has the same qualitative property as the one given above—the risky asset is sold if the date 2 price is lower than the date 1 price. However, the path of holdings in the stock is somewhat less extreme—all of the portfolio is not invested in the risky asset at date 1, and only part of the investment in risky assets is sold at date 2 if the price falls.[16]

Another form of portfolio insurance, called constant proportion portfolio insurance (CPPI) moves the investment in the risky asset linearly according to how much higher the value of the portfolio is than the insurance level (the insurance level is $900 in the above example).[17] This trading strategy also has the property that a fall in the stock price will lead the investor to reduce his holdings of risky assets.

In summary, the users of portfolio insurance will tend to have demands for stocks that are more price sensitive than those investors utilizing buy and hold strategies.

6.4 Market Equilibrium

In this section I tie the strategies of various investors together for the purpose of analyzing market equilibrium. I shall analyze three cases. In the first case, market timers at date 1 know the extent to which dynamic hedging strategies are being used. In the second case, market timers do not know the extent to which such strategies are being used, but real put options are traded at date 1. In the third case, market timers do not know the extent to which dynamic hedging strategies are being used, and there are insufficient real index options markets to convey this information.

A. Extent of Adoption of Dynamic Hedging Strategies Is Known

For expositional simplicity, I focus on the case where there are two possible public news announcements about fundamentals at both date 2 and date 3. Hence, a model of market clearing involves finding a date 1 price, P_1, and a date 2 price for each announcement, P_{2g} or P_{2b}, such that the securities market clears at each date and state. It is clear that, if the fractions f of investors using dynamic hedging strategies is known (and the types of strategies being used are also known), then it will be possible for all parties to forecast the volatility of date 2 prices, and hence there will be prices P_1, P_{2g}, and P_{2b} such that, if all traders anticipate these prices and if the dynamic hedging strategies are indeed feasible at these prices, then the stock market will clear at those prices.

Market clearing at date 2. The above remarks may be slightly clarified by the use of the following notations.

Market timers: let $X(P_2/P_2^*, M; N)$ be the demand function of market timers at date 2, which can be thought of as a function of the price P_2 relative to its normal level, the capital that market timers can commit M, and the public news about fundamentals N. As I noted earlier, if $P_2 = P_2^*$, then they demand no shares. As P_2 falls relative to the P_2^* that is appropriate for the information N, market timers increase their holdings.

Buy and hold investors: the demand function of the buy and hold investors is also a function $Y(P_2/P_2^*; N)$ of the price relative to its normal level. However, unlike the market timers, for the reasons given above, this demand will not be very sensitive to price changes. In the extreme case of a buy and hold investor, it will be totally insensitive. I assume that if $P_2 = P_2^*$, then $Y = 100\%$. That is, if the market was composed only of buy and hold investors, then these investors would demand 100% of the outstanding shares of stock.

Dynamic hedging strategy: the desired holdings of those investors who are using a dynamic hedging strategy is $Z(P_2; N)$. Their desired holdings of shares will fall as P_2 falls. There may even be a critical level beyond which they desire to hold no shares.

Given the news N, a market-clearing price P_2 will satisfy

$$X(P_2/P_2^*, M; N) + (1 - f) Y(P_2/P_2^*; N) + (f)Z(P_2; N) = 100\%. \tag{1}$$

This is the statement that P_2 will adjust until 100% of the outstanding stock is held by those people who, at price P_2, no longer desire to trade. We write the market-clearing price as a function of f and N:

$$P_2 = P_2(f, N),$$

Note that if $f = 0$, so that no dynamic hedgers are present, then the market-clearing price will be P_2^*. This means that if good news arrives, then $P_2 = P_{2g}^*$, and if bad news arrives, then $P_2 = P_{2b}^*$. The difference between P_{2g}^* and P_{2b}^* gives a measure of the *normal* level of volatility in the market.

Now consider the case where $f > 0$, so dynamic hedgers are present. In such a situation when bad news arrives, the market will no longer clear at P_{2b}^*. This is because the demand of the hedgers is lower than the demand of the buy and hold investors at P_{2b}^*. Market clearing will require a price lower than P_{2b}^*. How much lower depends on the impact of market timers. If market timers have a very large presence in the market, that is, M is very large, then even a very small deviation of P_2 from P_2^* will cause large trades by market timers. However, if M is small, then it will take a large deviation of P_2 from P_2^* to clear the market when f is large.

In summary, if V denotes the volatility of date 2 prices in response to news about fundamentals, then V will depend on f and M, which I write as $V(f, M)$. Volatility will rise with f and fall with M.

Market clearing at date 1. The above analysis of the market at date 2 can be used to analyze the behavior of market participants at date 1. Under the assumption that f is known at date 1, the market timers will be able to infer the volatility of date 2 prices and, hence, their potential benefits from committing their resources, M, to market timing activities. In particular, the function $V(f, M)$ generates an aggregate demand for market-timing services [which I denote by $M^d(V; f)$] since it implies a particular return to date 1 investments in obtaining capital commitments for the purpose of date 2 market-timing activities. As we noted earlier, there are costs of obtaining market-timing capital. These costs generate a supply curve for market-timing capital, M, denoted by $M^s(V)$. The intersection of these two curves [i.e., the M such that $M = M_d(V; f) = M_s(V)$] will generate an M and a V that depend on f, denoted respectively by $M(f)$ and $V(f)$.

The less costly it is to commit capital to market-timing activities, the larger will be M for a given level of f. That is, the more it will be the case that the demands of market timers offset the demands of investors using dynamic hedging strategies. Thus, date 2 price volatility, $V = V(f) = V(f, M(f))$, will be low if it is not costly to commit capital to market-timing activities at date 1.

The feasibility of portfolio insurance. Finally, M determines the feasibility of certain types of portfolio insurance. Recall that M determines the level of the date 2 price in the presence of bad news about fundamentals, P_{2b}. An insurer would not be able to offer a dynamic strategy that assured a price higher than P_{2b}. In the event that bad news arrives at date 2, the joint execution of all the portfolio insurance strategies will force the price down to P_{2b}, so that insurers would not be able to execute stop-loss orders at a price higher than P_{2b}. Of course, if it is known at date 1 that market-timer presence will be large at date 2, then it will be possible to offer insurance at levels almost as high as P_{2b} since P_{2b} will be almost as high as P_{2b}^*.

B.   Extent of Adoption of Dynamic Hedging Strategies Is Unknown, but Real Put Options Are Traded at Date 1

The previous analysis was predicated on the notion that the degree of date 2 price volatility was known at date 1. If this is not known, then it will be difficult, if not impossible, for market makers to know the benefits of their date 1 capital commitments and for date 1 insurers to know that their date 2 trading strategy can be implemented. This is exactly the type of situation where a real put options market may have a very important role.

If portfolio insurers implement their strategies via the purchase of put options at date 1, then the price of put options will reveal the fraction of investors who are using portfolio insurance strategies. Since the price of the put is a function of the anticipated volatility of the stock, the price will equivalently reveal the volatility of the stock.

To understand the ability of prices to aggregate information, imagine that a fraction f of investors decides to use portfolio insurance, and in a market where this is known, a volatility $V(f)$ would be implied. This in turn would imply a particular date 1 price for the put, say, $Q(V(f)) = Q(f)$. Now suppose that traders do not know what the volatility will be because they do not know f. Suppose, for example, that this leads to a put price below $Q(f)$. Could this really represent a market equilibrium? It could not, because the users of dynamic hedging strategies would find it cheaper to use real puts to execute their trades than synthetic strategies, and this would drive up the put price. A similar argument obtains on the downside when the put price is higher than $Q(f)$. It would then be optimal for some portfolio insurers to sell puts and cover this sale with a dynamic hedging strategy.[18] In the terminology of Grossman (1976), the put price is a sufficient statistic for the one-dimensional variable V.

After all investors have learned the information about the stock's volatility from observing the option price, the option can indeed be a redundant security (in the sense that its date 2 and date 3 value can be replicated using a dynamic hedging strategy in the risk-free asset and the stock). However, since the option is not informationally redundant, the volatility of stock prices can be substantially lower in an economy where real options are traded than it would be in an economy in which market timers have no way to forecast the extent to which their capital is in demand. This is because the option price will inform market timers about the profitability of committing their capital to volatility-reducing trades at date 2. A high option price is suggestive of a high date 2 price volatility, which is suggestive of a high expected return from committing capital to market-making activity at date 2.

The above analysis assumes that the only cause of variability in volatility is the variability in (i.e., the uncertainty regarding) the intensity of portfolio insurance usage. Of course, price volatility varies for many other reasons, such as variability in the volatility of interest rates, earnings, dividends, and so forth. If I let A denote the other factors that affect volatility, then I can write $V = V(f, A)$, and the put price is $Q = Q(f, A)$. [See equation (A1) in the appendix, where s represents the nonportfolio insurance volatility and s is determined by the factors called A above.] In this environment, where A is important, the put price will not be a sufficient statistic for f. Recalling that intense portfolio insurance usage causes reversals in the stock price (i.e., changes in expected returns), if A represents factors in price volatility that are not associated with expected return volatility, then it is f and not A that signals market-timing opportunities. Therefore, Q is a noisy signal about f. How much information will Q reveal about f? Clearly, if portfolio insurers use synthetic puts, then the real put price Q will contain very little information about f—it will primarily reveal information about A. However, if real puts are used rather than synthetics, Q will be much more informative about f, and market-timing capital will respond appropriately.

C.   Extent of Adoption of Dynamic Hedging Strategies Is Unknown, Insufficient Put Options Are Traded at Date 1

This is a situation where price signals about the extent of adoption of portfolio insurance strategies are absent or arrive too late.[19] At date 1, market timers must make capital commitments based on incomplete information, and investors choose dynamic hedging strategies under incomplete information. As a consequence, a put option will no longer be a redundant security; that is, it can be impossible to replicate the put option's payoff using a dynamic hedging strategy because the stock volatility is unknown.

If investors continue to use portfolio insurance strategies in the presence of uncertain volatility, then not only will volatility be uncertain but it also will be larger than it would otherwise have been. Recall that the capital commitments of market timers serve to reduce volatility. In particular, if option price or other information reveals the extent of portfolio insurance usage f, then in times of high usage market timers commit more capital. That is, capital commitments can be tailored to the anticipated volatility caused by adoption of portfolio insurance strategies. The inability to tailor capital commitments will reduce the average gain from such market timing investments. Therefore, average volatility can rise and be accompanied by a fall in market-timing capital commitments.

The above remarks can be better understood by the following example. Suppose 50% of the time no investors pursue portfolio insurance strategies at date 1, while the other 50% of the time most of the investors use portfolio insurance. (This is just a method for describing the uncertainty market timers have about the extent to which portfolio insurance strategies will cause date 2 trading.) At date 1, the market timers do not know which type of situation they are facing. If no investors are using portfolio insurance strategies, then date 2 price volatility will be very low, and the benefits from date 1 capital commitment to market timing will be low. The situation is reversed if many investors are using portfolio insurance strategies. If market timers knew which situation they were in, they would commit capital where appropriate, and actual volatility would be low. Lacking information about adoption, however, they commit an "average" amount of capital that is correct for the "average" situation. As a consequence, when adoption is low their capital is unnecessary, and when adoption is high their capital is inadequate to prevent excessive date 2—price volatility.

It should be emphasized that in a continuous time version of this model, market participants will discover information about the intensity of portfolio insurance usage by observing *realized* stock price volatility and the extent to which expected returns are variable. If stock price volatility is variable only because insurance adoption is variable, then realized volatility will be a very good signal for adoption intensity. Further, if adoption intensity changes slowly relative to the rate at which new information about fundaments arrives, market timers will be able to commit capital in response to observed changes in realized volatility in such a way that "excessive" volatility is reduced.

6.5   Index Arbitrage, Futures Markets, and Stock Price Volatility

The previous sections have not distinguished between trading activity in stock index futures and trading activity in common stocks. These issues are discussed next. Portfolio managers apply insurance strategies to cover a large basket of different stocks. In principle, they could trade individual stocks or packages of individual stocks in the stock market to implement their strategies. However, if they really want to trade in packages, they may be able to economize on transaction costs by using a futures market in a stock index.

The New York Stock Exchange (NYSE) is organized around specialists who make markets in small groups of individual stocks. There are no specialists in packages of stocks such as the Standard and Poor (S&P) 500. The S&P 500 futures market is a competitive market-maker environment where, in effect, packages of stocks can be traded. For example, if on a particular day one pension fund manager wants to decrease his holdings of the S&P 500 while another pension fund wants to increase its holdings by the same amount, then the former can take a short position and the latter can take a long position in index futures. Thus, the pension funds have transferred the price risk of the S&P 500 in a single transaction rather than in 500 separate transactions on a stock exchange. Further, if the trading times of the two institutions are slightly asynchronized, the market makers in the futures "pit" will take a position on their own account from the first arriving order and then liquidate that position when the offsetting customer order arrives later. Thus, the existence of a futures market insulates the NYSE market makers from having to bear risk associated with slightly asynchronized order flows in baskets of stocks.

In the above example, there was no net desire to sell S&P 500 stocks at the last price. However, now suppose that at the price of the last trade, many pension fund managers want to decrease their holdings of stock; that is, there is net selling of stock index futures. If futures markets are used to reallocate packages of stock among institutional investors, then what happens when they all want to sell? Who are the "natural" buyers? If there is a large net supply of futures because institutions want to sell stocks, then this will drive the futures price down. At that instant, index futures will be cheaper than the S&P 500 package of common stocks. Index arbitrageurs will view this differential as a profit opportunity. They will buy futures and sell common stock. They are the "natural" buyers of futures in situations where futures are being sold because investors, in net, want to hold less common stock.

In the above scenario, the index arbitrageurs are messengers. They merely take the sell orders from the futures market (i.e., buy futures) and bring them to the stock market (i.e., sell stock). If there were no futures market (and thus no index arbitrageurs), then the institutions would have sold the common stock directly on the stock market, rather than indirectly attempting to eliminate the downside risk by selling the stock on the futures market. In the short run, this selling pressure would have to be borne totally by NYSE market makers (given the absence of an arbitrageur-linked futures market).

It is crucial to recognize that the market makers on futures markets combine with market makers on the NYSE to enhance the overall liquidity of the equity market. A given amount of institutional selling faces the buying power of market makers on both markets. Index arbitrageurs take positions that unify both markets.

The use of portfolio insurance strategies by institutional fund managers will, to some extent, raise stock price volatility irrespective of the existence of futures markets. Futures markets, by permitting low transactions cost trades in packages of stocks, allow institutions to trade more gradually than would be the case if the stock market were used directly. A larger transactions cost will cause insurers to trade less frequently, but in larger amounts per trade. In the absence of a futures market, institutions would face a larger transactions cost, and the stock market would bear the full brunt of port-folio insurance trades—without any cushion provided by the futures market.

Index arbitrageurs and futures markets are not the crucial issue in understanding large price moves. The crucial phenomenon is that, when institutions *simultaneously* attempt to use a dynamic trading strategy to synthesize a security (thereby attempting to lock in past capital gains), they will fail. The failure is caused by the fact that the dynamic trading strategy is based on the Black-Scholes model that assumes that the underlying stock price is independent of how many investors use the strategy. In the case of synthetic puts this assumption is untenable.

6.6   Conclusions and Recommendations

The theoretical perspectives developed in this chapter show that a synthetic security puts informational burdens on market participants that are quite different from those put on a real security. If an investor chooses a dynamic trading strategy to synthesize a European put option, then he should be very concerned with the number of other investors who have chosen similar strategies. He may very well find his own strategy infeasible if a substantial number of other traders are using the same strategy. Even if his strategy is feasible, it may cost far more than anticipated. However, if an investor could buy a real European option with the desired strike price and expiration day, then the price of the option would reveal the cost of the trading strategy. He would not have to know what other traders are doing in order to know whether his strategy is feasible.

The above informational role of prices occurs in many contexts. Hayek (1945) wrote, "We must look at the price system as ... a mechanism for communicating information if we want to understand its real function.... The most significant fact about this system is the economy of knowledge with which it operates, or how little the individual participants need to know in order to be able to take the right action ... by a kind of symbol, only the most essential information is passed on." I have shown elsewhere how this view of prices helps illuminate the informational role of securities markets.[20] Focusing on the informational role of markets seems especially appropriate in attempting to forecast the consequences of substituting real securities for synthetic securities.

I have argued that market timers and other liquidity providers will find it difficult to engage in stabilizing trades when they have poor information about the desire for their services. In the absence of a real options market it will be difficult to forecast price volatility and, hence, difficult to forecast the effective demand for commitments of capital to market-timing activities. Equally important, portfolio insurers will not know the cost of their strategies when they do not know the intensity with which other investors are using similar strategies. If a substantial number of investors suddenly decide to use insurance strategies predicated on historical levels of stock volatility, then this will raise stock and stock index futures price volatility.

The above perspective suggests that index options play a role in providing information about the costs of insurance strategies. If investors trade in such markets, they face the true cost of their strategies. Hence, the common stock volatility problem would only be increased if the effectiveness of these markets is reduced by regulation. It should be noted that current Securities and Exchange Commission regulations impose a limit on the number of (traded) stock index option contracts that can be held by a given institutional investor. These position limits effectively force large institutional managers to avoid the use of real options and instead use synthetic strategies. Excessive capital and margin requirements (erroneously imposed to limit volatility caused by "speculation") reduce the ability of options, futures, and stock market traders from taking the opposite side from the insurance traders and, hence, increase volatility.

The above theoretical perspective should not be construed as suggesting that (a) portfolio insurance, or dynamic hedging strategies, are bad or that (b) the increased use of such strategies has caused an increase in stock and futures price volatility. First, dynamic hedging strategies clearly play an important and useful role in increasing the feasible set of payoffs available to investors. It is costly (both privately and socially) to have liquid, real markets in every imaginable security. Dynamic hedging strategies permit us to economize on the number of active markets. Second, even if dynamic hedging strategies have contributed (or will contribute as their importance grows) to stock price volatility, it does not follow that this is, in net, socially harmful or worthy of regulation. To say that the use of a strategy imposes costs hardly implies that these costs outweight their benefits.

How can the exchanges reduce the costs imposed if volatility increases with an increase in the adoption of dynamic hedging strategies? To answer this question, recall that the source of the problem is that market participants lack *current* information about the *future* trading plans of other participants. If many investors today adopt portfolio insurance strategies, then this implies that many will be sellers in the future when prices fall. This creates a *current* opportunity for market timers to commit resources, *if only they were aware of the existing plans of other traders.*

It hardly seems practical to solve this problem by suggesting that the exchanges require all members to publicize their plans and the plans of their customers. Aside from the obvious enforcement difficulties, it would have the effect of forcing those people who may not be "informationless" portfolio hedgers to reveal their strategies. How could the exchanges distinguish those investors who invest resources in the collection of market-timing information from those traders who are simply pursuing "informationless" trading for the purpose of synthesizing a put option? It surely will not help the informational efficiency of markets if the exchanges force individuals to reveal (legally obtained) information that they want to keep secret and that they have expended real resources to acquire. This would only reduce the amount of information collected in the first place and thus inhibit market-timing activities that are volatility reducing.

The maintenance of privacy for those investors who desire privacy is not a problem for our purposes if the disclosure is voluntary. An investor whose trades are for the purpose of synthesizing an option will have no need for secrecy in his trading plans. This is seen clearly in Kidder, Peabody's "sunshine" trades for the portfolio insurance strategy firm of Leland, O'Brien, Rubinstein & Associates (Kidder, Peabody & Co., 1986). They use preannounced trading to reveal themselves to be "information-less" and to enhance the number of investors willing to take the other side of their trades. It is interesting to note that Kidder, Peabody was unable to fully preannounce their trades because of the possible conflict with exchange rules against prearranged trading.

I think that the exchanges could avoid the problem of prearranged trading and also create a system conducive to voluntary disclosure by the following system. Each exchange could set up a system where stop-loss and other limited orders would be sent to a central computer where they are aggregated and the results made public continuously. For the NYSE a special system is feasible.[21] With many specialists already using an electronic "book," it is feasible to link the books across stocks and publicly display the size of the limit orders for various indexes in which there are futures or options. For example, the aggregate of buy orders could be computed under the hypothesis that each component in the S&P 500 falls in price by 1%. This can be done by looking at the "book" for each component stock, finding the number of shares to be bought on the specialist's book if the price for that stock falls by 1%, and computing the weighted sum across the stocks in the S&P index. A similar calculation could be performed for a range of percentage up moves and percentage down moves of the stocks in the index. The final result would be a chart indicating the total buy orders in the specialists' books for the index at various relative price moves in the index. A similar chart could be constructed for sell orders. Finally, a chart could be constructed for the net buy (buy minus sell) orders for the index.

The transmittal of information about size of net buy orders at prices for the index that are away from the current price will allow investors to gauge the *depth* of the market. If net sells are very high (due to stop-loss orders of portfolio insurers) at a price just below the current price, then market timers know that there will be opportunities for advantageous trades. They will have time to raise the capital (or contact their own brokerage customers), which will lessen the impact of the execution of the stop-loss orders.

There is another adaptation for the NYSE that would interact with the above system and also enhance the execution of index trades. The exchange could set up a system by which there is a limit order (and stop-loss order) electronic book in various stock indexes. For example, members could enter such orders on the electronic book for the S&P 500 that would specify that if the index hits a particular level, then, for example, 20 units of the index should be sold. When the index hit that level the computer would cross all of the buys and sells at the current index price if the buy volume equaled the sell volume. Otherwise, it would send those orders for the components of the index to the specialists' posts for execution. The aggregate positions in the electronic book would be made public so that the public would know how many index trades can be expected to be executed at various index prices. Again, the dissemination of such information would enhance the effectiveness of market-timing activities and reduce volatility.

It is somewhat more difficult to effect similar changes on futures exchanges. However, it is crucial to realize that the index futures and options markets do not exist in a vacuum. If futures contracts are sold by a portfolio insurer as a low (transactions cost) alternative to selling the portfolio's common stock holdings, then this must have an impact on the cash (i.e., stock) market. Index arbitrage will cause the cash prices to stay (roughly) in line with the futures prices. If the cash market is illiquid, the futures market will show an increase in volatility.

The relevant adaptation for futures markets would be a system by which brokers could commit themselves to execute orders at various prices, and the exchange would aggregate these commitments and display them on a screen to various interested parties.[22] To avoid liquidity-reducing prearranged trades, the screen need not even identify the source of the orders. The exchange would have to find some method of assuring that brokers carried out their commitments. It should be noted that the physical arrangement of most trading pits, and the hectic pace of activity may make it difficult for a broker to carry out his commitment. For example, a broker could always claim that he tried to carry out the commitment, but trading was too hectic. Some problems of implementation may be alleviated if a particular part of the trading pit is designated as the place where brokers with preannounced trades must stand. Of course, this may create prearrangement abuses. I do not believe that these problems are insurmountable; however, the creation of an electronic display of stop-loss and limit orders clearly creates special problems for futures markets.[23]

Finally, it should be emphasized that the suggested adaptations are for a "problem" that may not now exist and may never exist. The implementation of any proposal contained here should await careful measurement of the market impact of synthetic hedging strategies. The purpose of this section is to illustrate the potential application of a theoretical perspective that emphasizes the informational role of markets; it should not be construed as a practical guide for regulation or for the modification of exchange rules.

Appendix

The 3-period model discussed in the text obscures certain ideas that I attempt to clarify below. Consider a stock price process

$$\frac{dP}{P} = (u - x)\, dt + s\, db + dx, \tag{A1}$$

where $b(t)$ is a standard Brownian motion. If x is a constant, then rates of return follow a Brownian motion with drift $u - x$ and variance s^2. However, I assume that x is a diffusion with dynamics given by

$$dx = \left(\frac{dP}{P} - u\, dt\right) l, \tag{A2}$$

where $1 > l \geqslant 0$. The term "dx" represents the additional price move caused by portfolio insurers, and l is proportional to the intensity of portfolio insurance usage. Note that (A2) states that an unusually large (say upward) price move will be associated with a fall in the expected return on the stock. The hypothesis in the text is that, for example, a large sell order inflow by portfolio insurers will lower stock prices and increase expected return.

The easy case to analyze is where l, u, and s are known and constant. In this case, substitution of (A1) into (A2) yields

$$dx = g(s\, db - x\, dt), \tag{A3}$$

where $g \equiv l/(1 - l)$. Setting $x(0) = 0$, (A3) can be solved for $x(t)$:

$$x(t) = gs \int_0^t e^{-g(t-y)}\, db(y). \tag{A4}$$

Substitution of (A3) into (A1) yields

$$\frac{dP}{P} = \left(u - \frac{x}{1 - l}\right) dt + \frac{s}{1 - l}\, db, \tag{A5}$$

and substitution of (A4) into (A5) yields

$$\frac{dP}{P} = u\, dt + \frac{s}{1 - l}\, db(t) - \frac{gs}{1 - l} \int_0^t e^{-g(t-y)}\, db(y). \tag{A6}$$

In the text, intense portfolio insurance usage (i.e., a high f) causes increased volatility and a tendency for price reversals (e.g., expected returns at date 2 are high when the date 2 price is low). From (A5), the instantaneous conditional variance is

$$\text{Var}_t \frac{dP}{P} = \frac{s^2}{(1-l)^2}. \tag{A7}$$

and from (A6) the conditional expected rate of return is

$$E_t \frac{dP}{P} = u\,dt - \frac{gs}{1-l} \int_0^t e^{-g(t-y)}\,db(y). \tag{A8}$$

If $l = 0$ (and hence $g = 0$) we are in the standard Brownian motion case. However, as l grows (i.e., g grows), the price process becomes increasingly volatile, and expected returns move in the opposite direction from the sign of the previous price changes.

The hypothesis in the text is that l depends on the actual realization of f and on the amount of market-timing capital available, or M. With incomplete information about portfolio insurance usage, f should be modeled as a stochastic process. This causes l to be stochastic. The consequent stochastic volatility will make put options no longer redundant.

Notes

1. The seminal contribution is the Black-Scholes (1973) option pricing approach, whereby it is shown how a dynamic trading strategy in a stock and risk-free asset can reproduce a European call or put option on the stock.

2. See Grossman (1977) for an elaboration of the informational role of securities and futures prices. See Grossman (1988) for a summary of some of the points contained here.

3. In this article, "stock" is often used interchangeably with "stock index" to represent a portfolio of risky assets.

4. The cost of the strategy is the potential upside gains that are foregone to protect against downside losses. If the stock volatility is high, then this cost will be high. I shall argue below that the volatility will be higher the larger the number of investors using protfolio insurance strategies. Hayne Leland, commenting on an earlier draft of this chapter, pointed out that the benefits of portfolio insurance can rise when volatility rises. This implies that users of synthetic put strategies face both higher costs and benefits if there is an unanticipated rise in volatility.

5. In the Black-Scholes model, the volatility is assumed constant, so that an option of any strike price and maturity can be used to infer the volatility of the stock. Clearly, the situation considered here is one where the volatility is not constant. In

particular, the volatility of the stock price will be a function of the demand for put options. This is elaborated below.

6. This phenomenon shows not only that portfolio insurers are concerned about the price impact of their trades, but also that they think that the release of information *before* a trade can bring forth capital (and offset customer order flow) to enhance the liquidity of the market.

7. Date 3 is a theoretical device to tie down the equilibrium. The time between date 2 and date 3 is the length of time necessary for the temporary price impact of the date 2 trades to disappear. That is, the expected return from holding stocks from date 3 forward would be uncorrelated with the date 2 news event.

8. It should be emphasized that there may be incomplete information about more than just the fraction of investor capital managed with the use of portfolio insurance strategies. There may also be incomplete information about the type of strategy used; e.g., there can be incomplete information about the horizon and/or strike price of the implicit put options being used, or both. I focus on incomplete information about f for expositional simplicity alone. A very appropriate alternative definition of f is that it represents the "gamma" of the average synthetic put implemented by the insurance. The basic principle would be unaffected by more complex types of incomplete information.

9. Throughout this chapter, a price with a state subscript represents a random variable.

10. This is a crude description of the extent to which date 1 commitments enable date 2 trades. My argument requires only that the size of market timers' trades at date 2 is an increasing function of the volatility they anticipated as of date 1.

11. See Leland (1980) and Benninga and Blume (1985) for an analysis of the sources of demand for portfolio insurance.

12. See Cox and Rubinstein (1985) for an exposition of dynamic trading strategies that synthesize options and other contingent claims.

13. This form of portfolio insurance, where an objective is stated and a strategy is found that maximizes the objectives subject to constraints, is called "optimal portfolio insurance." See Grossman and Vila (1988).

14. The replication of such strategies in a complete market would require trading in *real securities* for which a buy and hold strategy would yield a path-dependent payoff.

15. See Rubinstein (1985) and Brennan and Schwartz (1987) for a discussion of these strategies.

16. At date 1, 68.97 shares of the stock are held, and if the price falls, then 34.48 shares are held at date 2, while if the price rises, then 97.18 shares are held at date 2.

17. See Black and Jones (1987), and Perold (1986) for a discussion of this strategy.

18. The above argument is true for situations where a given investor knows that his decision to use a portfolio insurance strategy is correlated with the decision of others, and, therefore, each investor has a little information about the overall fraction of users. One may wonder what would happen if each user of portfolio insurance did not know how many others were using it and thus would not know the volatility. This is irrelevant in a situation where the only variable that affects the put price is the volatility. In order for the put price to be below $Q(V)$, a substantial portion of the market must expect a volatility lower than V. A price below $Q(V)$, say, Q_1, would be consistent with a lower volatility than V, say V_1. Each investor desiring portfolio insurance who is *certain* that the volatility is V_1 will be indifferent between the appropriate dynamic hedging strategy and holding the option at a price of Q_1. However, if the investor is even slightly uncertain about his ability to execute the appropriate dynamic hedging strategy, then he will prefer the option. The number of people who prefer the option will be proportional to the number of investors who desire portfolio insurance strategies. This will cause the price of the option to reveal the intensity of investor desire for portfolio insurance.

19. I assume that the date 1 price of the stock price index does not reveal the intensity of date 1 adoptions. Date 1 is supposed to be the date at which market timers must make capital commitments in order to attempt to profit from date 2 price volatility caused by date 1 adoptions. If the price is already varying at date 1 from its normal level because of adoptions, then the dates should be relabeled and we should start the analysis at an earlier date. In general, as described in Grossman and Stiglitz (1976), there will be "noise" in the stock price that will prevent it from completely revealing such information.

20. See Grossman (1976).

21. The New York Stock Exchange (NYSE) recognizes the need for providing advance information about future order flow. Its experiments with (a) disclosing "market on close" orders prior to the close of trading and (b) disclosing order imbalances prior to the opening of trade (on index option and futures expirations) are examples of the type of mechanism I am proposing, and its motivation is similar to mine.

22. This suggestion goes somewhat beyond current proposals to enable "sunshine" trading. Current proposals are concerned with transmittal of information to market participants regarding a broker's commitment to execute a trade at some time in the near future. The purpose of such a proposal is to lower the market impact to a portfolio insurer for a trade that he has just decided to make. My proposal is to show the market the whole schedule of trades at prices away from the current price (aggregated over all customers who desire to participate). A floor trader could look at such a schedule and see that if the index price falls, then there will be heavy selling. This alerts the floor to the need for more liquidity *before heavy selling drives the price down*.

23. See Grossman and Miller (1988) for a discussion of some of the differences between futures markets and the NYSE.

References

Benninga, S., and Blume, M. 1985. On the optimality of portfolio insurance. *Journal of Finance* 40, no. 5 (December): 1341–152.

Black, F., and Jones, R. 1987. Simplifying portfolio insurance. *Journal of Portfolio Management* 14, no. 1 (Fall): 48–51.

Black, F., and Scholes, M. 1973. The pricing of options and other corporate liabilities. *Journal of Political Economy* 81 (May–June): 637–659.

Brennan, M., and Schwartz, E. 1987. Stationary portfolio insurance strategies. Research Report no. 2–87 (January). Los Angeles: University of California, Los Angeles, Graduate School of Management.

Cox, J., and Rubinstein, M. 1985. *Options Markets*. Englewood Cliffs, N.J.: Prentice-Hall.

Grossman, S. 1976. On the efficiency of competitive stock markets where traders have diverse information. *Journal of Finance* 31, no. 2 (May): 573–584.

Grossman, S. 1977. The existence of futures markets, noisy rational expectations and informational externalities. *Review of Economic Studies* 64, no. 3 (October): 431–449.

Grossman, S. 1988. Insurance seen and unseen: the impact on markets. *Journal of Portfolio Management* 14, no. 3 (Summer): 5–8.

Grossman, S., and M. Miller. 1988. Liquidity and market structure. *Journal of Finance* 43, no. 3: 617–637.

Grossman, S., and Stiglitz, J. 1976. Information and competitive price systems. *American Economic Review* 66, no. 2 (May): 246–253.

Grossman, S., and Vila, J. I. 1988. Optimal portfolio insurance. Mimeographed. Princeton, N.J.: Princeton University.

Hayek, F. 1945. The use of knowledge in society. *American Economic Review* (September).

Kidder, Peabody & Co. 1986. Stock index futures. *Weekly Commentary*. New York: Kidder, Peabody & Co. Financial Futures Department (November 4).

Leland, H. 1980. Who should buy portfolio insurance? *Journal of Finance* 35 (May): 581–594.

Perold, A. 1986. Constant proportion portfolio insurance. Mimeographed. Cambridge, Mass.: Harvard Business School, August.

Rubinstein, M. 1985. Alternative paths to portfolio insurance. *Financial Analysts Journal* (July–August): 42–52.

7

The Allocational Role of Takeover Bids in Situations of Asymmetric Information

7.1 Introduction

It is generally accepted that takeover bids help to bring about an efficient allocation of resources. However, the following argument is often suggested by those who want the government to restrict takeover bids: The acquiring firm may have special information about the target firm's resources indicating that the target is really worth more than its current market valuation. Hence, the acquiring firm, by paying only a small premium, is able to acquire these resources at a price below the true worth to shareholders indicated by the inside information. Thus shareholders are unable to capture the true benefits of their investments, and an inefficient amount of investment will take place. Therefore the government should restrict takeover bids.[1]

The above argument is clearly wrong if there is competition among informed bidders for the target firm's assets. However, proponents of the argument claim that some takeover bids occur exactly because only one agent has special, inside information about the target company's resources. In this chapter we show that the argument is false *even if there is only one bidder* as long as shareholders have rational expectations about the takeover bid process.

Though we think it important to point out the error in the above argument, this chapter's main purpose is to study the informational role of takeover bids. In the process of modeling the transmission of information, we provide a theoretical model that explains among other things the empirical result that firms subject to an unsuccessful takeover bid are (on average) revalued upward by the market even after the bid fails.[2]

7.2 The Model

There are various motives for takeover bids.[3] This chapter assumes that management acts in the shareholders' interest but does not necessarily have the best information about the status quo value of the firm or about the improvements in the firm that could be made by a change in production decisions. If an outsider has information indicating that a profit could accrue from a change in managerial decisions, then he may not be able to sell this information directly. The only way he can make a profit from his information may be to buy the firm and change the production decision. We call such a takeover "allocational." In this section, we shall develop a model of allocational takeovers. We shall assume that a typical firm's profit is given by a function $q = f(\theta, \varepsilon)$, where θ is a parameter specific to the firm and ε is a parameter specific to the firm's manager.[4] Both θ and ε will be assumed to be nonnegative real numbers that are bounded above: $0 \leqslant \theta \leqslant \bar{\theta}$, $0 \leqslant \varepsilon \leqslant \bar{\varepsilon}$. θ should be interpreted as representing factors such as the firm's location, the state of its capital stock, conditions in the markets it operates in, etc.—in other words, factors that would be faced by any manager of the firm. On the other hand, ε represents manager-specific factors, such as the manager's competence or ability, or the quality of his information. We shall assume that f is strictly increasing in θ and ε and that $f(0, 0) = 0$.

We assume that the firm's owners, i.e., its shareholders, know the distribution of θ and ε in the population of firms and managers, but do not know the value of their firm's θ or their manager's ε. An acquiring firm, on the other hand, is assumed to be able to determine both θ and ε at a cost of c_I (the cost of investigation).[5] We shall assume that takeovers become a possibility once the firm's profit under incumbent management, $q = f(\theta, \varepsilon)$, is observed. At this stage it is assumed that a single potential bidder arrives at the firm and, on the basis of the q observed, decides whether or not to incur the investigation cost, c_I. If an investigation is carried out and on the basis of it, the bidder makes a successful tender offer. It is assumed that he installs management of the highest quality $\bar{\varepsilon}$ and that profits equal to $v(\theta) \overset{\text{def}}{=} f(\theta, \bar{\varepsilon})$ are realized. On the other hand, if either no investigation is carried out or there is an investigation but no takeover bid, then it is assumed that incumbent management will retain power and that the firm's profits will equal $q = f(\theta, \varepsilon)$.[6,7]

We assume that shareholders do not know θ and ε because in general information about the quality of the firm or its management will not be publicly available and will be costly to acquire. We are particularly interested in firms with a large number of shareholders, each with a small holding, in which case the marginal benefit from acquiring extra information is likely to be very small relative to the cost.[8] Although information collection will generally not be worthwhile for small shareholders, this will not be the case for a potentially large shareholder such as one making the takeover bid. This is because a bidder, if he uses the information he collects to improve the firm, can—if exclusion is permitted (see later)—make a capital gain on a large number of shares. The takeover bid process serves as a mechanism by which agents may earn a return on information collection—this is analogous to the informational role of speculative markets. If a person collects information about how to better allocate the target firm's resources, then he can earn a return on this by buying the resources, improving their allocation, and making a profit out of the resulting price appreciation of the firm's shares.[9]

Note that, if there was only one source of randomness θ instead of the two sources, θ and ε, then the bidder (and also the shareholders) would be able to deduce $v(\theta)$ from observing q and there would be no need ever to investigate a firm. In the presence of two types of uncertainty, however, observations of q provide only probabilistic information about $v(\theta)$ and so investigations will in general be worthwhile (see also note 15).

Let P be the lowest price (per 100% of the firm's shares) at which the acquirer can get control of the firm. Below we shall analyze the determination of P. We assume that, if a takeover bid is carried out, the bidder, as well as incurring the investigation cost c_I, incurs an additional cost at the time of the bid, denoted by c. We shall regard c as including the cost of raising the funds to finance the bid, the administrative cost of the bid itself, etc.

Let us consider under what conditions a takeover occurs. Suppose that the bidder investigates the firm. Then, given the values (θ, ε) that he discovers, he will make a bid for the firm if and only if

$$f(\theta, \bar{\varepsilon}) - P - c = v(\theta) - P - c > 0. \tag{1}$$

His maximum profit at this stage is therefore given by $\max(v(\theta) - P - c, 0)$.[10]

Let the (objective) distribution function of (θ, ε) be given by $G(\theta, \varepsilon)$, i.e. $G(\theta, \varepsilon) = \text{Prob}[\bar{\theta} \leqslant \theta, \bar{\varepsilon} \leqslant \varepsilon]$. [Note that $G(\bar{\theta}, \bar{\varepsilon}) = 1$.] We assume that G is known both to the bidder and to the shareholders. We shall assume that G has a density function g and that θ and ε are independent, so that $g(\theta, \varepsilon) = g_1(\theta)g_2(\varepsilon)$. We also assume that $g_2(\bar{\varepsilon}) > 0$. Then at the time when the bidder has to decide whether to investigate the firm, his expected profit, given his information about the firm, i.e. given $q = f(\theta, \varepsilon)$, is $E[\max(v(\theta) - P - c, 0) \mid f(\theta, \varepsilon) = q]$. We shall assume that the bidder is risk neutral. Therefore he investigates the firm if and only if $E[\max(v(\theta) - P - c, 0) \mid f(\theta, \varepsilon) = q] > c_I$.

Let us consider now how the price P is determined. We shall assume that the bidder gets control of the firm if he obtains more than 50% of the firm's

shares. The bidder is assumed to acquire these shares by making an unconditional tender offer, i.e. by announcing his willingness to buy any shares
tendered to him at P. We also assume that shareholders are risk neutral and
that the firm's shares are widely held, so that the likelihood that any
individual shareholder's tender decision has a decisive influence over the
outcome of the bid is negligible. Finally, we assume as in Grossman and
Hart [1980a] that the corporate charter, written by the firm's initial shareholders, permits any successful acquirer to reduce the firm's posttakeover
profits by a designated amount equal to ϕ, which he pays to himself. That
is, shareholders who do not tender and thus free ride on the bidder's
improvement of the corporation are prevented from getting their pro rata
share of the improved firm by an aggregate amount denoted by ϕ.[11]

Under the above conditions, for the bid to succeed unambiguously, the
tender price P must satisfy the following two conditions:

$$P \geqslant E[v(\theta) - \phi \mid I], \tag{2}$$

$$P \geqslant q, \tag{3}$$

where I denotes all the information shareholders have about θ at the time
the bid takes place. Unambiguous success means that the bid should succeed if shareholders think it will succeed [which is what (2) requires] and the
bid should also succeed if shareholders think it will fail [which is what (3)
requires]. In (2), it is assumed that a shareholder who does not tender
receives a pro rata share of $v(\theta) - \phi$ in the posttakeover company. (For a
more detailed discussion of these issues, see Grossman and Hart [1980a].)

We shall confine our attention to bids that are unambiguously successful
in this chapter. We see then that the lowest price at which the bidder can
get control is given by the smallest P satisfying (2) and (3). Denote this
price by $\hat{P}$.[12] In order to solve for $\hat{P}$, we must know what determines I. First
it is clear that since the shareholders, like the bidder, have observed $q = f(\theta, \varepsilon)$, they will use this information in order to make deductions about θ.
However, this is not the only information which the shareholders possess.
In particular, they know also that the bidder has investigated the firm and,
on the basis of the θ and ε discovered, finds it profitable to make a bid at
price P. In other words, the shareholders know that $v(\theta) - P - c > 0$.
Putting the shareholders' two pieces of information together, we see that

$$I = \{(\theta, \varepsilon) \mid f(\theta, \varepsilon) = q \text{ and } v(\theta) - P - c > 0\}. \tag{4}$$

In particular, it is clear that the fact that a bid takes place at price P will in
general signal information to the shareholders of which they would otherwise not be aware.[13]

The condition that shareholders have rational expectations about the bidder's tender price has very strong implications. It implies in particular that bids can only occur if the dilution factor, ϕ, exceeds c. For if $\phi \leq c$, then $E[v(\theta) - \phi \mid I] \geq E[v(\theta) - c \mid I] > P$ by the definition of I in equation (4). Hence (2) can never be satisfied however high P is. That is, as the tender price is raised, the expected return from not tendering goes up sufficiently fast relative to P—because of the information about the maximized value of the firm contained in P—so as to keep $E[v(\theta) - \phi \mid I] > P$. This occurs because, where $\phi \leq c$, the worth to a shareholder from not tendering, $v(\theta) - \phi$, is always greater than the worth to the bidder of the acquired firm, $v(\theta) - c$. However, each shareholder knows that the bidder must value the firm by more than P (or else why would he be willing to pay P). Thus each shareholder knows that $v(\theta) - \phi > P$.

We see then how important exclusion is, i.e., how important it is to have $\phi > 0$. If there is no exclusion, there will (in our model) be no takeover bids since there is no price at which the bidder can get control of the firm. In fact, for bids to take place we must have $\phi > c$. We shall see below, however, that while $\phi > c$ is a necessary condition for bids to take place, it is not a sufficient one.[14]

Consider now the case where $\phi > c$. Then for P sufficiently large, the right-hand side of (2) < P. (For example, take P slightly below $v(\bar{\theta}) - c$, i.e. $P = v(\bar{\theta}) - c - \delta$, where $\delta > 0$ and small. Then $E[v(\theta) - \phi \mid v(\theta) - P - c > 0, f(\theta, \varepsilon) = q] \leq v(\bar{\theta}) - \phi < P$.) It follows that when $\phi > c$, two possibilities can arise. The first is where $P = q$ satisfies (2). In this case $\hat{P} = q$. The second possibility occurs when the right-hand side of (2) evaluated at $P = q$ exceeds q. In this case $E[v(\theta) - \phi \mid q, v > P + c] \equiv H(P)$ can be graphed as a function of P. $\hat{P}(\phi, q)$ will be the smallest number P such that $H(P) = P$ [i.e., where the graph of $H(P)$ intersects the 45° line].

We may summarize the analysis of this section as follows. For each q and each value of the exclusion factor ϕ, let $\hat{P} = \hat{P}(\phi, q)$ be the smallest P satisfying (2) and (3) [if $\phi \leq c$, write $\hat{P}(\phi, q) = \infty$]. Then, given ϕ, the bidder will investigate the firm if and only if

$$E[\max v(\theta) - \hat{P}(\phi, q) - c, 0 \mid f(\theta, \varepsilon) = q] > c_I. \tag{5}$$

If (5) is satisfied, bids actually take place when

$$v(\theta) - \hat{P}(\phi, q) - c > 0. \tag{6}$$

Note that (6) is satisfied in some events (θ, ε) and not in others; i.e., whether a bid occurs or not is a probabilistic event as far as the bidder and shareholders are concerned. If (5) is not satisfied, bids will never occur.[15]

It should be clear why $\phi > c$ is a necessary but not a sufficient condition for bids to take place. $\phi > c$ guarantees that $\hat{P}(\phi, q)$ is finite, but it does not guarantee that (5) is satisfied. For (5) to be satisfied, ϕ must be substantially in excess of c if c_I is large.[16]

7.3 Acquisitional Takeover Bids

In the last section, we considered bids that transfer resources from those whose productivity is low (inefficient managers) to those whose productivity is high (bidders). We now introduce a second type of bid, where a bidder takes over not to improve management. but because he has special information indicating that the firm is undervalued at its current price— we call such a bid *acquisitional*.

Acquisitional bids can be modelled by generalizing the model of section 7.2 to the case where the firm's profits are uncertain. Assume that profit is now given by $\bar{y} = q\bar{t}$, where $\bar{t}$ is a random variable representing the state of the world and $q = f(\theta, \varepsilon)$ as before. We shall assume that q is known to shareholders (as section 7.2), but that the realization of $\bar{t}$ is not. This assumption can be justified in the following way. Suppose that $\bar{t}$ represents current economic conditions faced by the firm and that the realizations of $\bar{t}$'s at different dates are independent. If shareholders have had experience of the performance of this manager-firm combination in the past under different economic conditions, then they can observe the mean of $\bar{y}$. If shareholders also know the mean of $\bar{t}$, this will allow them to compute q. On the other hand, there is no reason for shareholders to know the current realization of $\bar{t}$.

The sorts of current uncertainty that might be represented by $\bar{t}$ include whether the firm is about to discover oil and whether the firm is likely to win a lucrative export contract.

A bidder who becomes informed about the firm will be assumed to find out the value of $\bar{t}$ at the same time as he discovers θ (and ε). The value of the firm to him is then given by $v(\theta)\bar{t}$. We shall assume that $\bar{t}$ is a nonnegative, continuous random variable defined on $[0, \bar{t}]$ with mean 1 and that $\bar{t}, \bar{\varepsilon}$ and θ are independently distributed. The purely allocational model is then a special case of the present model in which $\bar{t} = 1$ with certainty.

How much must an informed bidder pay to get control of the firm? In the previous section we have argued that the bid price, P, must be no less than the value of the firm under status quo management, since otherwise shareholders who believe that the bid will fail will not tender their shares and the bid will indeed fail. In the present model, the value under current management is a random variable, $q\bar{t}$. It might be thought that it is appropriate to take the expected value of this random variable and write the above condition as $P \geqslant E[q\bar{t}] = q$. However, shareholders who use q as an estimate of the expected value of the firm's profit under current management are ignoring an important piece of information—in particular, that a bid is taking place at price P. For the fact that a bid is taking place at price P tells shareholders that $v(\theta)t - P - c > 0$. Hence the best estimate of the firm's profit under current management is given by $E[q\bar{t} \mid v(\theta)\bar{t} - P - c > 0, f(\theta, \varepsilon) = q]$. We see that the condition that shareholders tender their shares even if they think that the bid will fail must be written as

$$P \geqslant E[q\bar{t} \mid v(\theta)\bar{t} - P - c > 0, f(\theta, \varepsilon) = q]$$

$$= eE[\bar{t} \mid v(\theta)\bar{t} - P - c > 0, f(\theta, \varepsilon) = q]. \tag{7}$$

In deriving (7), we have assumed that shareholders have considerable foresight and knowledge about the takeover bid process—in particular, that they know the distributions of $\bar{t}$, θ and $\bar{\varepsilon}$. There is another justification of (7) that does not rely on such a high degree of shareholder intelligence. Suppose that the bid price P violates (7). For the bid to succeed, the price of the firm's shares on the open market cannot exceed P after the bid is announced (otherwise people will sell on the market rather than tendering to the bidder). But this means that it will pay a wealthy individual (a competing bidder possibly) to buy large numbers of shares on the open market. For if such an individual can get at least 50% of the shares, so that the bid is prevented from succeeding, then *by adopting a policy of leaving management unchanged*, he can make an expected profit proportional to $qE[\bar{t} \mid v(\theta)\bar{t} - P - c > 0, f(\theta, \varepsilon) = q] - P$.[17]

(7) tells us that a revision of the value of the status quo production plan occurs when a bid takes place. Before a bidder appears, the expected value of this plan is given by $E[q\bar{t}] = q$. On the announcement of a bid at price P, however, the value is revised to equal $qE[\bar{t} \mid v(\theta)\bar{t} - P - c > 0, f(\theta, \varepsilon) = q]$.

One would expect that this revision would be in an upwards direction. This is indeed the case. The proof of the following is available from the authors.

Proposition 1 $qE[\bar{t} \mid v(\theta)\bar{t} - P - c > 0, f(\theta, \varepsilon) = q] > q$.

It is interesting to note that the upward revision in the status quo value of the firm can be empirically quite substantial. Dodd and Ruback [1977], table 3, p. 368] found that target firms subject to unsuccessful bids had a permanent increase in value of about 15% due to the tender offer.

We see then that if acquisitional bids are possible, (3) must be replaced by (7). On the other hand, (2) becomes

$$P \geq E[v(\theta)\bar{t} - \phi \mid v(\theta)\bar{t} - P - c > 0, f(\theta, \varepsilon) = q]$$

$$= E[v(\theta)\bar{t} \mid v(\theta)\bar{t} - P - c > 0, f(\theta, \varepsilon) = q] - \phi. \qquad (8)$$

So if a bid is to succeed both when it is expected to succeed and when it is expected to fail, (7) and (8) must both be satisfied.

Consider conditions (7) and (8). If the set of P's satisfying these conditions is nonempty, let $\hat{P}$ be the smallest element of this set (a minimum exists since the right-hand side of (7) and the right-hand side of (8) are continuous functions of P). As before, we write $\hat{P} = \hat{P}(\phi, q)$. On the other hand, if there is no solution to (7) and (8), write $\hat{P}(\phi, q) = \infty$.

Given the above, we may now determine when a bid will take place. As before, two conditions must be satisfied. First: $\pi(\phi, q) \equiv E[\max v(\theta)\bar{t} - \hat{P}(\phi, q) - c, 0) \mid f(\theta, \varepsilon) = q] - c_I > 0$, where now the expectation is taken with respect to θ, ε, and $\bar{t}$. This simply says that it must pay a potential bidder to become informed about the firm. Second, having become informed, he must want to proceed with a takeover bid: $v(\theta)\bar{t} - \hat{P}(\phi, q) - c > 0$.

It is interesting to try to provide a formal distinction between an allocational bid and its antithesis, an acquisitional bid.

Definition   Consider a bid that takes place in event (θ, ε, t), i.e. when $\bar{\theta} = \theta$, $\bar{\varepsilon} = \varepsilon$, and $\bar{t} = t$, given q and ϕ. We shall say that this bid is

a. *purely acquisitional* if $v(\theta)t - c - qt \leq 0$;

b. *purely allocational* if $\hat{P}(\phi, q) \geq qt$;

c. *partly acquisitional* if $\hat{P}(\theta, q) < qt$;

d. *partly allocational* if $v(\theta)t - c - qt > 0$.

Of course, in all cases $v(\theta)t - c - \hat{P}(\phi, q) > 0$, since otherwise the bid would not take place.

Let us interpret these definitions. A purely acquisitional bid is one that would not take place if the bidder had to pay the true value of the firm under current management to get control, i.e., $P = qt$. In contrast, a purely allocational bid is one that takes place even though the bidder has to pay at least this true value. A partly acquisitional (respectively, allocational) bid is one that is not purely allocational (respectively, acquisitional).

It should be clear that any bid must fall into at least one of the above categories. Furthermore, the following are exhaustive and mutually exclusive possibilities: (1) the bid is purely acquisitional; (2) the bid is purely allocational; (3) the bid is partly acquisitional and partly allocational. Note that (1) and (2) are mutually exclusive since for a bid to take place it is necessary that $vt - c - P > 0$. But (a) and (b) imply $vt - c - P \leqslant 0$.

It cannot be that all takeover bids are purely acquisitional if shareholders have rational expectations. Instead, some bids must be purely allocational for, if no takeover bids are purely allocational, then for a given bid (i.e., a given realization of $\bar{\theta}, \bar{\varepsilon}, \bar{t}$), all shareholders know that the only reason that the bidder is willing to pay P dollars for the firm is that it is worth more than P dollars *under current management*. But then, of course, shareholders will not tender. Formally, we can prove

Proposition 2   *Assume that bids take place with positive probability. Then they cannot all be purely acquisitional, and some bids must be purely allocational.*

Proof   Suppose that no bid is purely allocational. Then

$$v(\theta)t - c - \hat{P}(\phi, q) > 0 \qquad \text{implies} \qquad \hat{P}(\phi, q) < qt \tag{9}$$

with probability one. Hence $\hat{P}(\phi, q) < E[\bar{q}\bar{t} \mid vt - c > \hat{P}(\phi, q), q]$. This contradicts (7). Hence $\hat{P}(\phi, q) = \infty$ and no bids take place. Contradiction. QED

We see then that to get a satisfactory theory of acquisitional bids, there must be at least one other motive for takeovers, such as the allocational motive. That is, it is false to claim that all bids take place because the bidder has inside information indicating that the market has undervalued the target firm. In particular, when acquisitional bids take place it is because shareholders cannot distinguish an acquisitional bid from an allocational one. It is for this reason that it is impossible for shareholders to restrict *only* acquisitional bids.

7.4   The Optimal Exclusion Factor

In the last two sections, we analyzed under what conditions takeover bids will occur. We saw that a crucial determinant of the likelihood of bids is the exclusion factor ϕ, since this has a direct influence on $\hat{P}$, the price the bidder has to pay to get control of the firm. In this section, we consider what is the optimal choice of ϕ, both from the point of view of the shareholders and of society. We study the optimal choice of ϕ both for the acquisitional model where $\bar{f}$ is a continuous random variable and for the allocational model in which $\bar{f} \equiv 1$.

We would expect that the higher are the permitted deductions that the bidder can make, i.e., the higher ϕ is, the lower will be $\hat{P}$. In fact, this is clear from (8). For if $\phi' > \phi$, then

$$E[v(\theta)\bar{f} \mid \hat{I}] - \phi > E[v(\theta)\bar{f} \mid \hat{I}] - \phi', \tag{10}$$

where $\hat{I} = \{(\theta, \varepsilon, f) \mid v(\theta)\bar{f} - P - c > 0, f(\theta, \varepsilon) = q\}$, and so if P satisfies (7) and (8) for some level of ϕ, then it also satisfies them for any higher level of ϕ. This proves

Lemma 1 $\hat{P}(\phi, q)$ *is decreasing in* ϕ.

It follows from (8) that the bidder's expected profits, given by

$$\pi(\phi, q) = E[\max(v(\theta)\bar{f} - \hat{P}(\phi, q) - c, 0) \mid f(\theta, \varepsilon) = q] - c_I, \tag{11}$$

are increasing in ϕ.

We shall assume that the exclusion factor must be chosen before any information about the firm is known, in particular, before $q = f(\theta, \varepsilon)$ is observed. Consider first the position of the firm's initial shareholders, who write the corporate charter. Since by assumption shareholders are risk neutral, they would like to maximize the expected return from investing in the firm. In order to calculate this, consider their position once the status quo profit of the firm $q = f(\theta, \varepsilon)$ is known. Then the shareholders' expected return given the particular realization q is

$$\begin{cases} q\bar{f} & \text{if there is no bid} \\ \hat{P}(\phi, q) & \text{if there is a bid.} \end{cases} \tag{12}$$

A takeover bid occurs in the event that $v(\theta)\bar{f} - \hat{P}(\phi, q) > c$. We denote such an event by $B(\phi, q)$. The occurrence of such an event gives shareholders information about $\bar{f}$. We denote the complement of such events (i.e., no bid) by $NB(\phi, q)$.

The shareholders' expected return, given that they observe q, is

$$r(\phi, q) = \begin{cases} E[q\bar{f}] = q & \text{if } \pi(\phi, q) \leqslant 0 \\ qE[\bar{f} \mid NB(\phi, q), q] \operatorname{Prob}(NB(\phi, q) \mid q) \\ \quad + \hat{P}(\phi, q) \operatorname{Prob}(B(\phi, q) \mid q) & \text{if } \pi(\phi, q) > 0. \end{cases} \tag{13}$$

This is because if there is no bid, the market value of the firm equals the firm's profit which equals $q\bar{f}$, while if there is a bid, the market value of the initial shareholders' shares equals the tender price, which equals $\hat{P}(\phi, q)$.[18] Moreover, we have seen that a bid takes place if and only if

$$\pi(\phi, q) > 0, \quad \text{and} \quad v(\theta)\bar{f} - \hat{P}(\phi, q) - c > 0. \tag{14}$$

Note that, as well as being the expected return accruing to initial shareholders, $r(\phi, q)$ is also the price at which the firm's shares in the market sell after q is discovered but before it is known whether or not a takeover bid is going to occur [we are assuming here that the market knows c and c_I and hence can deduce $\hat{P}(\phi, q)$].

It is now an easy matter to compute the expected return from investing in the firm before q is observed. This is just

$$r(\phi) = E_q r(\phi, q) = \int r(\phi, f(\theta, \varepsilon)) g_1(\theta) g_2(\varepsilon) \, d\theta \, d\varepsilon. \tag{15}$$

One result that follows immediately from (7), (13), and (15) is that shareholders cannot be made worse off *on average* by the occurrence of bids.

Proposition 3   *For all values of ϕ, $r(\phi) \geq Eq$, where the latter is the expected return to shareholders in the absence of bids.*

Proof   It suffices to show that $r(\phi, q) \geq q$. But this follows immediately from the definition of $r(\phi, q)$ given in (13) and the fact that, by (7),

$$\hat{P}(\phi, q) \geq qE[\bar{f} \mid v(\theta)\bar{f} - \hat{P}(\phi, q) - c > 0, q]. \quad \text{QED}$$

In other words, the fact that the tender price must be no less than the value of the firm under current management, given the information implicit in the fact that a bid is occurring, is sufficient to ensure that shareholders do not suffer on average from bids, whatever the value of ϕ may be. Note that propostion 3 does not imply that shareholders do not lose out from particular bids—in fact, any bid that is partly acquisitional will make shareholders worse off, i.e., if such bids could be identified, the shareholders would vote that they not be allowed to take place [this follows from the fact that $\hat{P}(\phi, q) < g\bar{t}$ in the case of a partly acquisitional bid].

Let us return to an analysis of the optimal choice of ϕ for the shareholders. As ϕ increases, $\hat{P}(\phi, q)$ decreases by lemma 1 and $\pi(\phi, q)$ and $\text{Prob}[v(\theta)\bar{f} - \hat{P}(\phi, q) - c > 0 \mid q]$ both increase. Hence the probability of a bid unambiguously rises. On the other hand, the amount that shareholders get out of a bid, $\hat{P}(\phi, q)$, declines.

Ceteris paribus, shareholders would like to encourage bids since they benefit from them [this follows from the fact that $\hat{P}(\phi, q) \geq E[q\bar{f} \mid v(\theta)\bar{f} - P - c > 0, q]$ by (7)]. However, the only way they can do this is by reducing the bid premium, and this leads to a fall in the gain they get from any particular bid.

When $\phi = \infty$, $\hat{P}(\phi, q) = qE[\bar{f} \mid v(\theta)\bar{f} - P - c > 0, q]$, and so, by (13), $r(\phi, q) = q$ and $r(\phi) = Eq$.[19] On the other hand, if $\phi \leq c$, we saw in section 7.2 that no bids occur and so $r(\phi)$ again equals Eq. In general, $r(\phi)$ will achieve a maximum for some $c < \phi < \infty$. Furthermore, this maximum will generally have the property that $\hat{P}(\phi, q) > qE[\bar{f} \mid v(\theta)\bar{f} - P - c > 0, q]$ with positive probability.

We turn now to a consideration of the social return from the firm's activities. In evaluating this return, we shall make some assumptions also used in Grossman and Hart [1980a]. First, we ignore distributional effects (equivalently we assume that lump sum taxes and transfers are possible). Second, we assume that perfectly competitive conditions prevail in the firm's product market(s), so that the social benefit from the firm's activities is represented by its profit (to put it another way, profits are pure rents). This latter assumption is obviously a strong one; it means that we are ruling out the case where one of the reasons for the takeover is to exploit monopoly power by restricting competition. Finally, we ignore any divergence between the private costs of becoming informed (c_I) and of taking over the firm (c) and the corresponding social costs.

Given q, the social return from the firm's activities equals

$$\begin{cases} q\bar{f} & \text{if the bidder does not become informed} \\ q\bar{f} - c_I & \text{if there is an informed bidder but no bid} \quad (16) \\ v(\theta)\bar{f} - c - c_I & \text{if there is a bid.} \end{cases}$$

Therefore the expected social return given q is

$$R(\phi, q) = \begin{cases} q & \text{if } \pi(\phi, q) \leq 0 \\ qE[\bar{f} \mid NB, q]\,\mathrm{Prob}(NB \mid q) & \quad (17) \\ \quad + E[v(\theta)\bar{f} - c \mid B, q]\,\mathrm{Prob}(B \mid q) - c_I & \text{if } \pi(\phi, q) > 0. \end{cases}$$

This is because if there is no bid, the return from the firm is simply its status quo profit q, while, if there is a bid, the return is the firm's posttakeover profit net of the cost of the bid, c. Whenever a potential bidder becomes informed, the cost of information, c_I, must be deducted from this gross return to get the net return.

It is now easy to calculate the expected social return from the firm's activities before q is known. This is simply

$$R(\phi) = E_q R(\phi, q) = \int R(\phi, f(\theta, \varepsilon)) g_1(\theta) g_2(\varepsilon) \, d\theta \, d\varepsilon. \tag{18}$$

Consider the relationship between $R(\phi, q)$ and $r(\phi, q)$. Obviously

$$R(\phi, q) = r(\phi, q) \qquad \text{if} \qquad \pi(\phi, q) \leqslant 0. \tag{19}$$

If $\pi(\phi, q) > 0$,

$$R(\phi, q) = qE[\bar{f} \mid NB, q] \operatorname{Prob}[NB \mid q] + E[v(\theta)\bar{f} - c \mid B, q] \operatorname{Prob}[B \mid q] - c_I$$

$$= qE[\bar{f} \mid NB, q] \operatorname{Prob}[NB \mid q] + \hat{P}(\phi, q) \times \operatorname{Prob}[B, q]$$

$$+ E[v(\theta)\bar{f} - \hat{P}(\phi, q) - c \mid B, q] \operatorname{Prob}[B \mid q] - c_I$$

$$= r(\phi, q) + \pi(\phi, q). \tag{20}$$

(19) and (20) imply that the social return always equals the private return plus the bidder's net profit [if $\pi(\phi, q) \leqslant 0$, the potential bidder does not investigate the firm and his net profit is zero]. It follows that the social return from the firm's activities is always at least as great as the private return.

Lemma 2 $R(\phi) \geqslant r(\phi)$.

Note that if there were competing bidders (rather than one bidder as we assume), then the bidder's profit would be zero and we would have $R(\phi) = r(\phi)$.

We have seen that $r(\phi)$ is not everywhere increasing in ϕ. The reason for this is that, as noted above, an increase in ϕ increases the probability of a bid but reduces the tender price $\hat{P}$. This reduction in the tender price has no effect on $R(\phi)$, however, since it simply involves a redistribution of income from the shareholders to the bidder.

On the other hand, the increase in the number of bids that results from an increase in ϕ will tend to raise $R(\phi)$ insofar as bids take place for allocational reasons and to lower $R(\phi)$ insofar as bids take place for acquisitional reasons. To see this, note that, by the definition given in section 7.3, in a purely allocational bid $v(\theta)\bar{f} - c > \hat{P}(\phi, q) \geqslant q\bar{f}$, which implies that the profit the bidder obtains from running the firm exceeds the profit under current management. But, given that competitive conditions prevail in the product market, this is a sufficient condition for a transfer of control to be socially desirable. Furthermore, an increase in ϕ that lowers $\hat{P}(\phi, q)$ will reduce the divergence between $\hat{P}(\phi, q)$ and $q\bar{t}$, thus permitting more of these socially desirable allocational bids to take place. [The exact argument is a bit more complicated since the cost of information c_I must be accounted for. As a result of this cost, some new bids that occur when ϕ is increased will reduce social welfare: those for which $v(\theta)\bar{t} - c - q\bar{t} - c_I < 0$. However, it can be shown that these bids are outweighed by those increasing social welfare.]

In contrast, purely acquisitional bids [those for which $v(\theta)\bar{t} - c < q\bar{t}$] reduce social welfare since the net value of the firm under the bidder is less than under current management. An increase in ϕ, by reducing $\hat{P}(\phi, q)$, will tend to increase the number of these undesirable bids. In fact, it is not difficult to construct examples where the decrease in social welfare caused by the greater number of acquisitional bids outweights the increase in social welfare caused by the greater number of allocational bids; i.e., an increase in ϕ reduces $R(\phi)$.

If we are prepared to make an additional assumption, however, then we can be sure that the good effect of extra allocational bids will dominate the bad effect of extra acquisitional bids, so that $R(\phi)$ is increasing in ϕ.

Proposition 4   *Assume that $E[\bar{t} \mid v(\theta)\bar{t} - P - c > 0, f(\theta, \varepsilon) = q]$ is an increasing function of P. Then $R(\phi)$ is increasing in ϕ. In particular, it is socially optimal to set $\phi = \infty$. The proof is available from the authors.*

The assumption that $E[\bar{t} \mid v(\theta)\bar{t} - P - c > 0, f(\theta, \varepsilon) = q]$ is increasing in P says that increases in $v(\theta)\bar{t}$ go together on average with increases in $\bar{t}$. While this seems reasonable if $\bar{\theta}$ and $\bar{t}$ are independent, there are cases where it is violated. One case where the assumption of proposition 4 clearly holds is when status quo profit is nonrandom, i.e., $\bar{t} = 1$ with certainty—this is the model of section 7.2. Proposition 4 tells us that $\phi = \infty$ is socially optimal in this case.

Proposition 4 implies that, if $E[\bar{t} \mid v(\theta)\bar{t} - P - c > 0, f(\theta, \varepsilon) = q]$ is increasing in P, then the privately optimal level of exclusion $\phi_p \leqslant$ the socially optimal level of exclusion $\phi_s = \infty$. That is, there is a divergence between what is privately optimal and what is socially optimal, with shareholders desiring to restrict bids more than is socially desirable by limiting exclusion in order to obtain premiums.[20] It is not at all surprising that there is a divergence, since we assumed that the bidder is always a monopsonist. If bidders competed for the firm's shares, then the shareholders would find it optimal to set $\phi = \infty$. This follows because a large ϕ

does not reduce the tender price if bidders compete for the shares, since the firm is worth $v(\theta)\bar{t} - c$ to all the (presumably) identical bidders. Note, however, that competition among bidders may be inconsistent with any of them earning a return on the information cost, c_I. This, in situations where c_I is large, the case where the bidder is a monopsonist may be empirically more relevant than the case where there are competing bidders.[21] In any case, our goal was not to show that a lack of competition leads to some distortion (that is obvious), but rather to point out the direction of the distortion. In this case the direction of the distortion is such that the government should encourage takeover bids more than the private sector, if it does anything at all.

7.5 Takeover Bids and the Incentive to Invest in Corporations

As we noted in the introduction, it is sometimes argued (often by incumbent directors'.) that the government should restrict takeover bids because they reduce the incentive to invest in corporations. That is, initial shareholders who set up the corporation anticipate that (acquisitional) bids will take place in states of nature when the market undervalues the firm relative to what inside information indicates the value to be. In these states of nature, the bidder's tender price will not reflect the inside information because there may be only one bidder who possesses this information. Hence, it is argued, the expected return to setting up the firm is lower than it would be in the absence of bids and this leads to underinvestment in the corporate sector by initial shareholders. To correct this distortion, it is argued that the government should discourage takeover bids.

In this section, we extend the results of the previous sections and show that monopsony in the takeover market implies that the government should *encourage* takeovers rather than discourage them. To model the possibility of distortion in investment, assume that shareholders possess an alternative investment with constant and exogenous rate of return given by s. Assume that if the aggregate amount of investment or capital, k, is forthcoming, then it is possible to set up $g(k)$ distinct corporate units, each with production function as in sections 7.2 and 7.3. Here g is a function with $g' > 0$ and $g'' < 0$, the concavity of g indicating that there are decreasing returns to scale in the setting up of new corporations. If $r(\phi)$ is the private rate of return per corporate unit, then the private rate of return from investing in corporations is given by

$$g(k)r(\phi) - sk. \tag{21}$$

Let ϕ_P be the optimal level of exclusion chosen by initial shareholders, i.e., ϕ_P maximizes $r(\phi)$. Then, in the absence of government intervention, investment will occur until

$$g'(k)r(\phi_P) = s. \tag{22}$$

Socially, the return per corporate unit is given by $R(\phi)$ rather than $r(\phi)$, as described in the last section. Thus social efficiency involves the maximization of $g(k)R(\phi) - sk$. The particular government intervention we shall consider is the following. We shall assume that the government can encourage or discourage takeover bids by dictating ϕ, but that the market is free to choose k. (Note that dictating ϕ is equivalent to regulating the ease of takeover bids in terms of the cost to the bodder.) That is, let $k(\phi)$ be the maximizer of $g(k)r(\phi) - sk$ for a given ϕ. Then $k(\phi)$ is the investment that would take place if ϕ were dictated by the government.

The government chooses ϕ to maximize $S(\phi) \equiv g(k(\phi))R(\phi) - sk(\phi)$. Let ϕ_s denote the maximizer of $S(\phi)$. Then it can be shown that $\phi_s \geqslant \phi_P$. That is, the government will want to choose a charter that allows more (not less) exclusion and thus encourages *more* takeovers than the private sector. We have already shown that ignoring the investment effect of this section, we have $\phi_s \geqslant \phi_P$. We have argued that the government wants ϕ large to encourage bids because on average bids improve the allocation of resources. In the previous sections the government did not care that making ϕ large reduces the return to initial shareholders, $r(\phi)$, by lowering the tender price. However, when private investment, $k(\phi)$, is sensitive to the expected rate of return on investment, $r(\phi)$, the government will want initial shareholders to share more than previously in the improvements of the corporation so that the right amount of investment is encouraged.

However, it is easy to see that the investment effect does not change our basic result that initial shareholders want to get more out of any improvement than is optimal from an efficiency standpoint. To see this, consider equation (22), which gives k as a function of ϕ. Differentiate both sides with respect to ϕ_P to get $g''k'(\phi_P)r(\phi_P) + g'r'(\phi_P) = 0$. But if ϕ_P is chosen optimally by shareholders then $r'(\phi_P) = 0$. Hence $k'(\phi_P) = 0$. That is, if the government raises ϕ just a little above ϕ_P, then k will not change, so at the margin the investment effect can be ignored. On the other hand, proposition 4 implies that $R'(\phi_P) \geqslant 0$ and so $g(k(\phi))R(\phi) - sk(\phi)$ increases when ϕ is raised a little above ϕ_P. Thus we can prove

Proposition 5 $\phi_s \geqslant \phi_P$; i.e., *the government should not want to restrict takeover bids even if investment is sensitive to the rate of return earned by initial shareholders.*

7.6   Conclusion

In this chapter we have developed a model of the takeover bid process. We have considered a firm with many shareholders, each of whom has a small shareholding. Under these conditions, we would not expect it to pay any shareholder to monitor the firm to find out whether a good performance is the result of good management or of, say, favorable market conditions. The job of monitoring the firm will therefore be left to a potentially large shareholder, such as a prospective bidder.

We have assumed that managers act on behalf of shareholders, i.e., maximize profits, but that they may be inefficient. One role of a potential bidder is to discover whether a firm is being run inefficiently and, if it is, to take it over and replace the current management by more efficient management. We call such a bid allocational. We have also considered a second type of bid—called an acquisitional bid. An acquisitional bid occurs when a bidder discovers information not available to other traders indicating that a firm is undervalued on the stock market relative to its true performance under *current* management. Under these conditions, a bidder may attempt to take over the firm simply because he uniquely has this information.

In contrast to allocational bids, (purely) acquisitional bids are bad from the point of view both of shareholders and of society. This is because they do not lead to a better allocation of resources, but simply involve a redistribution of income from the (uninformed) shareholders to the informed bidder—a redistribution, moreover, that is costly since resources will be used up in the bid. In addition, to the extent that shareholders cannot identify acquisitional bids, they get a lower return on their investments than they would get if such bids could be identified. Thus the existence of (partly) acquisitional bids will tend to reduce the incentives of investors of invest in the corporate sector—which is both privately and socially undesirable.

The undesirable consequences of acquisitional bids have led some to argue that the government should introduce provisions to restrict takeover bids. As noted by Aranow, Einhorn and Berlstein [1977, pp. 204−257], state takeover bid law seems designed explicitly to make bids more costly (and to protect incumbent management). Grossman and Hart [1980b] show that federal disclosure law can have the effect of reducing the exclusion of (free riding) minority shareholders and thus have the effect of restricting takeover bids. Further, required disclosure of all information would clearly prevent the bidder from earning a return to his information costs, and severely restrict bids. This chapter has argued that even if the bidder has monopsony power due to information possession, it is *not* the case that the government should restrict takeover bids. If acquisitional bids can be distinguished from allocational bids, then shareholders can prohibit acquisitional bids and government efforts to reduce their impact are unnecessary. On the other hand, if acquisitional bids and allocational bids cannot be distinguished—as we have assumed in this chapter—then shareholders can, through their own actions, restrict takeover bids sufficiently so that further restrictions by the government are undesirable—in fact, if anything, to correct the distortion associated with a monopsonistic bidder, the government should act so as to make takeover bids easier. The way that shareholders can restrict bids is by writing a corporate charter that limits the extent to which minority shareholders can free ride on the bidder's improvement of the company.[22]

As well as yielding normative results concerning the ease with which bids should take place, our analysis provides some explanation for the existence and magnitude of bid premiums. Premiums arise for two reasons in the model described here. First, if the exclusion factor ϕ is small, the value of not tendering to the bidder and becoming a minority shareholder in the posttakeover company will in general exceed the value of the firm under incumbent management. Thus, a bidder must offer a premium, since otherwise shareholders will hold on to their shares and the bid will fail. Second, both allocational and acquisitional bids are more likely to occur when a bidder has inside information indicating that the firm is currently undervalued on the market. Shareholders, with rational expectations, will realize this. Consequently, they will revise upwards their estimate of the *current* (status quo) value of the firm when they observe a bid. Thus, even if $\phi = \infty$, the bidder will have to offer a premium over the prebid market value of the firm because of this revaluation effect.[23,24]

Note that this revaluation effect will persist even if the bidder's bid fails.[25] Hence our model provides an explanation for the empirical evidence that a firm's shares sell at a premium after an unsuccessful takeover bid.

Notes

1. The Williams Amendment of 1968 to the 1933 Securities and Exchange Act contains federal regulations concerning takeover bids. This amendment was first proposed by Senator Williams, who stated, "In recent years we have seen proud old companies reduced to corporate shells after white collar pirates have seized control ..., then sold or traded away the best assets ..." [111 Cong. Rec. 29257, Oct. 22, 1965]. References to similar remarks by other legislators can be found in Aranow and Einhorn [1973, pp. 64–68]. The Federal Trade Commission, in its

Economic Report on Corporate Mergers (reprinted in Brudney and Chirelstein [1979, pp. 504–509]), notes that "... merger profits may arise if the acquired assets can be bought at bargain prices." The fear that shareholders will be bought out at too low a price is one of the reasons for the disclosure provisions of the Williams Amendment. The chairman of the Securities and Exchange Commission, in remarks reprinted in Brudney and Chirelstein, op. cit. pp. 720–722, argued that a company might be selling for $5 per share, but a person making the takeover bid thinks he can liquidate the company for $15 per share. It is suggested that if shareholders do not know the liquidation value is $15, then the takeover bid might succeed at $6. This is used to argue that there should be a disclosure law. Implicit in this argument is the assumption that there is not competition for the shares of the company among bidders who know that its worth is $15. The chairman of the SEC noted that "this disclosure required ... might discourage some tender offers, (but) it is a small price to pay for informed choice by shareholders ..." [op. cit., p. 722]. State law has had an even more important effect on restricting takeover bids. Many states require long delays and the approval of a state commission that certifies that shareholders get a "fair value" for their shares. It is generally agreed that these state regulations have the effect of making takeover bids much more difficult than in the past; see Aranow, Einhorn and Berlstein [1977, pp. 207–257].

2. See Dodd and Ruback [1977].

3. For a discussion of motives for making takeovers, including the allocational and acquisitional motives considered below, see Gort [1969], Mueller [1969], Lintner [1971], Dodd and Ruback [1977], Manne [1965], and Smiley [1976].

4. The number $f(\theta, \varepsilon)$ can also be interpreted as the firm's net present value or the market value of its shares—in this chapter we shall make no distinctions between profit, net present value, and market value.

5. The acquirer should be thought of as being an entrepreneur or another firm with a highly efficient manager.

6. It is being assumed that the higher productivity of superior management is not offset by the increased wages that must be paid. We also assume that status quo management is unwilling or unable to vote itself out of office and hire better managers to run the firm. One reason that hostile takeover bids (as opposed to friendly acquisitions) occur is that current management does not have the same information as the acquirer and disagrees with him about what decisions will maximize profit. Throughout this chapter we assume that the acquirer has strictly better information than the incumbent and so is able to extract a higher value out of the firm. In this interpretation ε parametizes the quality of the decision maker's information. We assume that the acquirer has the best information available, $\bar{\varepsilon}$.

7. We assume that no further bids by this bidder or other bidders occur.

8. The assumption that shareholders know nothing about their particular firm's characteristics is obviously rather strong. Our analysis would go through unchanged, however, if it was assumed that $q = f(\theta_1, \theta_2, \varepsilon)$ where θ_1 represents known characteristics about the firm and θ_2 represents unknown characteristics (θ_1

might, for example, be the book value of the firm's assets, profits, and sales in the last few years, etc.).

9. Grossman [1977] has emphasized that securities markets can serve as a place where traders earn a return on information collection, thereby facilitating a better allocation of resources as the price system aggregates and transmits information across traders.

10. We assume that if the bidder takes over the firm, he purchases all the shares. This assumption will be justified below (see note 12).

11. After a successful tender offer, the acquirer often votes to merge the target into the acquirer. This involves the acquirer (the new manager) stating what the "true value" of the target's assets are. Since it has voting control, it can attempt to mistreat minority shareholders in the target by having a poor appraisal of the assets if this is permitted by the corporate charter. In Grossman and Hart [1980b], we show that ϕ is related to the amount of disclosure (and the quality of the appraisal) that the acquirer is required to make to the minority shareholders of the target at the time of the posttakeover merger.

12. At this price $\hat{P}$ shareholders are just indifferent between tendering and not tendering their shares. We shall assume that all shares are in fact tendered.

13. Given this signaling effect, it may be wondered whether it might be in the bidder's interest to try to fool the shareholders by sometimes bidding in unprofitable states, i.e., when $v(\theta) - P - c \leqslant 0$. While this would lead to lower profits in some bids, it might through worsening the quality of the bid price signal increase profits in the long run. This fooling possibility is only important, however, if the same bidder takes over many firms during his life and is therefore prepared to sacrifice profits in the short run for profits in the long run. We shall avoid the fooling possibility by assuming that the bidder only makes one bid during his life, so that only current profit is important.

14. The above should not be confused with the bilateral monopoly problem that arises when a person A offers person B P dollars for the latter's stock. When this occurs, person B knows that his stock must be worth at least P dollars to A (and thus in general has an expected worth of more than P to A). Thus we might conclude that B holds out for more than P and thus no trade ever takes place— which is absurd. In our case there are many small sellers (i.e., shareholders) and each one assumes that he cannot sell and still share in the improvement of the corporation. That is, the bilateral monopoly problem concerns the trade of a private good [either A gets $v(\theta)$ or B does, but not both], while our problem concerns the trade of shares in a common property, the corporation, which is a public good among its shareholders.

15. One possibility that we have ruled out is that the bidder makes a takeover bid without investigating the firm; i.e., the bidder makes an uninformed bid and simply installs management of quality $\bar{\varepsilon}$ without incurring the cost c_I. One justification for ruling this out is the following. Suppose shareholders always assume that

bidders are informed. Then the tender price will be given by $\hat{P}(\phi, q)$ as determined in this section. If the bidder makes an uninformed bid, his expected profit is $E[v(\theta) - \hat{P}(\phi, q) - c \mid q]$. As long as c is large enough relative to c_I and $v(\theta)$ is sufficiently variable, however, this is less than $E[\max(v(\theta) - \hat{P}(\phi, q) - c, 0) \mid q] - c_I$, which is his expected profit if he investigates the firm. Thus uninformed bids will not occur under these conditions.

16. We assume that the bidder cannot charge shareholders directly for the true costs c_I and c incurred, as these cannot be directly monitored by shareholders. Another interpretation of ϕ is that it states the maximum amount that the bidder can charge shareholders for the takeover bid.

17. Alternatively, the wealthy individual can announce a counter tender offer at a price between P and $qE[\bar{t} \mid v(\theta)\bar{t} - P - c > 0, f(\theta, \varepsilon) = q]$.

18. We shall assume that if a bid takes place at all, it occurs almost immediately. Thus shareholders receive either $q\bar{t}$ or $\hat{P}(\phi, q)$ rather than some weighted combination of the two, with the weights being determined by the length of time incumbent management is in office.

19. For if (7) holds with strict inequality, then since the right-hand side is continuous in P, (7) will be satisfied for a slightly lower value of P. This contradicts the fact that $P(\phi, q)$ is the smallest P satisfying (7).

20. This is the same conclusion that was arrived at in the analysis of disciplinary bids given in Grossman and Hart [1980a]. The main differences between the two analyses are (1) in the present chapter, the ex ante information cost c_I and the bid cost c are treated separately, whereas in Grossman and Hart [1980a] they were lumped together; (2) in Grossman and Hart [1980a] the disciplinary effect of bids meant that making bids easier by increasing ϕ caused managers to work harder on the shareholders' behalf, i.e., to increase q. This effect on q is missing in the allocational model described here because inefficiency is due only to managerial inability and not to managerial discretion.

21. Further remarks on the case where bidders compete may be found in Grossman and Hart [1980a].

22. We are, of course, not claiming that government retrictions of takeover bids are never warranted. If, for example, most takeover bids occur in order to restrict competition in the product market, then government retrictions may be justified. All we are claiming is that the view that government restriction is justified because of the existence of acquisitional bids is unfounded.

23. There is a third reason for the existence of premiums. We have assumed throughout that only a single bidder investigates the firm and makes a bid. In general, however, a number of bidders may choose to monitor the same firm. One of these will discover the firm's secrets first—in the present model the secrets concern whether the firm has a good manager and a bad capital stock, say, or a bad manager and a good capital stock—and will make a bid. This bid will, however, signal information to others (including those who were not monitoring the firm)

that the firm is worth taking over, and this may induce others to make competing bids. If the process of making bids and counterbids is expensive, the bidder making the first bid may prefer to offer a sufficiently large premium to deter competing bids rather than to engage in a bid battle.

24. It is sometimes suggested that a further reason for premiums is that the demand curve for the firm's shares is downward sloping; that is, shareholders get consumer surplus out of the earnings stream provided by the firm. (This can occur when there is imperfect competition in the production of earnings streams) Then, e.g., in the simplest case where $\bar{t} \equiv 1$, the market price q of shares represents the *marginal* worth of a share rather than the total worth of 100% of the shares. It is claimed that in this case, in order to take over the firm, a bidder will have to "go up the demand curve." This is false, however. In fact, if $\phi = \infty$, the bidder can get the firm for q. For if he offers $q + \varepsilon$, where $\varepsilon > 0$, then if shareholders think that he will succeed, they tender, since their shares will be worthless if they hold on, while if they think he will fail, they also tender since they are being offered more than q now and can always repurchase their shares for q once the bid has failed. Now let $\varepsilon \to 0$.

25. In the model studied here, there are no unsuccessful bids. However, unsuccessful bids could easily be introduced by assuming that the bidder does not know shareholders' assessments of the potential value of the firm, $v(\theta)$, so that the bidder will sometimes offer too low a price and will not obtain a majority of the shares.

References

Aranow and Einhorn [1973], *Tender Offers for Corporate Control*; Columbia University Press: New York.

Aranow, Einhorn, and Berlstein [1977], *Developments in Tender Offers for Corporate Control*; Columbia University Press: New York.

Brudney, Y., and M. Chirelstein [1979], *Cases and Materials on Corporate Finance*, 2nd edition; The Foundation Press: Mineola, New York.

Dodd, P., and R. Ruback [1977], "Tender Offers and Stockholders Returns: An Empirical Analysis," *J. of Financial Economics*, 5, pp. 351–373.

Gort, M. [1969], "An Economic Disturbance Theory of Mergers," *Quarterly J. of Economics*, 83(4), pp. 625–642.

Grossman, S. [1977], "The Existence of Futures Markets, Noisy Rational Expectations, and Informational Externalities," *Rev. of Econ. Stud.*, vol. SLIV (3), Oct., pp. 431–449.

Grossman, S., and O. Hart [1980a], "Takeover Bids. The Free Rider Problem, and the Theory of the Corporation," *Bell. J. Econ.*, vol. 11 (1), Spring, pp. 42–64.

Grossman, S., and O. Hart [1980b], "Disclosure Laws and Takeover Bids." *J. Finance*, vol. XXXV (2), May, pp. 323–334.

Lintner, J. [1971], "Expectations, Mergers, and Equilibrium in Purely Competitive Securities Markets." *Amer. Econ. Rev.* 61(2), May, 101–111.

Manne, H. G. [1965], "Mergers and the Market for Corporate Control. *J. of Pol. Econ.*, 73, pp. 110–120.

Mueller, D. [1969], "A Theory of Conglomerate Mergers," *Quarterly J. Econ.*, 83(4), pp. 199–219.

Smiley, R. [1976], "Tender Offers, Transaction's Costs, and the Theory of the Firm." *Rev. Econ. and Stat.*, 58, pp. 22–32.

8

The Informational Role of Warranties and Private Disclosure about Product Quality

8.1 Introduction

A fundamental role of competition is to facilitate the allocation of resources. This is achieved by prices that, to some extent, reflect and transmit the underlying worth of resources. The ability of prices to reflect and transmit information derives from the attempt of economic agents to buy or sell based on their information. Competition among all those who want to buy wheat because they think that wheat will be scarce tomorrow drives up the price of wheat. Hence their information can be transmitted by the price system to those who store wheat but do not have direct access to information about next period's wheat demand. This mechanism works because there is some future state of nature that will lead to prices that reward those who buy or sell today.[1]

Unfortunately, there are situations where no such prices exist. An important case involves information about product quality. Sellers may know the quality of the item they sell but it may be in their interest to withhold that information. If there is no way for buyers to learn about the sellers' quality, then this will force all items to sell at the same price. If there is no way sellers of good-quality items can distinguish themselves from sellers of low-quality items, then the low-quality sellers will find it in their interest to hide their quality. This has been called the "lemons problem."[2]

In this chapter, we shall consider cases where good sellers have an incentive to distinguish themselves from bad sellers. Of particular interest is the case where there is a single seller. Consumer information is often quite poor about those products that are new. It is just these products where (temporary) monopoly is likely to be found. Thus, we shall be concerned with cases where a monopolist could have an incentive to reveal his quality even when it is low. In order for this incentive to exist, there must be some event that occurs after the sale that will reward sellers as a function of their true quality. We consider two cases.

In our first case, the seller can make statements about the product's quality that are *ex post* verifiable. For example, a diamond seller can disclose the weight of a diamond he is selling. He can give the buyer a warranty that states the weight of the diamond. That is, in section 8.2 we shall consider situations where sellers can make any disclosure about their product's quality and give a complete warranty that guarantees that the disclosure is true (for example, the diamond seller gives the buyer a written statement guaranteeing that the diamond can be returned if an objective party finds that its weight is less than specified).

The second case that we consider is where statements about product quality are too costly either to communicate or verify *ex post*. For this reason, the statements cannot be guaranteed. However, we assume that there is some characteristic that is observable *ex post*. For example, the quality of an automobile's construction is difficult to describe or verify *ex post*. However, it may be easy to verify *ex post* whether the auto "breaks down." If it is the case that low-quality items have a higher probability of breakdown than do high-quality, then warranties that guarantee against (the *ex post* cheaply observable) breakdown can substitute for guarantees regarding (the *ex post* very costly to observe) quality.

This chapter is primarily concerned with situations where consumers have had no experience and will have no further experience with the monopolist. This is the case where the monopolist will have the greatest incentive to mislead. Our basic result is, however, that the monopolist will *not* be able to mislead rational consumers about the quality of his product. In section 8.2, we assume that the monopolist has the ability to make *ex post* verifiable statements about his quality. We show that consumers with rational expectations will assume that the monopolist is of the worst possible quality consistent with his disclosure when he makes less than a full disclosure. The monopolist, realizing this, decides to make a full disclosure. This result generalizes the result in Grossman and Hart.[3]

In section 8.3, where verifiable disclosure is assumed to be impossible, the monopolist can offer warranties. It is assumed that the warranty is conditional on an event, the probability of which depends *only* on the seller's quality. Further, the consumer is assumed to be risk averse. In this case, we show that if a seller offers less than a full warranty, consumers with rational expectations will conclude that he is trying to mislead them about the product's quality. Each consumer knows that it is Pareto optimal for the seller to sell the item at the consumer's reservation price with a complete warranty. Hence a seller would only offer less than a complete warranty if it would make the seller better off than the complete warranty contract. But then it would have to make the consumer worse off than the complete warranty contract. But this would give the consumer less than his reservation price, so he does not make the purchase.

The above arguments are based upon adverse selection against sellers that makes consumers bear the risk associated with not knowing the quality of their product. This is to be contrasted with signaling arguments. Spence has presented a model with many different sellers who have marginal costs of production that depend on their quality.[4] In his model (where consumers differ in risk aversion), there is an equilibrium distribution of qualities and warranties outstanding at a given time. Further, high-quality firms offer a larger warranty than do low-quality firms, thus signaling their quality. This result is very different from mine. It requires that consumers have information about the statistical relationship between warranties and quality. He further requires that there are many competing sellers extant at a given moment. I have presented a much weaker equilibrium concept that is appropriate for markets with a *single* seller and many buyers. Further, because there is only a single seller, I am able to be more precise in defining consumers' conjectures about the seller's quality than is normally done in a signaling model. In a signaling model, consumers can only get information from the equilibrium contract schedule, while in my model it is the consumers' conjectures about the monopolist's quality *out* of equilibrium that forces the monopolist to choose a particular equilibrium. In my model, the monopolist is unable to mislead consumers because of the rational conjectures consumers have regarding what his quality must be if he deviates from a full-information Pareto optimal contract. In the equilibrium I present, consumers are *unable* to determine the seller's quality by inverting the equilibrium contract. This is what distinguishes the result and model presented here from Spence and other signaling models.

8.2   A Model of Private Disclosure

In this section we assume that it is possible for a seller to make *ex post* verifiable disclosures. For example, a diamond seller can specify the weight of the diamond; a doctor can specify the medical school he graduated from, his class standing, the number of malpractice suits he is engaged in, and so forth. In this section, we shall be concerned with disclosures that have negligible *ex post* verification cost and also negligible communications cost. For example, it would be very costly for a doctor to explain to a patient, in detail, his contribution to the study of ulcers. This might involve imparting four years' worth of medical school training to the patient. Yet, if the patient must choose between two doctors, this information gross of acquisition costs is very valuable (while net of acquisition costs it is of no value). Note further than the doctor may desire to substitute low communications cost information such as, "I am the best ulcer doctor in the world," but such a statement is not easily subject to verification (primarily because it is not sufficiently detailed—what does "best" mean?).

In this section we shall not model a consumer's decision about verifying *ex post* the truth of the statement made by the seller. Rather, for simplicity, we shall limit attention to situations where all of the seller's statements are costlessly verifiable *ex post*. A clear example is where the seller is selling boxes of oranges. If the seller states that there are ten oranges in a box, then this becomes verifiable *ex post* for free. It is important that the information be publically verifiable for the purpose of this section. In particular, if the seller states that a product will "make the buyer happy," then this fact is not open to easy third-party verification. When the seller states that the diamond weighs one ounce, this is very cheap to verify *ex post*.

There has been much recent interest in laws that require sellers to make particular disclosures. This is to be distinguished from antifraud laws that make it illegal for a seller to lie.[5] It is sometimes argued that there are disclosures that are of negligible cost but are not made by sellers in an attempt to mislead buyers. Hence a law is needed that requires such disclosures. This section focuses on cases of costless disclosure to derive insight about the issue of what a firm would voluntarily disclose.

We restrict attention to disclosures that are truthful. (For example, a seller who says nothing is making a truthful disclosure. A seller with a diamond that weighs one ounce who states that it weighs at least one-half ounce is making a truthful disclosure, while if the same seller said that his diamond weighs two ounces it would not be truthful.) We consider only truthful disclosures for two reasons. First, we are interested in analyzing the benefits of a positive disclosure law that are above and beyond those provided by a law against lying. Second, if there are zero *ex post* verification costs, sellers would warranty their disclosures. Any seller who did not warranty his disclosure would immediately be assumed to be lying: that is, saying nothing. As can easily be seen from the analysis to be given below, unwarranteed disclosures could easily be incorporated.

In situations where there is objective, costless *ex post* verification and no communications costs, we can most clearly elucidate the role of *positive disclosure*. In situations where sellers do not lie, the only issue is how much of the truth they will decide to tell. In particular, if a seller has a bad product, will he say nothing, leading consumers to believe his product is of average quality? Will adverse selection by the low-quality sellers drive out the high-quality sellers? If the market is competitive, then this will clearly not be the case. That is, if there is free entry into the sellers' activity, then good sellers will make disclosures to distinguish themselves from bad sellers. If any good seller should be lumped with the bad sellers due to nondisclosure, then the good seller could costlessly disclose his quality and be distinguished, getting a higher price.

The case of free entry is reasonably obvious. However, in many important cases involving consumer uncertainty, free entry may be an inappropriate assumption. Consumer information is relatively poor about new products. There may only be one firm selling a new product because of patent protection or because that firm is a particularly rapid innovator. Schumpeter has argued that an extremely important role of the competitive system is in encouraging innovation via the temporary monopoly power won by the fastest innovator.[6] Thus it is important to ask whether a monopolist would find it in his interest to make a full disclosure. It is remarkable that if the monopolist has customers with rational expectations, then it will be in his interest to make a complete disclosure. It will be shown that adverse selection works *against* a monopolist who makes less than a full disclosure. The idea of the analysis can be seen from a simple example. Suppose the monopolist is selling boxes of apples. He can label the boxes with an exact number of apples, but if he does then his must be the true amount under the above "no lying" assumptions. However, he could also put no label as to the quantity or he could state, "There are at least three apples in the box." Suppose that from the size of the box consumers can tell that the box holds between zero and 100 apples, and they also know that the seller knows how many apples are in the box. Suppose the seller says nothing about the number in the box. Then a consumer could rationally conclude that the box contains no apples, for if there were, say, three apples in the box, the seller could have said, "There are at least three apples in the box." Similarly, suppose a seller makes the statement, "There are at least six apples in the box." This must mean that there are *exactly* six apples in the box, for if there were really seven, then the seller could have made more profit by saying that there are at least seven apples in the box. This is because the expected number of apples in the box under the latter statement is higher than the former, so consumers will be willing to pay more. Thus there is a kind of adverse selection against a seller who does not make a full disclosure, even though he is the only seller. Consumers rationally expect a seller's quality to be the poorest possible consistent with his disclosure. The seller, knowing that consumers will only offer to pay the lowest amount consistent with his disclosure, finds it optimal to disclose the highest possible quality consistent with the truth; that is, he discloses the truth when he knows it. The remainder of this section is devoted to providing a formal model of the above.

Let q be a vector of characteristics that gives a consumer utility. A product of unknown quality can be modeled as a product where the consumer does not know which particular vector of characteristics the commodity contains (for example, see Leland for an analysis that uses characteristics to model product quality).[7] Let Q represent the set of all possible vectors of characteristics. Assume that if a consumer has income I, then his willingness to pay for a particular known vector q is given by the p such that

$$U(q, I - q) = \bar{u}, \tag{1}$$

where $\bar{u}$ is the utility he can get by not consuming the commodity. We shall sometimes call p "the consumer's reservation price." We shall take $\bar{u}$ as an exogenous description of the best alternative available opportunity for the consumer. We assume that the consumer is only interested in zero or one unit and that all consumers are identical. Assume that U is increasing in I.

This chapter is concerned with situations where sellers know more than buyers about the quality of a product. We represent the buyers' knowledge about the product by specifying a probability distribution on Q. For example, if there are only two possible qualities, q_1 and q_2, and γ is the probability that the consumer places on q_1, then the consumer's expected utility is $V(\gamma, p) \equiv \gamma U(q_1, I - p) + (1 - \gamma) U(q_2, I - p)$. In general, there may be many possible vectors of characteristics $\{q_1, q_2, q_3, \ldots\} \equiv Q$, where the consumer assesses γ_i to be the probability that q_i is the true quality. If we let $\gamma = (\gamma_1, \gamma_2, \ldots)$ be his probability assessment, then his expected utility is

$$V(\gamma, p) = \sum_i \gamma_i U(q_i, I - p). \tag{2}$$

Hence, if the buyer has beliefs γ, his willingness to pay will be $p(\gamma)$, which is the p such that

$$V(\gamma, p) = \bar{u}. \tag{3}$$

The seller wants to maximize the price he gets for the item. We assume that the seller has no long-term relationship with the buyer or with other buyers that a given buyer may communicate with. (I make this assumption to create the strongest case for nondisclosure.) The seller can choose to make a disclosure about q. We model this disclosure by assuming that the seller picks a set of q's denoted by D and states, "My q is an element of D (denoted by $q \in D$)." For example, if the seller states $D = \{q_1, q_2\}$, then this means that his quality is either q_1 or q_2. Note that the larger is the set D that a seller reports, the less a consumer can infer about his true quality. A seller could state $q \in Q$ and this is equivalent to making no disclosure, for then he is merely stating that his quality is any possible quality. Let $D(q)$ be the disclosure made by the seller if his true quality is q. Then it must be the case that

$$q \in D(q). \tag{4}$$

This is because we have assumed lying is impossible.

Equilibrium is characterized by the function $D(q)$, which describes the optimal disclosure set for a seller when his quality is q. There are two ways by which consumers can infer q from $D(q)$. First, the seller may reveal everything so $D(q) \equiv \{q\}$.[8] Second, the consumer may be able to reason that only a particular quality seller, say, q_i, would find it profit maximizing to make a disclosure $D(q_i)$. That is, the function $D(q)$ may be invertible. For example, suppose that the consumer convinces himself that only a seller of type q_i would make a disclosure like $D_i = \{q_i, q_{i+1}, q_{i+2}, \ldots\}$ (that is, the seller states, "My quality is at least q_i"); then in this case the quality of the seller can be inferred from D, even though D is not a one-element set.

In order to define a seller's profit-maximizing disclosure, it is necessary to decide how much a consumer is willing to pay for the item, given that a particular disclosure D is made. Let p_i denote the consumer's willingness to pay for an item of sure quality q_i; that is, p_i solves

$$U(q_i, I - p_i) = \bar{u}. \tag{5}$$

It is convenient to label the qualities in order of consumers' willingness to pay, so that

$$p_1 < p_2 < p_3 < \cdots. \tag{6}$$

(There is no loss generality in assuming that all the prices are different. For if $p_1 = p_2$, then at this price the consumer is indifferent between q_1 and q_2, so it does not matter to him which is the truth.)

If the seller discloses a set, say, $D = \{q_3, q_6, q_7\}$, then the consumer knows that the true quality is q_3, q_6, or q_7, but he may know more. Note that p_7 is larger than p_3 or p_6. The consumer reasons that if the seller's quality was really q_7, then the seller would have disclosed $D = \{q_7\}$ rather than $D = \{q_3, q_6, q_7\}$, since in that case the seller would have received more money by shifting the consumer's beliefs toward the better-quality item. Continuing this argument, the consumer concludes that the quality must be q_3.

To make the above idea precise, let $\gamma_i(D)$ denote the consumer's beliefs about the probability that the item has quality q_i after he observes a disclosure D. Let $\gamma(D) \equiv \{\gamma_1(D), \gamma_2(D), \ldots\}$. Note that, given the consumer's beliefs $\gamma(D)$, we can use (3) to find his willingness to pay $p[\gamma(D)]$. We now give necessary conditions for a particular $\gamma(D)$ to be a rational expectations inference function. Appendix A gives a rigorous definition of $\gamma(D)$ and proves that in equilibrium the seller's disclosure reveals his quality. In the remainder of this section, we give the basic idea.

The seller's disclosure must maximize his profit. Therefore it must be the case that the price he receives when he makes the disclosure, D, $p[\gamma(D)]$, must be as large as the price he would get if he made any other disclosure. One disclosure that is always open to a seller is to disclose his exact quality and receive p_i when he is of quality q_i. Hence, for $D(q)$ to be an optimal disclosure for a seller of quality q, when buyers have an inference function $\gamma(D)$, it must be the case that

$$p\{\gamma[D(q_i)]\} \geqslant p_i \qquad \text{for all qualities } i. \tag{7}$$

The right-hand side of (7) is the price the seller would receive if he reveals his true quality.

We now show that this implies that $p\{\gamma[D(q_i)]\} = p_i$, and that $D(q)$ reveals q. It must be the case that

$$V(\gamma[D(q_i)], p\{\gamma[D(q_i)]\}) = \bar{u} \tag{8}$$

for the consumer to buy the item and for the seller to have maximized profits. Note that if $D(q)$ reveals q, then (7) must hold as an equality. So suppose $D(q)$ does not reveal q. Then it must be the case that the seller would make the same disclosure for two different q's, say, q_i and q_j, with $p_i > p_j$. That is, (8) holds for the common disclosure $D = D(q_i) = D(q_j)$. [For if there was a distinct disclosure set for each distinct q, then the particular disclosure set would reveal q; see the example in the paragraph after equation (4).] Further, (8) states that the consumer's *average* utility is $\bar{u}$, but this means that either (a) the consumer gets $\bar{u}$ whether the quality is q_i or q_j—that is, $U(q_i, I - p\{\gamma[D(q_i)]\}) = U(q_j, I - p\{\gamma[D(q_i)]\}) = \bar{u}$—or (b)

$$U(q_i, I - p\{\gamma[D(q_i)]\}) > \bar{u} > U(q_j, I - p\{\gamma[D(q_i)]\}). \tag{9}$$

But (a) is impossible by the convention that different qualities are associated with different willingnesses to pay—see (6). Hence (b) must hold. But (9) states that the consumer is doing strictly better than $\bar{u}$ in the event of high quality q_i. This means that the seller is getting a lower price than he would if he revealed exactly that $q = q_i$ when his quality is q_i; that is, $p\{\gamma[D(q_i)]\} < p_i$. This contradicts (7).

We have shown that an equilibrium inference function $\gamma[D(q)]$ must reveal q to the consumer. The essence of the argument is the assumption that the seller could have always disclosed the exact quality. The only reason for the seller not to do so is that he could make higher profit by reporting a larger set. However, the only way he can get a higher profit is by making the same disclosure both when he has high quality and when he has low quality. But this is not optimal. When the seller has high quality, he should certainly reveal exactly what his quality is. Hence consumers know immediately that he has low quality when the seller does not make a full disclosure.

It is essential to note that we *do not* assume that consumers have had a lot of experience with the seller, and are thus able to learn the relationship between the actual disclosure $D(q)$ made by a seller of type q and his true quality q. Instead, we argue that, for example, if a seller says nothing about his quality, the consumers infer that he is of the lowest possible quality, because *only* a seller of the lowest quality would find it profit maximizing to say nothing. A seller whose actual quality is q_2 (just above the lowest quality) would have been better off saying, "My quality is at least q_2." With lying impossible, every rational consumer will be willing to pay more to a seller who says his q is at least q_2 than they will to a seller who says nothing. Hence only the worst possible seller would say nothing. A similar argument shows that only a seller of quality q_i would find it profit maximizing to state, "My quality is at least q_i."[9]

8.3   Warranties and Indirect Disclosure

The previous section considered commodities where disclosure about quality involves (a) negligible communication cost and (b) negligible cost of making *ex post* verifiable statements. As noted earlier, there exist situations where the seller has some information about a product, the disclosure of which would be costly. (For example, a used-car salesman can make statements about the kind of driver who previously owned the car, but the making of *verifiable* statements might be costly, as would an objective inspection of the car.) In this section, we consider the extreme case where

the cost to the seller of making relevant statements or of the buyer determining the quality before purchase is larger than the difference in value
between the best and worst possible commodity. We maintain the assumption that the seller knows the quality of the commodity, and this
quality is exogenous. As before, we consider a situation where buyers have
no experience with sellers and will have no future relationship with them.

Under the above assumptions, all sellers will be judged to be identical.
Each seller, whether his commodity is best or worst, will receive the same
price. There are two situations to consider. If there are no warranties or any
other device other than price to signal quality, then we will have the usual
"lemons" problem. There will be adverse selection against high-quality
sellers. Each high-quality seller will want to be distinguished from those of
average quality, but in this case there is no way for him to do so.

In some situations, sellers can attempt to distinguish their quality even if
disclosures are very costly. This can be done with warranties. It seems
intuitively plausible that a seller of a high-quality item can offer a better
warranty than can be offered by a low-quality seller. Of course, for this to
make sense, it is necessary that something be *ex post* objectively observable
by buyers and sellers. For example, a doctor can warranty a patient against
the recurrence of an illness, a manufacturer can offer a warranty against
breakdown, a lawyer can take a fee contingent on success, etc. In each of
these cases, it is observable *ex post* when the patient gets sick, the car
breaks, or the legal battle is lost. In many cases such events will be much
easier to verify *ex post* than will be the *ex ante* statements a seller makes
about his quality, and will have lower communication cost. For example,
the lawyer could try to tell the customer about all his previous cases, why
losing particular cases was not his fault, compare his record with the
records of other lawyers, and so on. Such statements are far more complicated and costly to the buyer and seller than a statement like "Pay me
$1,000 if I lose and $10,000 if I win." Sometimes the information is
impossible to convey in an *ex post* verifiable way. A doctor may know that
he is the best doctor in existence, but there is no way (at a reasonable cost)
that he can prove this to a prospective patient. In situations in which a
seller's information cannot be conveyed to a buyer, the seller's warranty
can, in effect, transmit that information to the buyer. There is a sense in
which the degree of warranty can be a sufficient statistic for the seller's
information.

To develop the warranty idea, we consider a special case of product
quality. In particular, for simplicity assume there are two states of nature: a
"good" state and a "bad" state. Let b_1 be the benefit the consumer gets in

the good state and b_2 his benefit in the bad state, where $b_1 > b_2$. Suppose that the only possible difference between products is the probability that the good state will arise. (For example, the only difference among cars is the probability of breakdown or among lawyers the probability that the case is won.) A warranty gives the consumer some payment w in state 2 only, while in the good state the consumer gets no payment from the seller. For notational simplicity, we consider a two-period model with a zero interest rate between the periods. In the initial period, a contract is signed and the consumer pays p dollars, while in the second period if state 2 arises the firm pays the consumer w, and in state 1 it pays nothing to the consumer. We *shall assume that there are no moral hazards on the consumer's part, so that the consumer cannot affect the probability of the states, and that the seller knows the buyer's benefits b_1 and b_2*. In this case, it does not matter whether a warranty involves a dollar payment or some repairs, or a combination of both.

We consider first what would happen if the buyer knows the quality of the seller's item. Let π be the probability of the good state and let the seller charge a price p with warranty w. If the seller sells many units of the product, his revenue per unit, by the law of large numbers, will be non-stochastic. His revenue per unit is

$$R(\pi, p, w) \equiv \pi p + (1 - \pi)(p - w), \tag{10}$$

since he gets p no matter what the state is, but must pay out w in the state that is bad for the consumer. If the consumer thinks the probability of the good state is π^e, then his expected utility is

$$V(\pi^e, p, w) = \pi^e u(b_1 - p) + (1 - \pi^e)u(b_2 - p + w); \tag{11}$$

b_i is the dollar value of the commodity in state i and $u(\cdot)$ is the consumer's von Neumann-Morgenstern utility function.

A Pareto optimal contract would involve choosing p, w to maximize $R(\pi, p, w)$ subject to the constraint that $V(\pi^e, p, w) \geq \lambda$, where λ is a number that determines the division of consumer surplus between the seller and buyer. Let $\bar{u}$ be the best utility level the consumer could attain elsewhere. Then monopoly is the Pareto optimal contract with $\lambda = \bar{u}$. If many firms with the same π competed and $\pi^e = \pi$, then the competitive equilibrium would involve a choice of p, w to maximize $V(\pi, p, w)$ subject to $R(\pi, p, w) \geq 0$ (where we take production as having already occurred and no more production is possible; more will be said about this assumption below). Clearly, for any λ, if the consumer is strictly risk averse ($u'' < 0$), then a Pareto optimal contract p^0, w^0 involves equalizing the consumer's net income in both states; that is, $b_1 - p^0 = b_2 - p^0 + w^0$—equivalently

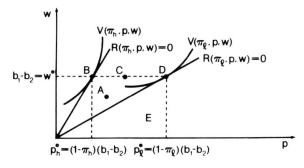

Figure 8.1

$$b_1 - b_2 = w^0. \tag{12}$$

In the case of a monopolist, p^0 would be chosen so that

$$V(\pi^2, p^0, w^0) = u(b_1 - p^0) = \bar{u}, \tag{13}$$

while perfect competition among sellers with an identical π will drive p^0 down to where $R(\pi, p^0, w^0) = 0$—that is, where

$$p^0 = (1 - \pi)w^0 = (1 - \pi)(b_1 - b_2). \tag{14}$$

We are interested in situations where consumers do not know π. To facilitate the analysis, consider figure 8.1, which is drawn for two types of firms: the firm with the highes π, denoted by π_h, and the firm with the lowest π, denoted by π_l. For each firm, the zero revenue line is drawn, and labeled $R(\pi, p, w) = 0$. The consumer's indifference curve, which is tangent to each revenue line, is also drawn, and labeled $V(\pi, p, w)$. The slope of the consumer's indifference curve is

$$\left. \frac{dw}{dp} \right|_{V = \text{constant}} = \frac{1}{1 - \pi} \left\{ 1 + \pi \left[\frac{u'(b_1 - p)}{u'(b_2 - p + w)} - 1 \right] \right\}, \tag{15}$$

while the slope of the firm's isorevenue line is

$$\left. \frac{dw}{dp} \right|_{R = \text{constant}} = \frac{1}{1 - \pi}. \tag{16}$$

When the firm and the consumer have the same beliefs about π, a tangency occurs at the full insurance point $w = b_1 - b_2$. Note that firm revenue is higher below and to the right of the isorevenue line, while the consumer's utility is higher to the left and above his indifference curve.

It is easy to dispose of the competitive cases when the consumer does not know a particular firm's π but where the consumer knows the distribution of π's across firms. (By competitive, we mean that there are more potential products than buyers, and sellers do not collude.) First, suppose all firms have the same π—for example, π_h. Suppose one firm offers a contract like the point A in the figure. Then another firm could offer a slightly higher warranty, and this would be purchased since the consumer would know that they are of equal quality. The only undominated contract is at the tangency point B.

Another competitive case that is easy to analyze is where there are, say, two types in the population, π_l and π_h, but consumers cannot identify which firm is of which quality. There are two subcases to consider, depending on which type is the marginal firm.[10] First suppose that the number of identical consumers, say, n, is such that the high-quality firms can satisfy all of demand. In this case, the equilibrium contract will be B in figure 8.1. For if a contract like A is offered, then it will be dominated by a full warranty contract on the line BC. Note that consumers do not have to make inferences about the quality of items sold with full warranty contracts. Hence a consumer will always prefer a contract like B to a contract like A or C. The other competitive subcase is when the lower-quality firms are the marginal quality; that is, the high-quality firms cannot satisfy demand, but all the potential firms together more than satisfy demand. In this case, the equilibrium contract will be D. (Note that because D involves full insurance, a consumer does not care about π.) To see this, note that the only contract firms that would prefer to offer to D would be to the right of the $R(\pi_l, p, w) = 0$ line. Suppose the best firm, π_h, switches from D to a point in the region labeled E. There will be points in E that are better for a π_h firm than is D. However, there is no point in region E that can be better for both the π_h firm and for the consumer than is D. This is because D is a Pareto optimal point; it involves full insurance. Hence a consumer offered a contract in E would know that it was worse than D if it knew that a good firm offered it. If a consumer would not buy the best firm's offer of something in E if he could get D, he surely would not buy any (unidentified) firm's offer of something in E when he can get D. All other points are also clearly worse than D since they involve higher prices and less warranty than D.

The previous results are based on the idea that when the consumer is offered contracts involving a complete warranty (that is, where $w = b_1 - b_2$), then he does not care about quality. If there are a sufficient number of firms, then competition among firms will drive out contracts that do not offer a full warranty. As we noted earlier, consumers will be least informed

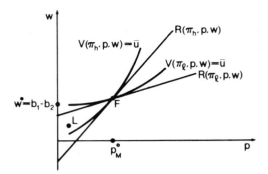

Figure 8.2

about those products that are new, and it is exactly the case of new products where monopoly is most likely to be found. Thus it is extremely important to see whether the results of this section generalize to the case of monopoly. In particular, will a monopolist of very low quality be treated as if he is of average quality by a consumer? Without disclosure or warranties, then, the answer is yes. However, we shall extend the results of the last section to show that there will be adverse selection against a monopolist who does not offer a full warranty, and thus even monopoly will be characterized by the same type of contracts that would arise as in the case where consumers know the monopolist's quality exactly.

Consider figure 8.2. We have drawn two indifference curves for the consumer. The steep curve is the (p, w) combination, which leaves the consumer indifferent when he knows the item is of high quality π_h. The less steep curve corresponds to an item of low-quality π_l. Both indifference curves are drawn to give the consumer a level of utility $\bar{u}$, which is the best he can do if he does not purchase the monopolist's product. Figure 8.2 also contains two isorevenue lines, each line tangent to its respective indifference curve. As we noted earlier, tangency occurs at the full insurance point. In figure 8.2, p_M^0 is the price such that $u(b_1 - p_M^0) = \bar{u}$. Both indifference curves and both isorevenue lines go through the point (p_M^0, w^0), which is labeled point F in figure 8.2. Thus, for example, $R(\pi_l, p, w)$ is the line with slope $(1 - \pi_l)^{-1}$ through the point (p_M^0, w^0). The point F is the contract that would arise if a monopolist of either quality maximized his revenue subject to the constraint that *a consumer knew his quality* and that the consumer must get an expected utility of $\bar{u}$.

We shall now use an argument similar to that of the last section to show that F is also the outcome even if the consumer does not know π. An optimal contract for a monopolist of type π is a pair (p, w) that maximizes his revenue subject to the constraint that a rational consumer is willing to buy it. In order to describe the set of contracts that a consumer is willing to purchase, it is necessary to describe what a consumer expects a firm's quality to be as a function of the contract offered—that is, to define $\pi^e(p, w)$. First, note that if a firm offers a contract with a complete warranty, then it does not matter what $\pi^e(\cdot)$ is; the consumer will purchase the contract if and only if $p \leqslant p_M^0$. However, suppose a consumer sees a contract like L in figure 8.2. [In figure 8.2, L is a point (w, p) just above and to the left of the indifference curve $V(\pi_h, p, w) = \bar{u}$.] Should the consumer buy it? Note that it is below his $\bar{u}$ indifference curve if it is the low quality, while it is above his $\bar{u}$ indifference curve if it is the high quality (that is, he would not buy it if he knew it was of low quality). Note further that a low-quality firm will make more profit offering L than it will offering F. Hence, in order to see whether F is an equilibrium, it is necessary to see whether the consumer would be willing to buy L.

It is rational for the consumer to reason as follows. Suppose the firm offering L was a high-quality firm; then, from the figure, the point L gives a high-quality firm strictly less revenue than the point F. A high-quality firm knows that if it offered F then the consumer would buy it, since F involves complete insurance and thus the consumer knows he will get $\bar{u}$. Hence why would a high-quality firm offer a contract like L rather than F? It would not. Thus if a firm offers L it must be of lower quality.

If there were exactly two qualities possible, the consumer would infer from L that the firm is of quality π_l and would not purchase the contract since it puts him on a π_l indifference curve below $\bar{u}$. However, there may be other possible qualities. Consider an isorevenue line through L and F. That is, if $L \equiv (p_L, w_L)$, the isorevenue line is the set of p, w such that

$$\frac{p - p_L}{w - w_L} = \frac{p - p_M^0}{w - w^0}.$$

Such a line would have slope $(w^0 - w_L) \div (p_M^0 - p_L)$. That slope can be used to define the quality π_L at which a firm would get the same revenue offering (p_L, w_L) and (p_M^0, w^0). All firms with quality below π_L will get higher revenue offering L than F. This is illustrated in figure 8.3. Hence the consumer knows that if the firm offers L its quality is below π_L. Consider the consumer's $\bar{u}$ indifference curve for a product of known quality π_L. That indifference curve must be tangent to the revenue line LF at the point F. Therefore L is below the indifference curve $V(\pi_L, p, w) = \bar{u}$. It follows immediately that L is also below all $\bar{u}$ indifference curves for qualities less

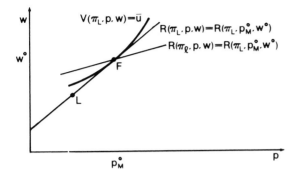

Figure 8.3

than π_L, since these curves are less steep. Hence the consumer knows for sure that if he purchases L and L was profit maximizing for the firm offering it, then he will get less than $\bar{u}$. Hence he does not buy it.

The above argument holds for any contract L that is not on the $R(\pi_h, p, w)$ isorevenue curve in figure 8.2. Therefore the only candidates for equilibrium are points on that isorevenue line. Consider a firm with quality less than π_h. Such a firm would get strictly higher revenue at F than any other point on the $R(\pi_h, p, w)$ line, since its isorevenue line is flatter than is $R(\pi_h, p, w)$. Hence any firm of quality less than π_h will offer F. Consider a firm of quality π_h. That firm is indifferent about anything on $R(\pi_h, p, w)$, so F is an optimal policy for it. However, if the firm should choose anything but F on its isorevenue line, the consumer would immediately know that its quality is π_h and thus that the consumer's expected utility is less than $\bar{u}$. Hence F is strictly optimal for even the highest quality firm.

We have shown that the full insurance point will be the monopoly solution even if consumers do not know product quality. All other contracts can be eliminated because consumers would infer that they are being offered only by firms that are offering qualities insufficient for the consumers to attain a utility level of $\bar{u}$. Such policies would only be offered by low-quality firms that wanted to be thought of as high-quality firms. One way to think of our argument is that the consumer knows that the point F is Pareto optimal. Hence he knows that any other point can only make the firm better off if it makes the consumer worse off than F. Since the consumer can do as well as F elsewhere (he can get $\bar{u}$ by not buying the product), he knows that he should not buy the product as a contract that gives the firm higher revenue than F gives the firm.[11]

Appendix B gives a formal definition of equilibrium and a proof of the above statements.

8.4   Extensions and Conclusions

We have analyzed the question of whether a monopolist can mislead consumers about his quality. Our basic principle can be described as follows: Consider the best contract that the monopolist could offer in a world where the consumers know the monopolist's quality ("the known-quality contract"). This contract extracts all the consumer surplus from the consumer and makes the monopolist as much profit as he can get. Consumers are left indifferent between buying and not buying the item. In a world where there is incomplete information, a monopolist with low quality has the potential of doing even better. If he can mislead consumers into thinking he is of high quality, then he can make the consumers worse off from buying his product instead of their next best alternative. In section 8.3 we showed that this is impossible if consumers can make "rational inferences." If the "known-quality" contract does not depend on the monopolist's quality (as it does not when it involves a complete warranty), then the consumer knows that anything that makes the monopolist better off than the full information contract must make him worse off, so he does not purchase anything else.

To prove the above result, we assumed that there are no moral hazards on the part of consumers; that is, the firm solely determines the probability of breakdown of the item. It is clear that our result will still hold when there are consumer moral hazards of the following type. Suppose the consumer can affect the probability of breakdown, so that even if the firm and the consumer knew the quality of the item, full insurance would not be Pareto optimal. However, suppose the known-quality contract that is best for the monopolist provides a level of insurance that is independent of his quality. In this case, the previous argument will go through unchanged and the "unknown-quality" contract will be the same as the "known-quality" contract. Similarly, if there are production costs that depend on quality, then the "known-quality" contract will still be independent of the quality for all produced qualities (there will be a full warranty and a price set to extract all of consumer surplus). Thus, in this case, our result will be true.

There is a problem in generalizing the results of this paper to situations involving many types of consumers. As Salop has shown, if consumers who differ in their willingness to pay for an item also have different risk aversions, then random prices can help the monopolist sort consumers by willingness to pay.[12] This increases the surplus he can extract. In our model, the monopolist, by making less than a full disclosure, or offering less than a full warranty, makes consumers bear some excess risk. Thus he may be able to increase his profit via this sorting mechanism. However, it is probably the case that there are better random devices (like random price reductions) that the monopolist can use for sorting high elasticity from low elasticity of demand consumers than incomplete disclosure or incomplete warranties.

We have tried to give some examples of situations in which firms will have an incentive to communicate their quality. Warranties seem like an incredibly useful device for getting around asymmetric information about product quality. There are many products sold with warranties, but I find it surprising that they are not used even more often. The reader might think that the answer lies with moral hazard. Yet there are many risks that are insured by insurance companies but not by sellers. A person can purchase health insurance but not usually from his doctor. I can buy theft insurance, but I cannot purchase it from the seller of burglar-alarm systems. It is very important that the insurance be sold by the commodity seller so that the terms of the insurance vary by seller. This would not matter if the insurance company knew the quality of sellers and sold insurance for products sold by different sellers at different prices. However, this also seems rare.

This chapter has been concerned with showing that when firms have tools available that they could use to convey information, they will do so. It is not in a monopolist's interest to withhold information about product quality. If information transmittal or warranties are costless, then there is no role for government intervention to encourage disclosure. Thus, the argument that there should be a positive disclosure law or government-mandated warranties cannot be justified on the grounds that these tools have negligible social and private cost, and high benefits through giving consumers more information about product quality or less risk about product quality. One might conclude that a positive disclosure law does no harm as well. Unfortunately, disclosure laws are often very broad. Securities law requires the issuer of a new stock to disclose all facts that are *material* to a purchaser.[13] This requirement may have disadvantages relative to what would arise if there is no positive disclosure law. After the purchase bad events do occur that were not perfectly predictable. Buyers can always bring suit claiming that a material fact was not disclosed regarding the possibility of the bad event. The buyer can then attempt to search the seller's records for evidence. Since this can make the seller bear costs, the seller, anticipating this, discloses an enormous amount of information in the first place. Some of this information may also surely be irrelevant but could be costly to disclose. The seller, by making excessive disclosures, makes the buyer bear more costs in trying to interpret the disclosure. This can convert a situation that involves costless disclosure of truly material facts into a situation where both the buyer and seller must bear costs. An important negative consequence of this is that disclosures may no longer reveal the quality of the seller because they have become so noisy. Thus in the case where disclosure of the (truly) material facts are costless, we are better off without a positive disclosure law.

It would be useful to see how far this policy conclusion can be extended to cases where disclosure or warranties are costly. I disclose that the voluntary disclosure theorem will not be true when disclosure is costly. Further, there are important externalities involved when search or disclosure is costly. Thus the reader should view this policy conclusion with extreme caution.

Appendix A: Formal Definition of Disclosure Equibrium

We define jointly the equilibrium disclosure function $D(q)$ and the equilibrium inference function $\gamma(D)$. For those to form an equilibrium, it must be the case that

for each q, $p\{\gamma[D(q)]\} \geq p[\gamma(D')]$ for all sets D' with $q \in D'$;   (A1)

$\gamma_i(D) = \text{Prob(seller } i \text{ would find it optimal to make a disclosure } D)$.   (A2)

Condition (A1) just states that a seller of type q must find it optimal to disclose $D(q)$. Recall that costs are zero, so the seller's profit is just the price he receives for the item. The next condition is quite vague. If this was a screening model, then buyers would try to invert $D(q)$ to discover q. That is, if from experience buyers knew the joint distribution of q and $D(q)$, they could learn something about q from a disclosure D by finding the set of q's such that $D(q) = D$.

However, the function $\gamma(D)$ must be well defined for *all* D, since the monopolist can choose any D (as long as he does not lie). For example, if there are just three possible qualities q_1, q_2, q_3, then in equilibrium there would be at most three disclosure sets $D_1 \equiv D(q_1)$, $D_2 \equiv D(q_2)$, $D_3 \equiv D(q_3)$. But a monopolist with quality q_1 can choose *any* D. In order to show that D_1 is profit maximizing, we must define his profit for all D, not only D_1, D_2, and D_3. For this reason we have had to go beyond signalling to define a rational inference function. Thus (A2) states that the consumer knows that D was optimal for the seller.

With this in mind, we make (A2) more precise. First, given a disclosure set D and a disclosure function $\gamma(\cdot)$, define a set of qualities (that is, the integer labels of the qualities) $J(D; \gamma)$ as follows: $J(D; \gamma)$ contains all integers l such that

$q_l \in D;$ (A3)

if $q_i \in D'$, then $p[\gamma(D)] \geqslant p[\gamma(D')]$.   (A4)

We further require that if D is a one-element set, say, $D = \{q_l\}$, then $J(D; \gamma) = \{l\}$:

$$J(\{l\}, \gamma) = \{l\}. \tag{A5}$$

Conditions (A3) and (A4) state that $J(D; \gamma)$ is the set of indexes of qualities q_l with the property that a seller of quality q_l would find D to be his optimal feasible disclosure (recall that lying is impossible, so that a disclosure D' is feasible for a seller of type q_l if and only if $q_l \in D'$), If $\bar{\gamma}_i$ is the buyer's prior probability that the seller is of type i, then (A2) can be written as

$$\gamma_i(D) = \begin{cases} \bar{\gamma}_i \div \sum_{l \in J(D; \gamma)} \bar{\gamma}_l & \text{if } i \in J(D; \gamma) \\ 0 & \text{if } i \notin J(D; \gamma). \end{cases} \tag{A6}$$

Note that (A6) gives a condition that $\gamma_i(D)$ must satisfy; it is a functional equation since $\gamma(\cdot)$ appears on both sides of the equation. Any $\gamma(D)$ that satisfies (A6) for all D is called a *rational inference function*.

The first result is the one given in the text:

Theorem 1 *If $\gamma(D)$ is a rational inference function and $D(q)$ is the best disclosure for a seller of type q (in the sense of [A1]), then*

$$p\{\gamma[D(q_i)]\} = p_i \qquad \text{for all } i.$$

Proof If $D(q)$ is an optimal disclosure, it must be at least as good as a complete disclosure. Hence

$$p\{\gamma[D(q_i)]\} \geqslant p_i \qquad \text{for all } i. \tag{A7}$$

Suppose (A7) holds with strict inequality for some i. Now simply follow the argument in the text of section 8.2. That is, (8) must hold and this contradicts (9).   QED

It is easy to see that a rational inference function exists. For example, define

$$\gamma_i^e(D) = \begin{cases} 0 & \text{if } q_i \text{ is not the lowest quality in } D \\ 1 & \text{if } q_i \text{ is the lowest quality in } D. \end{cases} \tag{A8}$$

To see that (A5) holds, all we must do is show that $J(D; \gamma^e)$ is the index of the lowest quality in D. To see this, let q_i be the lowest quality in D. Suppose a seller has a higher quality, say k; that is, $p_k > p_i$. Then a seller with quality k would get a higher price by announcing $D' = \{q_k\}$ rather than D under the function γ^e in (A8). This shows that only seller i would find it optimal to choose the set D. Thus $J(D; \gamma^e) = \{i\}$ when q_i is the worst quality in D.

Appendix B: The Monopolist's Optimal Warranty under Asymmetric Information

We want to define an equilibrium policy for each possible product quality π. That is, we want to define a function $[p(\pi), w(\pi)]$ that gives the policy that a firm of type π would offer. Further, it is necessary to define an inference function $\pi^e(p, w)$ that states what a consumer thinks π is when he observes a particular contract. Given a contract function $[p(\pi), w(\pi)]$, we can define a policy set $\delta = \{(p, w) \mid [p(\pi), w(\pi)] = (p, w) \text{ for some } \pi\}$. Note that δ need not be a very large set. In particular, $\pi^e(p, w)$ must be defined for all p, w, even those not in δ. Assume that consumers know the distribution of possible π's. Let $G(\pi)$ be the cumulative distribution function of qualities. If consumers know that the equilibrium (as yet undefined) is $p(\cdot)$, $w(\cdot)$, then they can compute the set δ. If they observe a $(p, w) \in \delta$, they can make an inference about π as follows. They can compute the conditional expectation of π given that $\pi \in \{\pi \mid [p(\pi), w(\pi)] = p, w\} \equiv M_e(p, w)$. However, if the consumer observes a $(p, w) \notin \delta$, then $M_e(p, w)$ is empty so another definition must be given. When the consumer observes (p, w), he knows that p, w must be the best policy for the firm in the class of all feasible policies. Given a $\pi^e(\cdot)$ function, a policy is feasible if $V[\pi^e(p, w), p, w] \geq \bar{u}$. Hence a firm of type π will offer a policy (p, w) if and only if

$$R(\pi, p, w) \geq R(\pi, \hat{p}, \hat{w}) \text{ for all } (\hat{p}, \hat{w}) \text{ such that } V[\pi^e(\hat{p}, \hat{w}), \hat{p}, \hat{w}] \geq \bar{u}. \quad (B1)$$

Hence, given $\pi^e(\cdot)$, the consumer knows that if $(p, w) \notin \delta$ is observed, then π must satisfy the above inequality. Let the set of π's that satisfy the above inequality be given by $M(p, w)$. Note that the inequality must also be true if $(p, w) \in \delta$. Hence $\pi^e(p, w)$ is a rational inference function if, for all p, w,

$$\pi^e(p, w) = \begin{cases} E\{\pi \mid [\pi \in M(p, w)] \text{ and } [\pi \in M_e(p, w)]\} & \text{if } (p, w) \in \delta \\ E\{\pi \mid [\pi \in M(p, w)]\} & \text{if } (p, w) \notin \delta. \end{cases}$$

Note that (p, w) will be in the equilibrium policy set if and only if (A1) is satisfied. Hence we define $\pi^e(p, w)$ to be a rational inference function if

$$\pi^e(p, w) = E\{\pi \mid [\pi \in M(p, w)]\} \qquad \text{for all } (p, w). \tag{B2}$$

From (B1), $M(p, w)$ depends on the function $\pi^e(\cdot)$ so that (B2) is a functional equation in the mapping $\pi^e(\cdot)$. Define $p(\pi)$, $w(\pi)$ to be an equilibrium policy when, for each π, (B1) holds at $[p(\pi), w(\pi)] = (p, w)$; that is, p, w maximizes $R(\pi, p, w)$ subject to $V[\pi^e(p, w), p, w] \geq \bar{u}$.

Before proving the existence of an equilibrium policy function and inference function, we show that for any equilibrium inference function there will be only one policy function—namely, full insurance.

Theorem 2   *Assume that $u(\cdot)$ is strictly concave and $G(\cdot)$ is such that $\pi = 0$ and $\pi = 1$ have zero probability. If equilibrium policy and inference functions $\pi^e(\cdot)$ exist, then $p(\pi) \equiv p_M^0$ and $w(\pi) = w^0$, where those numbers are given in the text by $u(b_1 - p_M^0) \equiv \bar{u}$ and $w^0 \equiv b_1 - b_2$.*

Proof   Suppose $(p, w) \neq (p_M^0, w^0)$; we derive a contradiction. If (p, w) maximizes $R(\pi, p, w)$ so that $V(\pi^e, p, w) \geq \bar{u}$, then it must be the case that

$$R(\pi, p, w) \geq R(\pi, p_M^0, w^0), \tag{B3}$$

since p_M^0, w^0 gives the consumer $\bar{u}$ irrespective of π^e. It must also be the case that

$$E\{[\pi u(b_1 - p) + (1 - \pi)u(b_2 - p + w)] \mid \pi \in M(p, w)\} \geq \bar{u}. \tag{B4}$$

Note that since $u(\cdot)$ is strictly concave for each π, there is no $(p, w) \neq (p_M^0, w^0)$ such that (B3) holds and $\pi u(b_1 - p) + (1 - \pi)u(b_2 - p + w) \geq \bar{u}$, since p_M^0, w^0 is Pareto optimal. Hence for all π such that (B3) holds, $\pi u(b_1 - p) + (1 - \pi)u(b_2 - p + w) < \bar{u}$. If $\pi \in M(p, w)$, then (B3) holds. Hence (B4) is impossible.   QED

It is easy to show that a rational inference function exists.

Theorem 3   *Define $\pi(p, w) \equiv E[\pi \mid R(\pi, p, w) \geq R(\pi, p_M^0, w^0)$; then $\pi(p, w)$ is a rational inference function.*

Proof   It must be shown that (B2) holds. We need only show that if $R(\pi, p, w) \geq R(\pi, p_M^0, w^0)$, then $R(\pi, p, w) \geq R(\pi, \hat{p}, \hat{w})$ for all $(\hat{p}, \hat{w})$ satisfying $V[\pi(\hat{p}, \hat{w}), \hat{p}, \hat{w}] \geq \bar{u}$. Equivalently, we must show that there is no $(\hat{p}, \hat{w})$ such that $R(\pi, \hat{p}, \hat{w}) > R(\pi, p_M^0, w^0)$ and $V[\pi(\hat{p}, \hat{w}), \hat{p}, \hat{w}] \geq \bar{u}$. As in the proof of theorem 2, if there was such a $\hat{p}$, $\hat{w}$ then $E[\pi u(b_1 - \hat{p}) + (1 - \pi)u(b_2 - \hat{p} + \hat{w}) \mid R(\pi, \hat{p}, \hat{w}) \geq R(\pi, p_M^0, w^0)] \geq \bar{u}$, but this implies that there exists some π such that $\pi u(b_1 - \hat{p}) + (1 - \pi)u(b_2 - \hat{p} + \hat{w}) \geqslant \bar{u}$ and $R(\pi, \hat{p}, \hat{w}) > R(\pi, p_M^0, w^0)$ which contradicts the Pareto optimality of p_M^0, w^0. QED

Notes

1. Sanford J. Grossman, Existence of Futures Markets, Noisy Rational Expectations, and Informational Externalities, 44 Rev. Econ. Stud. 431 (1977).

2. George A. Akerlof, The Market for "Lemons"; Qualitative Uncertainty and the Market Mechanism, 84 Q. J. Econ. 488 (1970), and Charles Wilson, The Nature of Equilibrium in Markets with Adverse Selection, Bell J. Econ. 11(2) p. 108 (1980).

3. Sanford J. Grossman and Oliver Hart, Disclosure Laws and Takeover Bids, 35 J. Finance 323 (1980).

4. Michael Spence, Consumer Misperceptions, Product Failure, and Producer Liability, 44 Rev. Econ. Stud. 561 (1977).

5. The best examples of positive disclosure laws occur in the buying and selling of securities. See Grossman and Hart, *supra* note 3, for an analysis of tender offers, when the offerer is required to state his purpose for buying shares in a company. See also Stephen Ross, Disclosure Regulation in Financial Markets, in Issues in Financial Regulations (Franklin Edwards ed. 1978), for an analysis of the incentive role of positive disclosure.

6. Joseph Schumpeter, Capitalism, Socialism, and Democracy (3d ed. 1950).

7. Hayne E. Leland, Quality Choice and Competition, 67 Am. Econ. Rev. 127 (1977).

8. $\{q\}$ is the set with a single element, namely q.

9. See Paul Milgrom, Good News and Bad News: Representation Theorems and Applications, Discussion Paper 407R Northwestern School of Management, October (1980), for a game-theoretic version of the same argument, and possible generalizations.

10. Note that in this model there is no production. Further, to insure that firms supply competitively, we assume that all firms together can more than supply the n identical consumers, each of whom wants at most one unit. For this reason, if consumers observe π, equilibrium will be characterized by a zero net price: $R(\pi^*, p, w^0) = 0$ for the marginal quality π^*. The only issue is which firms will sell their products. If we assumed that there was a production cost c, then competitive equilibrium with full information would be characterized by $R(\pi^*, p, w^0) = c$ for the marginal quality π^* (as long as this contract gives consumers at least $\bar{u}$).

11. Joseph Stiglitz in Monopoly, Non-Linear Pricing and Imperfect Information, Rev. Econ. Stud., vol. LXLIV, no. 138 pp. 407–432, has analyzed markets where a monopolist selling insurance chooses contracts which attempt both to price dis-

criminate and screen out bad risks. In his model, all customers know the qualities of the monopolist, but the monopolist does not know the qualities of the buyers. This is the reverse case from what I have considered. The basic equilibrium concept is very similar, however.

12. Steven C. Salop, The Noisy Monopolist: Imperfect Information, Price Dispersion, and Price Discrimination, 44 Rev. Econ. Stud. 393 (1977).

13. It is no accident that positive disclosure laws are very broad. If there were a few very specific pieces of information relevant to a buyer, then the theorem of this chapter would apply: a buyer would simply ask the seller about these pieces of information. A positive disclosure law appears to have benefits when the characteristics of product quality are so vague that a consumer literally has no idea of what to ask. For example, there are so many possible defects in a house that the information costs of disclosing that each possible characteristic works well is much higher than having a seller make a disclosure only in the event that he is aware that there is a specific defect. This is presumably what a positive disclosure law is trying to remedy. By requiring the seller to disclose any information *material* to a buyer, the law attempts to reduce disclosure costs by, for example, requiring the seller to disclose only defects in his product. However, for reasons described below in the text, these laws can actually raise disclosure costs.

9   Unemployment with Observable Aggregate Shocks

A general equilibrium model of optimal employment contracts is developed where firms have better information about labor's marginal product than workers. It is optimal for the wage to be tied to the level of employment, to prevent the firm from falsely stating that the marginal product is low and cutting the wage. It is shown that an observed aggregate shock that leads to an interindustry shift in labor demand and that would have no effect on total employment under symmetric information leads to a reduction in employment when firms and workers have asymmetric information.

9.1   Introduction

Recent theories of the business cycle have emphasized the misallocations associated with unobserved aggregate shocks.[1] Agents are assumed to have insufficient information to distinguish changes in their relative position from those in their absolute position. Here we develop an equilibrium model in which an aggregate shock (which, e.g., affects the price level or aggregate unemployment) is observed by everyone. However, the shock increases workers' uncertainty about their marginal value products. We show that this increase in uncertainty causes employment to fall below the complete information level.

Grossman and Hart (1981) and Azariadis (1983) analyzed the optimal labor contract between a firm and its workers in a partial equilibrium model where the firm has better information than workers about the real profitability of employment. If the firm is risk averse, optimal risk sharing implies that it should cut its real wage bill when it suffers from low profitability. When the firm's profitability, $\tilde{s}$, is unobservable to workers, however, the wage bill cannot depend directly on $\tilde{s}$. Instead, if the wage bill is to be reduced, the firm will have to reduce employment as "proof" that labor's marginal product has fallen. In particular, the firm and workers will agree ex ante to a labor contract $w(l; \tilde{n})$ that ties the wage bill w to employment l, and the realization of a random variable $\tilde{n}$ denoting public information.

Suppose that when $\tilde{n} = n_1$, workers have complete information about their marginal value product, while $\tilde{n} = n_2$ denotes an aggregate shock that creates uncertainty about the marginal value product of labor. When $\tilde{n} = n_1$, the optimal labor contract will involve productive efficiency (since there is complete information), and hence the marginal wage bill $w_l(l, n_1)$ and labor's marginal disutility of effort, say, R, will be equated. On the other hand, if $\tilde{n} = n_2$, it can be shown that risk sharing dictates that $w_l(l, n_2)$ exceed R. Hence there will be underemployment in low marginal product firms (but there will not be overemployment in high marginal product firms). This implies that total employment will be lower when $\tilde{n} = n_2$ than if information were complete or labor were allocated through Walrasian spot markets. Consequently, shocks that move the economy from n_1 to n_2 but do not affect total employment with complete information or with labor allocation through spot markets lower total employment when there is asymmetric information.

Section 9.2 reviews optimal asymmetric information contracts for a single firm. Section 9.3 presents an introductory general equilibrium model in which an observed economy-wide shock affects the physical productivity of labor. Workers know only the cross-sectional distribution of productivities across firms that the shock induces. For example, workers may know that an oil price shock lowers labor productivity by 75% in half the firms and raises it by 75% in the other half. However, a given worker does not know which half his firm is in. This captures the idea that workers know how the total demand for labor varies with the observed shock but not how their own firm's demand for labor is affected by the shock. We show that the relatively lucky firms do not increase employment more than they would if their workers had perfect information, while the unlucky firms decrease employment more than they would if their workers had perfect information.

Section 9.4 extends the analysis to demand shocks. We consider an economy in which there are three final consumption goods, of which two, X and Y, are produced from intermediate goods, K_1 and K_2, while the third is not produced using current resources (e.g., it represents real balances or the capital stock). The economy is subjected to two types of shocks, only one of which is observable to workers. First, the distribution of endowed wealth changes, which changes the demand for the final goods X and Y. This results in an observable change in prices of the final goods. Second, there are shocks θ to the technology of transforming intermediate goods into final goods. These shocks are not observed by workers and change the intensity with which a particular final goods industry uses each intermediate good. Workers produce only intermediate goods but do not observe intermediate good prices.

When workers in a particular intermediate good industry, say, industry 1, observe a shock to the relative prices of X and Y, they do not know how that affects their marginal value product, because they do not know whether X or Y is intensively using the output K_1 they produce. Note, however, that when relative prices are not very dispersed, it does not matter as far as the workers' marginal value product is concerned whether X or Y is using K_1 intensively. The model, therefore, has the property that an observed increase in the dispersion of relative final goods prices causes an increase in the uncertainty workers have about their own marginal value products. This situation, where each worker knows more about general economic conditions than about conditions in his own industry (since each consumes goods produced in many industries), is in contrast to Lucas's (1972) assumption that workers know more about their own firms' price than they know about the economy-wide price level.

Using the results of sections 9.2 and 9.3, section 9.4 shows that an increase in the dispersion of relative prices that leaves the complete information Walrasian equilibrium unchanged causes a fall in employment under asymmetric information. This is proved under the assumption that, ex ante, workers and firms write an optimal labor contract that appropriately is conditioned on everything that will be observable to both parties. Therefore, the contractionary effect of aggregate shocks occurs despite the fact that contracts are conditioned on these shocks. This is in contrast to models such as Taylor (1980) or Blanchard (1979) where observable shocks affect output because wage contracts cannot be conditioned on them.

Section 9.5 contains our interpretations, conclusions, and some references to evidence. In particular we suggest the importance of publicly observed but unanticipated changes in the price level (or rate of inflation) in a monetary economy. When a large percentage of individual wealth is held in the form of nominally denominated assets or liabilities, then changes in the price level will cause a redistribution of wealth between nominal borrowers and nominal lenders. This wealth redistribution can be the source of shocks to the relative demands for goods if borrowers and lenders have different tastes. Output can contract as a consequence of an increase in the relative price dispersion created by the wealth redistribution. A wealth redistribution that would have no effect on total employment when agents have symmetric information will cause employment to fall when they are asymmetrically informed.

9.2 The Optimal Employment Contract

We begin by analyzing the optimal contract between a single firm and its workers. For now, we do not distinguish physical productivity shocks from relative demand shocks. Thus we let $\tilde{s}$ represent a shock to the marginal value product of labor; that is, output q is given by

$$\tilde{q} = \tilde{s} f(l), \tag{1}$$

where l is total employment in the firm, and f is a production function satisfying $f' > 0$, $f'' < 0$, $f'(0) = \infty$, and $f'(\infty) = 0$. We regard $\bar{q}$ as "real" output or revenue.

We adopt a 2-period model. At initial date 0 the firm and workers have the same information. Neither party knows s (s denotes the realization of $\tilde{s}$), but both know the distribution of s. At date 1 the firm observes s, but the workers do not. This asymmetry reflects the reasonable presumption that management knows more about relevant demand and cost conditions than do workers. Because of the asymmetry, the wage bill cannot depend on s directly (if the firm were asked to report s, it would claim the s that minimized total wages). However, the workers and firm both observe l and some public information n. Hence the total wage bill w can depend on n and l. We assume that q is not observed by the workers.

Labor is supplied perfectly elastically at a real wage rate of R per unit at date 1; that is, a worker's utility of real income I and labor l is $U(I - Rl)$, where $U' > 0$ and $U'' \leq 0$. Let $\bar{U}$ be the expected utility at time 0 that a worker at this firm could obtain elsewhere. We shall suppose, for simplicity, that the firm can hire only one worker (Grossman and Hart [1981, p. 304] show that real values are unaffected if the firm can have many identical workers).

An optimal contract specifies a wage rule $w(l, \tilde{n})$ and an employment rule $l(\tilde{s}, \tilde{n})$ that maximize the firm's expected utility given that the worker's expected utility is at least $\bar{U}$. Note that since the worker cannot observe s directly, the contract must induce the firm to choose $l = l(s, n)$, given $w(l, n)$, when $\tilde{s} = s$ and $\tilde{n} = n$. The firm will do so if

$$sf[l(s,n)] - w[l(s,n),n] \geq sf(\hat{l}) - w(\hat{l},n) \tag{2}$$

for all s, $\hat{l}$, n—that is, if $l(s, n)$ maximizes ex post profit for the firm at date 1 when $\tilde{s} = s$, $\tilde{n} = n$, given the wage rule $w(l, \tilde{n})$.[2] We assume that the owners of the firm are risk averse and have a utility of profit $V(q - w)$, where V is strictly concave.[3] Thus an optimal contract maximizes

$$EV\{\tilde{s}f[l(\tilde{s}, \tilde{n})] - w[l(\tilde{s}, \tilde{n}), \tilde{n}]\} \tag{3}$$

subject to (2) and

$$EU\{w[l(\tilde{s}, \tilde{n}), \tilde{n}] - Rl(\tilde{s}, \tilde{n})\} \geqslant \bar{U}. \tag{4}$$

Expectations are taken with respect to the joint distribution of $\tilde{s}$ and $\tilde{n}$, which is assumed to be known to both the firm and worker at time 0.

If the worker could observe s, then an optimal employment contract would set the marginal value product of labor equal to the value of the marginal disutility of effort R and choose the wage bill to share risk optimally between the firm and the worker. We denote this complete information employment rule by $l^*(\tilde{s})$, where

$$sf'[l^*(s)] = R \qquad \text{for all } s. \tag{5}$$

Grossman and Hart (1981) showed that when the worker has no information $\tilde{n}$ about the realization of $\tilde{s}$, the optimal employment function $l(s)$ is everywhere below $l^*(s)$ except at the highest s. This result extends to the case where workers can observe n at time 1. In the following proposition, $[\underline{s}(n), \bar{s}(n)]$ denotes the support of the conditional distribution of s given n.

Proposition 1 *If $l^0(s, n)$ and $w^0(l, n)$ form an optimal contract, that is, maximize (3) subject to (2) and (4), then $l^0(s, n) \leqslant l^*(s)$ for all s and n, with equality if $s = \bar{s}(n)$. Furthermore, if, for each n, either (a) the conditional distribution of $\tilde{s}$ is continuous or (b) it is discrete and the worker is risk neutral, then $l^0(s, n) < l^*(s)$ almost surely for those realizations s less than $\bar{s}(n)$.[4]*

The first part of proposition 1 is established in Hart (1983). Part (b) is also proved there, while (a) follows from an application of the results of Grossman and Hart (1981).

To illustrate this proposition, suppose that $\tilde{n}$ takes on two possible values, n_1 and n_2. Assume that when $n = n_1$, $\tilde{s} = s_1$ always, so there is no uncertainty; whereas when $n = n_2$, $\tilde{s}$ can assume two values $\underline{s}$ and $\bar{s}$. Clearly the conditionally optimal contract for $n = n_1$ entails efficient employment, $l^*(s_1)$, since there is no uncertainty. On the other hand, when $n = n_2$, $l(\underline{s}, n_2) < l^*(\underline{s})$ (assuming risk neutrality for the worker) by proposition 1.

To understand proposition 1 in this case, suppose instead that a labor contract induced the full information employment rule, $l^*(s)$. From the incentive constraint (2),

$$\overline{s}f[l^*(\overline{s})] - w(\overline{s}) \geq \overline{s}f[l^*(\underline{s})] - w(\underline{s}).$$ (2')

The difference in the firm's profit across the two states is

$$\pi_2 - \pi_1 = \overline{s}f[l^*(\overline{s})] - w(\overline{s}) - \{sf[l^*(s)] - w(\underline{s})\},$$ (2'')

which, by (2'), is positive, since $l^*(\overline{s}) > l^*(\underline{s})$. Thus the firm bears risk. Now if (2') held with strict inequality, we could raise $w(\overline{s})$ and lower $w(\underline{s})$ to keep the mean wage the same. This would not affect the worker if he were risk neutral but would help the firm by reducing its risk. Hence (2') must hold with equality (it is immediate that, if [2'] holds with equality, the other incentive constraint for $s = \underline{s}$ holds). From (2') and (2''), it is clear that the only way to reduce $\pi_2 - \pi_1$ while still maintaining (2') with equality is to reduce $l(\underline{s})$ below $l^*(\underline{s})$ and raise $w(\overline{s}) - w(\underline{s})$. Moreover, such a change is desirable, assuming the worker is risk neutral, since the consequent loss of output is a second-order effect (starting from efficiency) but the gain in risk reduction for the firm is of the first order. Note also that since deviations in $l(\overline{s})$ from $l^*(\overline{s})$ do not affect $\pi_2 - \pi_1$, it is optimal to set $l(\overline{s}) = l^*(\overline{s})$.

For the remainder of the paper, when applying proposition 1, we shall suppose that either case (a) or case (b) holds.

9.3   General Equilibrium with Physical Productivity Shocks

We now embed the partial equilibrium model of section 9.2 in a very simple general equilibrium model of contracts. In this model aggregate shocks affect the marginal physical productivity of labor.

As in section 9.2, each firm i has a production function

$$q_i = s_i f(l_i).$$ (6)

We imagine that there is a steady state for the economy in which firms earn no rents. In this steady state, all firms find labor equally profitable; that is, $s_1 = s_2 = \cdots = s^*$. Now imagine that the economy is hit by a shock that induces a nondegenerate distribution of $\overline{s}$ across firms. We assume that the owner of each firm knows his own s but that his worker knows only the cross-sectional distribution of $\overline{s}$. Lacking any further knowledge, each worker assumes that his firm's s is a random drawing from that distribution.

In the notation of the previous section, let $\tilde{n}$ be the signal observed by firms and workers about the economy-wide shock. Let $F(s|n)$ be the cross-sectional distribution of productivities associated with the realization $\tilde{n} = n$. Denote the news that no shock has occurred by $\tilde{n} = n^*$; that is, this is the steady state where $s_i = s^*$ for all i. We assume that every $n \neq n^*$ leads to a nondegenerate distribution of s in the sense that

$$\text{Var}(\bar{s} \mid n) > 0 \qquad \text{for all } n \neq n^*. \tag{7}$$

It is useful to consider the Walrasian (or complete information) employment level associated with a particular cross-sectional distribution of $\bar{s}$. A firm with $s_i = s$ sets

$$sf'(l^*) = R. \tag{8}$$

This defines the employment level $l^*(s)$. Thus for a given cross-sectional distribution $F(s \mid n)$, economy-wide employment is

$$L^*(n) = \int_{\underline{s}(n)}^{\bar{s}(n)} l^*(s) \, dF(s \mid n), \tag{9}$$

where $\underline{s}(n)$ and $\bar{s}(n)$ are the bounds on the realization of s. Note that for the no-shock situation, total employment is

$$L^* \equiv L^*(n^*) = l^*(s^*)N, \tag{10}$$

where N is the number of firms.

Suppose now that the worker in firm i can observe l, and n but not s_i. Appealing to proposition 1 of section 9.2, we see that when the cross-sectional distribution of $\bar{s}$ is not degenerate, employment $l^0(s, n)$ satisfies

$$l^0(s, n) < l^*(s) \qquad \text{for } s < \bar{s}(n) \tag{11}$$

almost surely. Hence the economy's total employment under asymmetric information is

$$L^0(n) = \int_{\underline{s}(n)}^{\bar{s}(n)} l^0(s, n) \, dF(s \mid n) < \int_{\underline{s}(n)}^{\bar{s}(n)} l^*(s) \, dF(s \mid n) = L^*(n) \quad \text{for all } n \neq n^*. \tag{12}$$

On the other hand.

$$L^0(n^*) = L^*(n^*) = L^*, \tag{13}$$

since the asymmetry of information is irrelevant when there is no shock.

Using (12) and (13) we may compare the asymmetric and full information employment levels. In the steady state, total employment equals L^* under both symmetric and asymmetric information. Assume now that a shock hits the economy inducing a nondegenerate cross-sectional distribution of $\bar{s}$. In general, some firms gain from this shock while others lose. The lucky firms will raise employment, whereas the losers will diminish it.

If the move from n^* to n causes total Walrasian employment to fall below L^*, (12) and (13) imply that, under asymmetric information, the decline in total employment is greater, that is, it is multiplied. On the other hand, if total Walrasian employment rises when n^* goes to n, the increase must be smaller under asymmetric information; there is a "divider" effect. Finally, any movement from n^* to n that keeps the total level of Walrasian employment constant will lead to a decrease in aggregate employment under asymmetric information.

We see, therefore, that the effect of the asymmetry of information is itself asymmetric between "up shocks" and "down shocks" (where these are defined relative to total Walrasian employment). In the case of down shocks, the fall in Walrasian employment is exacerbated, whereas in the case of up shocks the rise is diminished. The model thus contrasts with that of Lucas (1972), in which asymmetric information has a (symmetric) multiplier effect on both up and down shocks.

Note that there is some reason to believe that the non-Walrasian effects of our model will be short run. For if the shock is permanent, there should be a flow of resources from adversely affected firms or industries to beneficially affected ones. This reallocation will tend to equalize the profitability of labor, returning the economy to a steady state.

9.4   Relative Demand Shocks

We next study uncertainty caused by relative demand shocks. Such uncertainty is more difficult to formalize than that from productivity shocks. The additional complication is rewarded, however, by a richer model. Moreover, relative demand shocks are arguably more important in practice as a source of uncertainty.

One possible cause of relative demand shocks is redistribution of wealth (induced, perhaps, by unanticipated changes in inflation). If workers do not know how a shift in demand affects their own firm, a redistribution of wealth may increase their uncertainty about their marginal value product. This uncertainty may cause a decline in aggregate employment relative to the Walrasian level.

There are a number of difficulties in formalizing this idea. First, the process we are trying to capture is intrinsically dynamic: A demand shift alters prices, which in turn influence employment, which then further affects demand, and so on. Ideally, we should use an intertemporal, monetary model. Instead, ours is nonmonetary and static.

Second, there is a special problem with modeling shocks to demand rather than to productivity, namely, that if firms operate in competitive product markets, the demand they face is completely summarized by the relative prices of their products. If workers buy these products, they cannot have imperfect information about their firm's demand.[5]

To get around this problem, we assume that some firms produce intermediate goods at prices that consumers do not observe. Thus a worker does not know how a change in the demand for a final consumption good affects the demand for the particular intermediate good produced by his firm. All he knows is that his firm's price is a random drawing from the current cross-sectional distribution of all intermediate good prices.

Consider a competitive economy with two produced consumption goods X and Y and two intermediate goods K_1 and K_2. There is also an unproduced third consumption good Z. There are firms that produce good K_1 (type 1 firms) and others that produce good K_2 (type 2 firms). Both types have the same concave, differentiable production function, $f(l)$, where l is labor input, as in section 9.2. Goods X and Y are produced *without labor* according to the linear production technologies

$$X = (1 - \theta)K_1 + \theta K_2, \tag{14}$$

$$Y = \theta K_1 + (1 - \theta)K_2, \tag{15}$$

where θ is the realization of a random variable $\bar{\theta}$. We assume that $\bar{\theta}$ takes two values:

$$\bar{\theta} = \begin{cases} \frac{1}{2} + b & \text{with probability } \frac{1}{2} \\ \frac{1}{2} - b & \text{with probability } \frac{1}{2}, \end{cases} \tag{16}$$

where $0 < b < \frac{1}{2}$. When $\theta > \frac{1}{2}$, industry Y finds K_1 a more productive input than K_2, while industry X finds the opposite true. The roles are reversed when $\theta < \frac{1}{2}$. We will see that, when $\theta > \frac{1}{2}$, industry Y uses only K_1, and industry X uses only K_2. Thus, when $\theta > \frac{1}{2}$, an increase in the final demand for X relative to Y is beneficial for type 2 firms, whereas when $\theta < \frac{1}{2}$ it is adverse. That is, the benefits that intermediate good firms derive from changes in final demand depend on the realization of $\bar{\theta}$.

We normalize the price of the third consumption good Z to be 1. For the rest of this section all prices are measured in terms of Z. Let v_i be the price of intermediate good K_i. Let P_x and P_y be the prices of X and Y, respectively.

There are two cases to consider:

CASE 1: $\theta < \frac{1}{2}$. In this case,

$$\frac{\theta}{1 - \theta} < \frac{1 - \theta}{\theta}. \tag{17}$$

If $v_2/v_1 > (1 - \theta)/\theta$, neither consumption good industry will demand K_2. But, as will become clear, a positive quantity of K_2 is always supplied—a contradiction of equilibrium. Similarly, $v_2/v_1 < \theta/(1 - \theta)$ is also impossible. Hence

$$\frac{\theta}{1 - \theta} \leqslant \frac{v_2}{v_1} \leqslant \frac{1 - \theta}{\theta}, \tag{18}$$

and industries X and Y specialize in K_1 and K_2, respectively. Competition implies that if X and Y are produced, their prices must equal unit resource costs:

$$v_1 = P_x(1 - \theta) = P_x\left(\frac{1}{2} + b\right), \qquad v_2 = P_y(1 - \theta) = P_y\left(\frac{1}{2} + b\right). \tag{19}$$

CASE 2: $\theta > \frac{1}{2}$. Symmetrically, we have

$$\frac{1 - \theta}{\theta} \leqslant \frac{v_2}{v_1} \leqslant \frac{\theta}{1 - \theta} \tag{20}$$

and

$$v_1 = P_y\theta = P_y\left(\frac{1}{2} + b\right), \qquad v_2 = P_x\theta = P_x\left(\frac{1}{2} + b\right). \tag{21}$$

Notice that the cross-sectional distribution of final good prices is mirrored by the cross-sectional distribution of intermediate good prices. A worker who observes the prices (P_x, P_y) and has only this information views his own firm's price v as a random drawing from the distribution

$$\bar{v} = \begin{cases} P_x(.5 + b) & \text{with probability } \frac{1}{2} \\ P_y(.5 + b) & \text{with probability } \frac{1}{2}. \end{cases} \tag{22}$$

Thus the worker can make good inferences about his own firm's price if the dispersion of P_x and P_y is small but correspondingly poor inferences for large dispersions.[6]

We next study optimal labor contracts between firms and workers in the intermediate good industries. To do so we first specify agents' preferences.

Workers and Firms in the Intermediate Good Industries

There are m intermediate good firms and m workers. All workers are identical and have ordinal preferences represented by the utility function $X^{\lambda_1}Y^{\lambda_2}Z^{\lambda_3} - RL$, where R is the marginal disutility of effort, $\lambda_i \geqslant 0$ for i, and $\lambda_1 + \lambda_2 + \lambda_3 = 1$. Workers' risk preferences are represented by the concave von Neumann-Morgenstern utility function U, so their utility over consumption is $U(X^{\lambda_1}Y^{\lambda_2}Z^{\lambda_3} - RL)$. Collectively, they have en-dowment e_w of the nonproduced good Z. Firms' owners (we identify firms with their owners) have the same tastes for consumption goods as workers; they have the utility functions $X^{\lambda_1}Y^{\lambda_2}Z^{\lambda_3}$. They have the strictly concave von Neumann–Morgenstern utility function V, and so their overall utility is $V(X^{\lambda_1}Y^{\lambda_2}Z^{\lambda_3})$. Owners have an aggregate endowment e_f of the un-produced good. Aggregate worker and firm demand for X and Y is

$$X^d = \frac{\lambda_1}{P_x}(I_w + I_F), \qquad Y^d = \frac{\lambda_2}{P_y}(I_w + I_F), \tag{23}$$

where I_w and I_F are the aggregate incomes for workers and firm owners, respectively. Define $\delta \equiv \lambda_1^{\lambda_1}\lambda_2^{\lambda_2}\lambda_3^{\lambda_3}$. Then the indirect utility functions of workers and firms are, respectively,

$$U\left(\delta P_x^{-\lambda_1}P_y^{-\lambda_2}\frac{I_w}{m} - Rl\right), \qquad V\left(\delta P_x^{-\lambda_1}P_y^{-\lambda_2}\frac{I_F}{m}\right). \tag{24}$$

The aggregate income of workers and owners together automatically nets out wage payments, so it equals total income from sales of intermediate goods plus aggregate endowment of the nonproduced good Z:

$$I_w + I_F = v_1 K_1 + v_2 K_2 + e_f + e_w = P_x X + P_y Y + e_f + e_w. \tag{25}$$

We model the economy as if there were two dates, 0 and 1. At date 0 the workers and firms meet according to some competitive process to sign contracts. From the equal numbers assumption each firm employs one worker. Everyone knows the distributions, but not the realizations, of $\tilde{\theta}$, $\tilde{P}_x$, and $\tilde{P}_y$. Since the distribution of $\tilde{\theta}$ is symmetric about $\frac{1}{2}$, workers are indifferent between signing contracts with K_1 and K_2 firms. Let $\tilde{n}$ de-note $(\tilde{P}_x, \tilde{P}_y)$. Then workers and firms write a contract that makes the wage bill paid at date 1 a function $w(\tilde{l}, \tilde{n})$. At date 1 the firm observes n and its own price v and chooses l, whereas the worker observes only l and n.

Other Consumers

There are other consumers who neither work nor own intermediate goods firms. The only source of wealth these consumers have is their (random) aggregate endowment $\tilde{e}_0$ of the nonproduced good. They have Cobb-Douglas utility functions but with parameters different from those of firms and workers, namely, $\gamma_1, \gamma_2, \gamma_3$. Their demands are

$$X_0^d = \frac{\gamma_1}{P_x} e_0, \qquad Y_0^d = \frac{\gamma_2}{P_y} e_0. \tag{26}$$

The only role of the other consumers is to generate changes in relative prices when the wealth distribution changes. We could alternatively have considered a wealth redistribution between firms and workers, but it is more difficult to characterize the optimal labor contract when workers and firms have different tastes for consumer goods.

Equilibrium

Let $\tilde{e} \equiv (e_f, e_w, \tilde{e}_0)$. In equilibrium, consumption prices $n \equiv (P_x, P_y)$ are functions of e. In turn, intermediate goods prices, from (19) and (21), are functions of n and θ. Thus, given the distribution of $\tilde{n}$ and $\tilde{\theta}$, the optimal labor contract $[w_i(\tilde{l}, \tilde{n}), l_i(\tilde{v}_i, \tilde{n})]$ for firms in industry i maximizes

$$EV \left\{ \frac{v_i f[l_i(\tilde{v}_i, n)] - w_i[l_i(\tilde{v}_i, \tilde{n}), \tilde{n}] + (e_f/m)}{\delta^{-1} \tilde{P}_x^{\lambda_1} \tilde{P}_y^{\lambda_2}} \right\} \tag{27}$$

subject to the constraints that $l_i(v_i, n)$ maximizes

$$v_i f(l_i) - w_i(l_i, n), \tag{28}$$

for all n and v, and

$$EU \left\{ \frac{w_i[l_i(\tilde{v}_i, \tilde{n}), \tilde{n}] + (e_w/m)}{\delta^{-1} \tilde{P}_x^{\lambda_1} \tilde{P}_y^{\lambda_2}} - Rl_i(\tilde{v}_i, \tilde{n}) \right\} \geq \bar{U}. \tag{29}$$

The expectations in (27) and (29) are taken ex ante over the prospective market-clearing prices $P_x(e)$, $P_y(e)$, and $v_1(e, \theta)$, $v_2(e, \theta)$. Because firms in the two intermediate goods industries are ex ante identical, we shall henceforth drop the subscript i and refer to the optimal contract as a pair $w(l, n)$, $l(v, n)$.[7]

In equilibrium P_x and P_y must clear spot markets at date 1. In view of (23), (25), and (26), we have

$$\frac{\lambda_1}{P_x} (P_x X + P_y Y + e_f + e_w) + \frac{\gamma_1}{P_x} e_0 = X \tag{30a}$$

and

$$\frac{\lambda_2}{P_y} (P_x X + P_y Y + e_f + e_w) + \frac{\gamma_2}{P_y} e_0 = Y, \tag{30b}$$

where X and Y are outputs of the two produced goods. Manipulating (30a) and (30b) yields

$$X = \frac{E_x}{P_x}, \qquad Y = \frac{E_y}{P_y}, \tag{31}$$

where E_x and E_y are given by[8]

$$E_x \equiv (e_f + e_w)\left[\frac{\lambda_1}{\lambda_3}(\lambda_1 + \lambda_2) + \lambda_1\right] + e_0\left[\frac{\lambda_1}{\lambda_3}(\gamma_1 + \gamma_2) + \gamma_1\right], \tag{32a}$$

$$E_y \equiv (e_f + e_w)\left[\frac{\lambda_2}{\lambda_3}(\lambda_1 + \lambda_2) + \lambda_2\right] + e_0\left[\frac{\lambda_2}{\lambda_3}(\gamma_1 + \gamma_2) + \gamma_2\right]. \tag{32b}$$

Let l_x and l_y be employment in the intermediate good industries supplying industries X and Y, respectively. Then, from (22),

$$l_x = l\left[\left(\frac{1}{2} + b\right)P_x, n\right], \qquad l_y = l\left[\left(\frac{1}{2} + b\right)P_y, n\right]. \tag{33}$$

Outputs X and Y are given by

$$X = (1 - \theta)K_1 = (1 - \theta)f(l_x), \qquad Y = (1 - \theta)K_2 = (1 - \theta)f(l_y),$$

if $\theta < \frac{1}{2}$, and

$$X = \theta K_2 = \theta f(l_x), \qquad Y = \theta K_1 = \theta f(l_y),$$

if $\theta > \frac{1}{2}$. Since $\theta = \frac{1}{2} - b$ or $\frac{1}{2} + b$, this simplifies to

$$X = \left(\frac{1}{2} + b\right)f(l_x), \qquad Y = \left(\frac{1}{2} + b\right)f(l_y). \tag{34}$$

Combining (31) and (34) gives us

$$(.5 + b)f(l_x) = \frac{E_x}{P_x} \qquad \text{and} \qquad (.5 + b)f(l_y) = \frac{E_y}{P_y}. \tag{35}$$

Conditions (22), (27)–(29), and (33)–(35) characterize a contract equilibrium under asymmetric information. To summarize the features of this equilibrium, a price function $P(\tilde{e}) = [P_x(\tilde{e}), P_y(\tilde{e})]$ maps each realization of the random endowment vector $\tilde{e} = (e_f, e_w, \tilde{e}_0)$ into a pair of prices. This function determines intermediate goods prices $v_1(e, \theta)$, $v_2(e, \theta)$ according to (22). Given these price functions, optimal labor contracts maximize (27) subject to (28) and (29). These contracts determine output through (33) and (34). Finally, for the system to be in equilibrium, these supplies must clear markets, that is, satisfy (35).[9]

It is useful by contrast to examine the Walrasian equilibrium as a function of $E \equiv (E_x, E_y)$.[10] Walrasian wages in each industry are equal to marginal value products of labor. This implies that the Walrasian equilibrium prices and employment levels, $\bar{v}_x, \bar{v}_y, \bar{P}_x, \bar{P}_y, \bar{l}_x, \bar{l}_y$, satisfy

$$\frac{\delta \bar{v}_x f'(\bar{l}_x)}{\bar{P}_x^{\lambda_1} \bar{P}_y^{\lambda_2}} = \frac{\delta \bar{P}_x(.5 + b) f'(\bar{l}_x)}{\bar{P}_x^{\lambda_1} \bar{P}_y^{\lambda_2}} = R, \tag{36}$$

$$\frac{\delta \bar{v}_x f'(l_y)}{\bar{P}_x^{\lambda_1} \bar{P}_y^{\lambda_2}} = \frac{\delta \bar{P}_y(.5 + b) f'(\bar{l}_y)}{\bar{P}_x^{\lambda_1} \bar{P}_y^{\lambda_2}} = R, \tag{37}$$

$$X = (.5 + b) f(\bar{l}_x) = \frac{E_x}{\bar{P}_x}, \tag{38}$$

$$Y = (.5 + b) f(\bar{l}_y) = \frac{E_y}{\bar{P}_y}, \tag{39}$$

where (38) and (39) are the market-clearing conditions for the two produced goods industries (see the derivation of [31]).

We now apply proposition 1 to the asymmetric information contract equilibrium. For a given realization of $\tilde{n} = (\tilde{P}_x, \tilde{P}_y)$, there will be a "lucky" intermediate goods industry (one whose output price is high) and an "unlucky" industry (i.e., if $P_x > P_y$, industry 2 is lucky if $\theta > \frac{1}{2}$ and unlucky if $\theta < \frac{1}{2}$ and conversely for industry 1). One difference between (27)–(29) and (2)–(4) is that workers and firms are interested in real income $\delta I P_x^{-\lambda_1} P_y^{-\lambda_2}$ rather than in I. Given that P_x, P_y are publicly observable, however, proposition 1 generalizes to this case (for details, see Hart [1983]). Hence, we may conclude that a firm in the lucky industry will equate the marginal value product of labor and the marginal disutility of effort, whereas a firm in the unlucky industry will set the marginal product of labor above the marginal disutility of effort. Specifically, when, say, $P_x \geqslant P_y$, employment satisfies

$$\frac{\delta P_x}{P_x^{\lambda_1} P_y^{\lambda_2}} (.5 + b) f'(l_x) = R, \tag{40}$$

$$\frac{\delta P_y}{P_x^{\lambda_1} P_y^{\lambda_2}} (.5 + b) f'(l_y) = R(1 + \alpha), \tag{41}$$

where $\alpha \geqslant 0$, and $\alpha = 0$ if and only if $P_x = P_y$. Thus, the crucial difference between the asymmetric information and Walrasian equilibrium conditions is the α in (41).

We now show that if the distribution of wealth induces prices that create uncertainty for workers about their marginal value products, then total employment is lower than with complete information. Furthermore, the prices of both produced goods are higher and the outputs are lower than their Walrasian levels.[11]

Proposition 2[12]   *Consider a Walrasian equilibrium with prices $\overline{P}_x$, $\overline{P}_y$ satisfying $\overline{P}_x > \overline{P}_y$ and employment levels $\overline{l}_x$, $\overline{l}_y$. The corresponding asymmetric information contract equilibrium P_x, P_y, l_x, l_y satisfies $P_x > \overline{P}_x$, $P_y > \overline{P}_y$, $l_x < \overline{l}_x$, and $l_y < \overline{l}_y$.*

Proof   Comparing (31) with (38) and (39) shows that it suffices to prove that $P_x > \overline{P}_x$ and $P_y > \overline{P}_y$. Suppose one of these inequalities failed. Define $P \equiv P_x^{\lambda_1} P_y^{\lambda_2}$, $\overline{P} \equiv \overline{P}_x^{\lambda_1} \overline{P}_y^{\lambda_2}$.

CASE (a): $P_x \leqslant \overline{P}_x$. The market-clearing conditions (38) and (31) yield $l_x > \overline{l}_x$. Thus, the marginal productivity conditions (40) and (36) imply that

$$\frac{P_x}{P} \geqslant \frac{\overline{P}_x}{\overline{P}}. \tag{42}$$

But since $P_x \leqslant \overline{P}_x$, (42) implies that $P_y \leqslant \overline{P}_y$. Market clearing requires that output of Y be higher in the contract equilibrium, so $l_y > \overline{l}_y$. But the marginal conditions (37) and (41) then imply that

$$\frac{P_y}{P} > \frac{\overline{P}_y}{\overline{P}}. \tag{43}$$

Now raise (42) to the power λ_1, (43) to the power λ_2, and multiply. This yields $P > \overline{P}$, which is inconsistent with $P_x \leqslant \overline{P}_x$, $P_y \leqslant \overline{P}_y$.

CASE (b): $P_y \leqslant \overline{P}_y$. Market clearing implies that $l_y \geqslant \overline{l}_y$. Then (41) and (37) imply that $P_y/P \geqslant \overline{P}_y/\overline{P}$. This gives $P_x \leqslant \overline{P}_x$. The contradiction now follows exactly as in case *a*.   QED

Notice that although only one intermediate goods industry is unlucky in the sense of setting marginal product above marginal disutility, both are unlucky in suffering employment levels below the Walrasian level. Thus, there is something resembling a multiplier that, through general equilibrium effects, transforms the sub-Walrasian output and employment of one sector into a general "recession."

As in section 9.3, proposition 2 implies that, if we start in the steady state $P_x = P_y$, (1) a demand shock that creates price dispersion and keeps total Walrasian employment constant will reduce total employment under asymmetric information; (2) a shock that reduces Walrasian employment will reduce employment under asymmetric information by more; and (3) a shock that increases Walrasian employment will increase employment under asymmetric information by less.

We see that changes in the distribution of wealth will cause relative price movements, which create uncertainty on the part of laborers about their marginal value product. We have used the convention that unequal final goods prices are associated with uncertainty about the marginal value product of labor within each industry. To see that this is just a convention, note that in a world of perfect certainty free entry leads resources to be allocated across industries in such a way that prices are determined by minimum average costs. When firms have identical production functions, minimum average costs are the same. If we instead began with industries that had different cost functions, then the steady-state (no shock) situation would lead to final goods prices that are unequal. However, the profitability of labor would be equalized across industries. A shock that changed relative demands would, in the short run, cause the profitability of hiring labor to be unequal across industries. If workers knew only the *distribution* of profitabilities across industries and they thought their firm's labor profitability were a random drawing from that distribution, then a shock that changed demand from its steady-state value would cause uncertainty about labor productivity within each industry. By the arguments of this section, this would cause a drop in employment relative to the Walrasian level.

9.5 Evidence and Conclusions

A. Relative Price Variability as a Cause of Aggregate Output Variability

In section 9.4 we outlined a model in which relative price shocks make workers uncertain about their marginal value products. Firms have superior information about marginal products but are risk averse; when the profitability of employing labor in a given firm is low, it would like to reduce the wage bill. Because of the asymmetry of information, it cannot do this directly but must also reduce the employment level to persuade workers that their marginal products really are low.

Before discussing potential sources for the relative price shocks, we offer some evidence that is consistent with the implication that relative price shocks affect aggregate output. Note that proposition 2 implies that relative demand shocks that leave employment unchanged under full information will lower employment under asymmetric information. Thus, assuming that, on average, the actual relative demand shocks that impact on our economy would be neutral under symmetric information, our major empirical implication is that aggregate employment will fall, on average, in response to relative demand shocks.

Lilien (1982) has presented evidence that the level of unemployment tends to be high when the cross-sectional variability of net employment is high. He found that the cross-sectional variability of employment can explain at least as much of the unemployment as can unanticipated decreases in the money supply. Unfortunately, Lilien does not examine the relationship between relative price shocks and the cross-sectional variability of net employment.

Fischer (1982) surveys the literature on relative price variability. He also studies the time-series behavior of aggregate output, relative price variability, and other macroeconomic variables. In a vector autoregression, relative price variability, when "put first," explains as much of the variability of output as interest rate, money, or inflation innovations (see his table 8), that is, about 10% of the total variability of output. When relative price variability is "put after" interest rates, money, and inflation, it does as well as inflation and money but worse than interest rates.

The comparatively high explanatory power of relative price variability for output is, of course, consistent with models other than ours. For example, all Fischer's results are consistent with a Walrasian model in which agents receive information that future output will fall but that components of output will fall in differing proportions. With a conventional money demand model this implies that prices will rise in the future in differing proportions, in turn raising present prices in differing proportions. Thus, the future decrease in output induces increases in expected inflation, variability of inflation, and nominal interest rates, which is exactly what Fischer finds. Fischer also suggests three other models that are consistent with his observations.

B.   The Causes of Relative Price Variability

The model presented in section 9.4 assumes that a shift in the distribution of wealth creates a change in relative prices. There are clearly many sources of relative price variability other than changes in the distribution of wealth, for example, variability in technology, tastes, and the prices of imports and exports. We have focused on wealth redistributions to allow for comparisons with existing macroeconomic models.

In particular, assume that there is a wealth redistribution between nominal borrowers and lenders after an unanticipated movement in the price level. (Although our model has no money, it would not be difficult to append an additively separable utility of real balances to preferences. Furthermore, we could model borrowing and lending associated either with life-cycle effects or random shocks to income.[13]) In such a model with nominal borrowing and lending, unanticipated inflation has important effects on the distribution of wealth.

In the United States, 50% of "wealth" is held in the form of nominal debt.[14] If the economy is composed of two types of individuals, nominal borrowers and lenders, who share other wealth equally, then a 10% permanent drop in the price level increases the real wealth of lenders by 50% of 10%, or 5%. Borrowers' wealth falls by the same amount. To the extent that the permanent drop of 10% in the price level is associated with expected deflation, there will be a second effect in the wealth distribution in the same direction: namely, the real price of long-term nominal debt will rise due to the decrease in the nominal interest rate. People over 55 (the "old") tend to be nominal creditors while people under 55 (the "young") tend to be nominal debtors. Fischer and Modigliani (1978) estimate (to within an order of magnitude) that a 1% unanticipated increase in the price level will transfer wealth with a flow value of about 1% of GNP.

Wealth redistributions have no effect on relative prices if wealth is redistributed between groups that have the same homothetic preferences. However, there is some evidence that there are systematic differences by age among individuals in their preferences. Michael (1979, p. 41) used the Bureau of Labor Statistics' consumer expenditure survey to find that there are systematic and significant differences among individuals' consumption proportions by age. The classification of borrowers and lenders by age may not be the most useful for tracing the consequences of the wealth redistribution. We mention it here because it is the only classification for which there is evidence that individuals are jointly sorted by desired consumption proportions and debt positions.

There are some other obvious sources of wealth redistributions that may be of sufficient magnitude to have caused observed output fluctuations. For example, unanticipated changes in nominal interest rates due either to real or to nominal factors redistribute wealth between long-term borrowers and lenders, and this could be a source of relative price variability. Alternatively, large decreases in the real value of assets such as houses and stocks can cause substantial redistributions of wealth between the young and the old. Finally, exogenous changes in the productivity of capital could be the cause of a change in the real value of assets.

C. Relative versus Aggregate Demand Shifts

The previous discussion may obscure some of the difference between our model and aggregate demand models of the business cycle. To the extent that changes in aggregate demand cause wealth redistributions that induce employment fluctuations, there is some similarity between our model and aggregate demand models. One important difference, however, is that there is no reason in our model why the *sign* of the aggregate demand shock should matter. A large unanticipated inflation can cause the same relative price shift as a large unanticipated deflation.[15] Hence there is no presumption that unanticipated inflation is expansionary whereas unanticipated deflation is contractionary. To a first approximation (i.e., where the Walrasian equilibrium total output is independent of the wealth distribution), the *absolute value* of the unanticipated price level change should be negatively correlated with output in our model. Furthermore, if relative price variability is an independent variable explaining output, then unanticipated inflation should have little incremental explanatory power.

Blejer and Leiderman (1980) and Fischer (1982) use innovations in inflation and relative price variability as explanatory variables for output. Their results suggest that each variable has some independent explanatory power for output in the post–World War II United States. Fischer (1982, figure 3) and Sims (1980, table 3) both find that in the post–World War II period positive price innovations precede a *decrease* in output. We conclude from this evidence that, in the post–World War II period, although the data suggest an independent effect of price innovations, the signs are the reverse of those predicted by the models of Sargent, Lucas, or Barro (see Barro [1981] for a survey of models in which unanticipated inflation causes an increase in output).

The period before World War II is likely to be favorable to the unanticipated inflation model. Sims (1980, table 3) finds that negative price innovations precede decreases in output in the period between World War I and World War II. Unfortunately, we have not been able to find any evidence that distinguishes the relative price variability hypothesis from the unanticipated inflation hypothesis in that period. In the pre–World

War II period, large unanticipated deflation may well be a proxy for high variability of relative prices. This is consistent with the data of tables 2 and 6 in Parks (1978).

Thus it seems that further empirical research is needed to distinguish the hypothesis that unanticipated falls in money (or prices) decrease output from the hypothesis that monetary or price level shocks of any sign decrease output. In addition, further theoretical research is required to develop models in which the sign of the publicly observed shock, as well as its size, affects output. One such contribution is that of Holmstrom and Weiss (1982), who suggest that when individuals confuse idiosyncratic and aggregate shocks, as in Lucas (1972), the direction of aggregate shocks matters.

Notes

1. See Barro (1981) for a survey of the literature on unobserved money supply shocks, and Grossman and Weiss (1982) for a model with unobserved real productivity shocks.

2. It is sometimes convenient to express a contract as a pair $[w(\tilde{s}, \tilde{n}), l(\tilde{s}, \tilde{n})]$ with the property that for all $s, \hat{s}, n$

$$\hat{s}f[l(\hat{s}, n)] - w(\hat{s}, n) \geq \hat{s}f[l(s, n)] - w(s, n). \tag{2*}$$

This formulation is equivalent to (2′) in the text because from (2*), $w(s_1, n) = w(s_2, n)$ whenever $l(s_1, n) = l(s_2, n)$; i.e., $w(s, n)$ depends on s only through l. That we may use this alternative expression is an instance of the revelation principle (see Dasgupta, Hammond, and Maskin 1979; Myerson 1979; or Harris and Townsend 1981]. Inequalities (2) and 2*) are often called incentive or self-selection constraints.

3. The assumption that we can treat the firm as risk averse makes sense if either (a) the owners cannot diversify away the riskiness of their shares in the firm or (b) the firm is run by a risk-averse manager who supplies an unobserved input (e.g., "entrepreneurial effort") and whose salary depends on the firm's performance. For elaborations of the second justification, see Holmstrom and Weiss (1982) and Hart (1983).

4. Risk neutrality of the worker is a stronger assumption than is necessary. All that is required is that the worker be not too risk averse.

5. If there are no futures markets, and labor at time t is used to produce goods at time $t + 1$, then it might appear that workers and firms could have different information about the value of employing labor at t. However, if the workers' wage at date $t + 1$ can depend on the date $t + 1$ spot prices that the firm learns at t, then one can show that employment in an optimal contract is the same as if both the firm and workers observed the date $t + 1$ spot price at date t.

6. We want to model the idea that workers know general labor market conditions better than conditions in their own firm. Thus workers observe the cross-sectional mean and variance of employment from newspaper reports on the economy-wide and regional unemployment rates. They do not know the state of demand for their own firm's product. Further, if there are many firms in a given industry, then the employment level of other identical firms will provide a useful signal to workers in a given firm. We *assume that no such signal is available.* To the extent that firms in the same industry are not completely identical but are subject to idiosyncratic shocks to demand, the employment level of other firms in the same industry may be a poor signal about a given firm's demand.

7. It is not difficult to show that under our assumptions the optimal contract is unique.

8. Note that when $\lambda_i = \gamma_i$ for all i, changes in the distribution of wealth have no effect on E_x or E_y and so none on prices.

9. We must also add the condition that $U^{**} \leqslant \bar{U} \leqslant U^*$, where U^* is the level of utility at which a firm is indifferent between signing a contract with a worker and not operating at all, and U^{**} is the level of utility at which a worker is indifferent between signing a contract with a firm and not working; i.e., $U^{**} = EU[\delta \bar{P}_x^{-\lambda_1} \bar{P}_y^{-\lambda_2} (e_w/m)]$. Equilibrium depends, in general, on the particular value $\bar{U}$ (not, however, if U and V exhibit constant absolute risk aversion; see Grossman and Hart 1983). It can be shown that a contract equilibrium exists.

10. Alternatively, we could examine the contract equilibrium with complete information. Such an equilibrium gives rise to the Walrasian employment levels.

11. Note that if a monetary contraction causes the change in the distribution of wealth, then prices of goods relative to the nonproduced good (money) will fall rather than rise. An implication of our result is that the decrease in supply associated with the increased uncertainty will cause prices in terms of money to fall less than they would under complete information.

12. We must emphasize that proposition 2 depends importantly on the ordinal (i.e., Cobb-Douglas) preferences we have assumed (although we could have assumed any number of goods). The result generalizes to utility functions over X, Y, and Z of the form $\phi(X, Y)^\lambda Z^{1-\lambda}$, where goods X and Y are gross complements.

13. See Grossman and Weiss (1982) for an example of a mechanical transformation of an asymmetric information real economy to a nominal economy. An almost identical transformation could be made here. An essential difference is that our model of section 9.4 will not work with complete endowment insurance. If the two different types of traders have perfectly insured each other, then the particular realization of the endowment distribution will not affect the relative wealth position. Similarly, unanticipated price movements will have no real effects if all contracts are indexed.

14. See Friedman (1982). By "wealth" we mean the value of total assets held by those who save. Thus, while inside debt is not usually considered net wealth, it is

net wealth to the consumers who are saving. If those people who pay the taxes to finance government debt interest payments are the same as the holders of government debt, then the wealth redistribution will only be associated with inside debt.

15. Of course in a Walrasian model it is possible that a wealth redistribution from group A to group B will cause an expansion of output while the reverse redistribution will cause a contraction. However, we prefer to maintain the presumption that the wealth redistribution has no effect on the Walrasian equilibrium.

References

Azariadis, Costas. "Employment with Asymmetric Information." *Q.J.E.* 98 (suppl.; 1983): 157–172.

Barro, Robert J. "The Equilibrium Approach to Business Cycles." In *Money, Expectations, and Business Cycles: Essays in Macroeconomics*. New York: Academic Press, 1981.

Blanchard, Olivier J. "Wage Indexing Rules and the Behavior of the Economy." *J.P.E.* 87 (August 1979): 798–815.

Blejer, Mario I., and Leiderman, Leonardo. "On the Real Effects of Inflation and Relative-Price Variability: Some Empirical Evidence." *Rev. Econ. and Statis.* 62 (November 1980): 539–544.

Dasgupta, Partha S., Hammond, Peter J., and Maskin, Eric S. "The Implementation of Social Choice Rules: Some General Results on Incentive Compatibility." *Rev. Econ. Studies* 46 (April 1979): 185–216.

Fischer, Stanley. "Relative Price Variability and Inflation in the United States and Germany." *European Econ. Rev.* 18 (May/June 1982): 171–196.

Fischer, Stanley, and Modigliani, Franco. "Towards an Understanding of the Real Effects and Costs of Inflation." *Weltwirtschaftliches Archiv* 114, no. 4 (1978): 810–833.

Friedman, Benjamin M. "The Changing Role of Debt and Equity in the United States." Manuscript. Cambridge, Mass.: Harvard Univ., 1982.

Grossman, Sanford J., and Hart, Oliver D. "Implicit Contracts, Moral Hazard, and Unemployment." *A.E.R. Papers and Proc.* 71 (May 1981): 301–307.

Grossman, Sanford J., and Hart, Oliver D. "Implicit Contracts under Asymmetric Information." *Q.J.E.* 98 (suppl.; 1983): 123–156.

Grossman, Sanford J., and Weiss, Laurence. "Heterogeneous Information and the Theory of the Business Cycle." *J.P.E.* 90 (August 1982): 699–727.

Harris, Milton, and Townsend, Robert M. "Resource Allocation under Asymmetric Information." *Econometrica* 49 (January 1981): 33–64.

Hart, Oliver D. "Optimal Labour Contracts under Asymmetric Information: An Introduction." *Rev. Econ. Studies* 50 (January 1983): 3–35.

Holmstrom, Bengt, and Weiss, Laurence. "Managerial Incentives, Investment, and Aggregate Implications. Part I. Scale Effects." Mimeographed. Evanston, Ill.: Northwestern Univ., 1982.

Lilien, David M. "Sectoral Shifts and Cyclic Unemployment." *J.P.E.* 90 (August 1982): 777–793.

Lucas, Robert E., Jr. "Expectations and the Neutrality of Money." *J. Econ. Theory* 4 (April 1972): 103–124.

Michael, Robert T. "Variation across Households in the Rate of Inflation." *J. Money, Credit and Banking* 11 (February 1979): 32–46.

Myerson, Roger B. "Incentive Compatibility and the Bargaining Problem." *Econometrica* 47 (January 1979): 61–73.

Parks, Richard W. "Inflation and Relative Price Variability." *J.P.E.* 86 (February 1978): 79–95.

Sims, Christopher A. "Comparison of Interwar and Postwar Business Cycles: Monetarism Reconsidered." *A.E.R. Papers and Proc.* 70 (May 1980): 250–257.

Taylor, John B. "Aggregate Dynamics and Staggered Contracts." *J.P.E.* 88 (February 1980): 1–23.

Author Index

Subject Index